LIVES OF MUSEUM JUNKIES

Norma Jean & Henry—
For continuing a life
of purpose and
creativity.

Marilynne Eichinger

PRAISE FOR *LIVES OF MUSEUM JUNKIES*

"Marilynne Eichinger has created a very worthwhile contribution with her thorough analysis of science museums. Her book will bring added interest to museums and what they can offer now and in the future."

Jean Auel, author Earth's Children series.

"Marilynne shares the experiences and insights of many who shaped the field, along with her personal reflections. Her engaging book will help you see science museums in a new light."

David Ucko, Museums+More LLC

"The book is very well written and easy to enjoy. This topic requires a "storytelling" approach, and it has been captured well. Those recognized in the chapters should be honored for your treatment of their many accomplishments. The book concludes with a valuable perspective on the future of museums. That future will be a function of the leaders who take to heart the many "lessons" that are offered."

Bud Rock, Executive Director Association of Science and Technology Museums.

"This great read tells the story of the beginning of science museums through the eyes of early pioneer Marilynne Eichinger. She includes lessons from her life and the lives of other pioneers in museums of experience. Recommended for those who care about museums, libraries and society today."

Ginnie Cooper, Past director of Washington D.C., Brooklyn, and Portland Library systems

"People interested in museums as real educational environments, parents interested in their children's education, and people seeking to find themselves in a positive way could all benefit from reading this book. I love the way the bios of major contributors are interspersed through-out—most thoughtful. A terrific story!"

Ronald C. Rosenberg. Professor, Associate Dean Emeritus, Michigan State University.

"Marilynne Eichinger has embraced the past to give a lively behind-the-scenes description of the evolution of interactive science museums and why these science playgrounds should be part of your life."

Michelle Marquart, Past VP Marketing, Oregon Coast Aquarium; General Manager, Mount Hood Railroad.

THE STORY OF AMERICA'S HANDS-ON EDUCATION MOVEMENT

MARILYNNE EICHINGER

INKWATER
PRESS

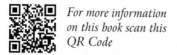

*For more information
on this book scan this
QR Code*

Publisher: Inkwater Press | www.inkwaterpress.com
ISBN-13 978-1-62901-382-4 | ISBN-10 1-62901-382-X

Printed in the U.S.A.

1 3 5 7 9 10 8 6 4 2

CONTENTS

SECTION I
IN THE BEGINNING

SECTION II
WHY SCIENCE CENTERS WORK

SECTION III

LEADING THE CHARGE

SECTION IV

THE PRACTICAL SIDE

SECTION V
CONTINUING THE EXPERIENCE

SECTION VI
SUMMARY AND CONCLUSION

SECTION VII
REFERENCES

Acknowledgements

Lives of Museum Junkies was made possible by a lifetime of family and friends willing to put themselves out to help educate a young woman. I thank my early loves, Dr. Ronald Rosenberg and Martin Eichinger, and my partner for the past twenty years, Ray Losey; my children Ryan, Kara, Julia, Jessica, Talik, and my honorary son Seth. They remain an inspiring part of my life and continue to assist me with many ventures. A special acknowledgment goes to Dee Pumplin who was there at the beginning, helping to turn a dream into a reality.

It is with appreciation that I mention editors Kristin Thiel and Karen Segal who cut, slashed and marked reams of paper, making me think about what I really wanted to say. I also am thankful for the support I received from Portland's chapter of 9 Bridges Writers Group for providing a critique as pages were read aloud. All budding writers could benefit by being part of this type of experience.

The eleven men and women whose mini-biographies are included were generous with their time and emotional support by reading, correcting, and approving their sections. We experienced great sadness and loss to the museum field when Alan Friedman, first president of the New York Hall of Science, died a few weeks after his biography was completed.

Helping to fill gaps in Frank Oppenheimer's life story were Sally Duensing, educator and past executive at the

Exploratorium in San Francisco and Sheila Grinell, Frank's first assistant director. To better understand the future possibilities of interactive museums, I spoke with Nancy Stueber, president of the Oregon Museum of Science and Industry; David Heil, an internationally known educator and museum consultant, and Al DeSena, a National Science Foundation program officer. Al has shown me how creative the next generation of educators are in their ongoing mission to inspire youth. Lastly, thanks to everyone who read copies of my early manuscript. Their suggestions were invaluable.

Introduction

———————————————————————————————

"It always seems impossible until it's done."
-Nelson Mandela

———————————————————————————————

Fifty years ago only a dozen or so science centers existed in the United States, and fewer in Europe. Today, there are many thousands dotting countries around the globe, all focused on raising science literacy.

As a young wife and mother I started a science museum in my basement. The year was 1972, and founding Impression 5 Science Museum in Lansing, Michigan, heralded the beginning of an adventure that would change a timid, naive woman into one capable of running one of the nation's foremost institutions, the Oregon Museum of Science and Industry (OMSI).

A wise man once advised me, "When the time feels right, go for it! Don't wait for everyone else to agree because that never happens. Grab your own opportunity." And that is what I did. But I was not the only one. In *Lives of Museum Junkies*, I share my joys and difficulties as well as the stories of eleven other men and women who were on the leading edge of an international movement to build experiential museums dedicated to science. Some of the names you might recognize;

others you will be glad to discover; all demonstrated from a young age a special curiosity and way of seeing the world that stimulated a lifetime of creative actions.

One theme common to all of the men and women described in this book is that we evolved from the culture of the times to become *change agents* affecting multiple aspects of our country's education ethos. As free spirits of creative energy, we combined artistry with science, engineering, and technology. We saw ourselves as promoters of lifelong self-improvement, practitioners of creative problem-solving, believers in equal opportunity, disseminators of the latest scientific information, and teachers who made learning so much fun that there could be no substitute for asking the next question and wanting to know more. Our passions were fired by psychologists, educators, and scientists such as Jean Piaget, Maria Montessori, Jonathan Kozol, John Hart, A. S. Neil, Carl Rogers, and Frank Oppenheimer.

Putting our lofty goals into practice was not without mishaps. When starting our museums we were not very sophisticated and did not understand the intricacies of fund-raising, board development, or staff management. We were artless in constructing interactive displays and did not understand how chauvinism and class structure in America would affect us. One important goal of this book is to offer "lessons learned" that will help anyone trying to establish a new creative venture.

Inside these pages, you'll learn how the director of the New York Hall of Science fought with Mayor Rudolph Giuliani on behalf of the Brooklyn Museum of Art, as well as suggestions on how to deal with deadly accidents, a devious press, and even more slippery insurance companies. I share what it is like to run a multimillion-dollar auction that became the best party of the year, as well as heartwarming tales of staff adopting street kids. You'll be delighted by the dedication shown by volunteers and board members, like author Jean Auel of *The Clan of the Cave Bear* fame, and appreciate the important role played by the National Science Foundation (NSF) in building new centers (including a story of how one NSF director saved *Nova* and then was instrumental in developing new science centers throughout the country).

Interwoven through these pages is my own story of growing up in Philadelphia at a time when women weren't expected to find professional careers, let alone seek advanced education. I have no doubt that it was my early access to museums that later unleashed my potential. Whether I was enrolled in classes in the basement of the Philadelphia Museum of Art or listening to the crackle of gigantic electric sparks that resounded throughout the science hall of the Franklin Institute, it was in museums that I learned about the nature of passion and the euphoric feeling that comes from total immersion in something you love. Exhibits introduced me to the creative expression of artists, historians, and scientists, and I realized that I wanted to be like them—inventive, clever, dedicated.

Later in my career I took another risk by leaving my comfortable nonprofit cocoon in order to create a thriving educational catalog company. During my years as museum president, I realized with increasing clarity that education starts in the home, so in 1995, with the help of twenty-two national museums, I left OMSI to start the *Museum Tour Catalog* in order to reach out to two million households. Parents who shop the catalog are provided tools with which to help their own children stay engaged and creative in an Internet-based world. Though I sold the company in 2013, it continues to provide museum-quality educational toys and materials to the nation.

Mostly though, *Lives as Museum Junkies* demonstrates how perseverance can overcome obstacles when you follow your dreams. As Norman Stiles implied in his book *Everything in the Whole Wide World Museum*, the entire universe is everyone's museum and we just have to organize our lives and psyches to embrace and take advantage of all that we see. I hope that this book will encourage you to do just that.

WOYAYA

We are going,
Heaven knows where we are going,
But we know within.
And we will get there,
Heaven knows how we will get there,
But we know we will.
It will be hard, we know,
And the road will be muddy and rough,
But we'll get there.

From a song by Loughty Amoa, Solomon Amarfio, Robert M. Baily, Roy Bedeau, Francis T. Osei, Whendell K. Richardson and Mac Tontoh Copyright 1993 Chappell & Co., Inc Warner Bros. Publications US, Inc. Miami, FL 33014 song ID WW009785370000. Reprinted with permission.

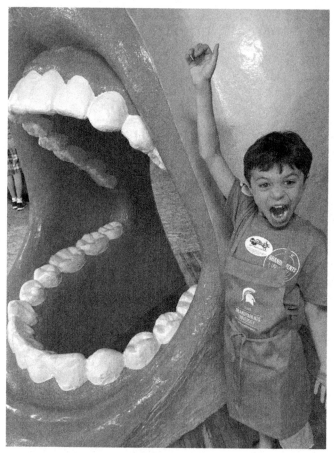

Dentistry at Impression 5

SECTION I
In the Beginning

CREATING AN INTERACTIVE MUSEUM: NAÏVE BEGINNINGS

"Stop running and making so much noise!" I shouted to five rambunctious children playing hide-and-seek in closets throughout the house. It was a cold day and my friend Dee Pumplin was visiting with her son. She and I were having a difficult time hearing each other as we chatted animatedly in the kitchen. It was during this conversation that my homemaker days started to end, when over coffee in my suburban house we brewed up the idea of a hands-on museum that emphasized science. Children are not always polite, studious little creatures set on this planet to impress and please their parents. Instead they are balls of energy who love to run, scream, and create bedlam. In short, they can drive a parent crazy, especially on a rainy day. As Dee and I talked, our children shouted and squealed, ignoring the storm roaring outside. The increasing noise level was like a drum roll announcing a new idea. We started imagining what it would be like to take our kids to an indoor playground.

"Wouldn't it be magnificent to have a great big barn," we fantasized, "and fill it floor to ceiling with ramps, poles, and climbing apparatus? What fun it would be for the children and their friends. They would get rid of their energy away from home and our houses would be preserved." Dee and I started to wonder where we could find a barn and even took the next step of contacting a realtor.

As we learned more, the vision for an indoor play structure grew. The immense dimensions of a working barn inspired our ideas to expand to include interactive learning activities inserted into climbing areas. We imagined children swooping down a sliding board and finding a light table, colored filters, and projectors to use for experimentation. The colored light could be projected on the next child speeding down the slide. We embraced the idea of physical play being integrated with academic challenges in a never-ending cycle of learning.

After months of talk and concept development we finally located a barn, but it wasn't long before we faced a dose of reality. The cost to acquire the property was more than we anticipated and building the inside play structure seemed monumental. The barn needed to be heated, insulated, electrified, bathroomed, and water sprinkled, and once it was upgraded, the cost of ongoing utilities would be astronomical. The permitting process was overwhelming. We began to wonder if the city would even allow this type of play-barn to exist. Insurance was bound to be phenomenal, not only because we were dealing with a wooden structure but because we were planning to let children run throughout. We especially liked the idea of fire poles descending from one level to the next. Sound safe? Costs mounted, reaching an enormous number before we had even considered the price of exhibits and staffing.

We did not give up; instead, we changed direction. The more Dee and I chatted the more we talked ourselves out of the play-barn idea and into the concept of a more permanent facility. During these early discussions our enthusiasm increased, and we came up with the concept of an inquiry-based science and art museum. It would be a "yes, you can touch" kind of place. We created an opportunity to turn the books we had read about self-directed schooling and learning through sensory experimentation into our own institutional brand.

Our first assignment was to select a name. In front of a fire with an open bottle of wine, Dee and I lay on the floor giggling while throwing out possibilities. We wanted the center to be open-ended, exploratory, and adventurous. The word "museum" sounded "fuddy-duddy old world" to our way of thinking, so we eliminated it from our vocabulary. Though Dee and I both loved classical art and history museums, they were not the type of institutions most young children enjoy. We were not interested in amassing a collection of objects, but rather in developing interactive challenges. Finally the word "impression" emerged. Our new center would make an impression on its visitors, and those visitors would be invited to leave an impression with us. The name seemed perfect, though we discovered later that it was difficult to brand Impression as a hands-on science center. To others it sounded more like a place to go for embossing paper. Still, Dee and I felt like proud parents who had given birth to a good concept, and we had a strong sense of accomplishment. Impression was going to be fun! Developing it would be easy.

At the time, few national museums were anything more than collections of antiquities and artifacts. A smattering were filled industrial displays that permitted a modicum of interaction rather than just passive viewings of objects placed behind glass. These museums, or centers of science and industry as they were often called, dabbled with sensory approaches to exhibitions. Pioneering institutions, such as Chicago's Museum of Science and Industry, The Franklin Institute, and the Los Angeles Science Center were supported in part by big businesses that controlled the messages presented in their exhibitions. Essentially, they were advertisements for specific industries. Visitors pushed buttons to view automated procedures that took place behind glass. A few expensive immersion exhibits

included a coal mine in Chicago, a steam locomotive in Philadelphia, and a walk-through a heart in Portland, Oregon. There
was even a sprinkling of hands-on physics experiments, though
these were the exception rather than the rule.

Thus when Dee and I started Impression there were few
models for the type of institution we were interested in creating. We mulled through ideas in a vacuum. We focused on
basic science and art activities and wanted children involved in
a comprehensive way. During this early brainstorming stage we
were open to ideas from anyone who would listen to us. Many
suggestions came from our science and engineering friends.

Our initial goal was not to operate Impression ourselves but
to establish it as a community organization complete with board
of trustees and a managing director. At the time both of us were
pursuing other career paths. Dee was looking for a job as a paralegal and I, afraid to work, was enrolled as a graduate student in
counseling psychology. We felt confident that university parents
in East Lansing would jump to embrace the science center concept, so we set about identifying our first tasks. Dee's assignment
was to develop a logo, print business cards, and create stationery.
With the donated services of our newly acquired attorney, we
were sure that we would be ready to operate successfully in a few
months with a paid managing director.

Marilynne's Lesson #1: Nothing ever occurs as
you might imagine.

A major problem emerged right from the start. Our lawyer
informed us that there already was a business in Michigan
with the name Impression. We had neglected to check corporate registration records in those pre-computer years and
wondered what we should do. Design costs were significant to
our nonexistent budget and we were reluctant to throw away
the work that had been completed only to start over. Instead

of spending another night brainstorming by the fire, we simply added the number 5 to the word Impression, five standing for the five senses. Impression 5 would develop science and art displays organized around the theme of sight, sound, touch, taste, and smell. The museum would focus primarily on science but be integrated with the arts and humanities. Now we really were on our way. Success was in sight and execution was going to be a snap.

___ ___ ___ ___ ___ ___ ___ ___ ___ ___ ___ ___

Marilynne's Lesson #2: Talk alone does not make an organization succeed.

___ ___ ___ ___ ___ ___ ___ ___ ___ ___ ___

While my children were in school, I continued to conceptualize Impression 5 in a place called Synergy, a drop-in center with an unusual purpose. The founder, whom I simply remember as Bob, had the dream of establishing a country club-like facility in a wooded area where there would be meeting rooms, photography and pottery studios, shops filled with tools, and a rich lending library overflowing with books covering every topic from inspirational teachings to crafts and politics. His concept included an abundance of relaxation areas where people could either sit and talk quietly or dance and move about. The thought behind Synergy was similar to the Maker Movement currently spreading throughout the country today. The notion, then as it is now, is for creative people to meet regularly in equipped spaces in order to develop crafts in community. At today's Maker gatherings you might find welding equipment, electronic boards, computer tablets, 3-D printers, sewing machines, and wood working tools all for use by members. Often a sponsor is sought to help defray material expenses. In those early days of Synergy we were less technologically astute and had little money to pay for the printing presses and darkrooms we wanted to share, so most of us came together with hope that Bob's dream would get realized. We continued to meet in our bare basement room located under a restaurant across the street from MSU.

Bob envisioned a for-profit organization with members purchasing shares in Synergy and paying monthly fees to support ongoing operations. There would be no particular agenda and members would not be pressured to produce a product or be required to help staff the organization. Bob's idea was that if we just chilled out in the company of friends, good things would happen. Alliances would be formed, friendships solidified, businesses initiated, and most important for this peace-loving generation, the world would become a better place—synergistically. Bob's dream was contagious, for he was an eloquent communicator.

Synergy's actual situation was not so elegant. Bob talked, espousing an idea that went nowhere, and we groupie types listened while reclining in an empty, though softly carpeted, large basement room near Michigan State University's main drag. Bob refused to work because he believed his vision would "just happen synergistically." I thought the man was just plain lazy and learned a lesson through observing the lack of energy he brought to bear in achieving his goal. Yet watching him was transformative because he showed me the value of co-action and underscored the need for leadership and hard work.

Perhaps Bob understood more than I did, for as people wandered in and out of the room I played with ideas for Impression 5 and discussed them with many visitors. One day a local newspaper reporter stopped by to interview those of us who were hanging around the basement. The reporter had even heard of Impression 5 and asked to speak to me about the fledgling concept for a hands-on science museum. In this relaxed atmosphere I was able to chat freely about the philosophy of play in a stimulating environment where kids would learn in their own way, in their own time frame. I spouted forth in what must have been a somewhat cohesive manner for much to my surprise, after a few days an article appeared in the newspaper. This publicity is what made Impression 5 a reality.

— — — — — — — — — — — — —

Marilynne's Lesson #3: When a concept is in print, it transforms brainstorming into action.

— — — — — — — — — — — — —

People started asking how they could get involved. Talk, as the saying goes, is cheap, but putting an idea into action takes commitment. I was not sure I was ready for this type of responsibility, but I suddenly found myself too embarrassed to back out.

To initiate and promote the new museum Dee and I decided to develop a small demonstration exhibit. Michigan State University employed many brilliant and creative engineers, mathematicians, scientists and artists who were ready to help. Since my husband was on the faculty of the college of engineering and Dee's was a physics professor, our friends and acquaintances were largely drawn from the more scientific end of the spectrum. Dee and I enjoyed discussing our new science center at the many parties we attended. Everyone was willing to give advice (that came easy for this erudite crowd), and in many instances some came forward to make displays explaining principles of physics and mechanics. Constructions were challenging and included devices such as swing pendulums upon which kids could sit on boards held up by short, medium or long lengths of chain in order to experience variations in the period of each movement. Gordon, a friend of Dee's, devised a large mobile of balancing bowling balls that appeared to defy gravity as additional balls were added without toppling the structure. This massive display was a perfect demonstration of how science and art could be imaginatively united. Gordon was a powerfully built man who looked like the type of person to think of a bowling ball mobile. He was as strong and as massive as the exhibit and enjoyed demonstrating how the mind can be fooled. When not volunteering to help our museum project, he ran his own free school, one that Dee's son attended, fashioned after Britain's Summerhill. Gordon, with his MS in Psychology, understood and embraced the value of participatory, self-directed education and was quite an encouraging presence.

I too had my hand in making exhibits. With determination I learned how to use shop tools and invited my eleven-year-old son Ryan to spend hours in our home basement making crude tabletop exhibits. We built light tables, Newton's cradles, and a variety of optical displays to explain basic scientific principles. Though we were enthusiastic about our primitive accomplishments, it was good that in later years we could afford to hire professional craftsmen. Carpentry was never our forte.

Dee and I gained access to military surplus and visited flea markets and secondhand shops where we acquired used oscilloscopes, strobe lights, and balance scales. We obtained two styles of wheelchairs enabling us to demonstrate the difference in mechanical advantage between those with wheels in the front and those with wheels in the back (the latter are the old fashioned kind). Visitors would use the chairs on an obstacle course, testing how easy it was to maneuver corners, go up or down ramps, and turn doorknobs. I discovered how difficult it was to turn a knob and open a door while swerving backwards in order to put the chair into position for entry.

In short time, we assembled challenging though interesting science puzzles, optical illusions, and mechanical devices but we didn't quite know what to do with our assemblage. Though none of the exhibits were professionally executed due to lack of funds, they were disguised by bright cheerful paint. Cardboard tube ends from cement footings became the bases for tables. Tops were salvaged and wooden wheels recycled from their original job of holding cable. My basement filled quickly with an odd collection of objects.

It was time to get the word broadcast to a larger circle of people. The local mall struck us as a fine place to install our contraptions so we asked management if we could have free space for a weekend showing and were rewarded with a welcoming yes. Friends, children, and I filled cars for the temporary move. For two days we took turns monitoring the floor and promoting the fledgling museum. Professors and their spouses talked to mall customers about science and art education, encouraging them not only to try our exhibits but to get involved as volunteers. We became euphoric by watching young visitors play with the displays as anticipated, believing fully that Impression 5 would be successful. It was time to take the next step. We needed to expand the size of the board of directors and locate a building. This would require cash.

In the late 1960's and early 1970's, students and faculty in most university towns were involved in Vietnam protests, experimenting with drugs, listening to loud rock music and sharing partners. Free sex was in vogue as were key parties, where women selected a key from a bowl to determine the evening's sleeping arrangements. Some of my friends blatantly shared stories about partner swapping, and were not embarrassed talking about venereal problems that occasionally resulted. As a protected young woman I was fascinated by their encounters. During this time of "anything goes" my home decorating style exemplified the off-beat living style then fashionable. The only items in our plushly carpeted living room were one low table and several fluffy pillows. The expanse was available for rolling, playing music, dancing and acting. One time during our gathering we ordered in pizza for our long-haired group. I remember the shocked look on the delivery man's face when he peered into the doorway of our outwardly classic suburban home to see people lounging on the floor. "Cool," was his comment.

Living without furniture is a freeing experience. An empty

room can serve many purposes, as it did when it became a launching site for my husband's band, the Bluegrass Extension Services. Our house provided a perfect practice setup for this group of long-haired MSU professors who were skilled in so many more ways more than just their professions. The band became a local success story when a pub hired them for a weekly gig. Students and faculty arrived early and stayed late to listen to them play. I loved the atmosphere filled with friends and students clogging, philosophizing, and drinking their way through the evenings.

I played the flute and was in a minor competition with my husband for practice time and space. Two of the band members were also in my chamber music group. In addition to bluegrass our living room became a site for Renaissance evenings attracting our classical musician friends to join together in costume, song, and dance. The period food we shared was delicious and our children enjoyed being full participants in our festivities. Several of us were adept at the recorder, which resounded throughout the house with ancient festival tunes. After a night of partying we would tuck the kids into beds upstairs.

Most of the time Dee and I were in the habit of wearing hippy haute-couture clothing. This meant long paisley skirts or bell bottom pants, beads, dangling earrings, and sandals. But once we found ourselves thrust into the job of marketing Impression 5 we reconsidered the question of what to wear. What image did we want to portray?

Grand plans had to be shared with people outside of our immediate circle and that meant visiting influential members of the community. Meetings had to be arranged with the president of Michigan State University, the superintendent of Lansing and East Lansing schools, the president of Oldsmobile, state and local politicians, real estate moguls, and community businessmen of wealth and power. These power brokers were all men and I was greatly intimidated by their standing in the community. I had never talked to anyone in an official capacity, was awed by these prominent figures and worried about our presentation. But by then Dee and I were hooked on the museum concept and knew that we had to proceed despite our insecurities.

For these meetings I decided to wear my most mainstream professional clothes, jewelry, and heels. The short hemlines on these outfits made them not exactly fit for business ensembles, but they were good enough, I decided. Dee on the other hand stayed true to her nature, choosing comfortable sandals, long skirts that accentuated her tall graceful figure, and tops that were accented by strands of beads. In this manner, the two of us, mismatched as we were, made appointments to promote this important new institution for Lansing, Michigan. Looking back I see that we must have been quite a sight going into those wood-paneled staid offices looking like female versions of Arnold Schwarzenegger and Danny Devito in the movie *Twins*.

Much to my surprise it was easy to get appointments and once we were inside the business offices there was usually an animated sharing of information and ideas. Asking for money was not part of the agenda, but as all fundraisers know, the first step of any project is to take the temperature of the community. Initial meetings help uncover potential monetary sources that will give a campaign a boost. I was new at fundraising and did not understand this concept until many years later, but my instinct to meet with community leaders was a good one.

— — — — — — — — — — — — —

Marilynne's Lesson #4: The person at the top does matter.

— — — — — — — — — — — — —

The mayor's office stands out in my memory because it was such a negative place. The mayor's assistant grudgingly gave us an allotted amount of time before acknowledging that we would have to get in line behind a long list of other projects. It might take four or five years before the city could even consider our proposal or offer assistance, we were told. With a plastered smile and a firm good-bye the unwelcoming woman walked us to the door. Under that particular mayor, city hall rarely encouraged community applicants. His overworked staff was unfriendly and cold, supporting the attitude of the "we cannot do" mayor. It was evident that whatever we set out to accomplish was going to happen without the assistance of city hall, so we put on our hard shell and continued on. Until there was a change at the top we would be without local government support.

Several years later a new mayor, Terry McKane, was elected and within only a few months the atmosphere changed. His administration was welcoming and helpful. It was hard to believe that many of the civil servants were the same people we had spoken with just months before. Watching this transformation taught me a lesson in how the person at the top has the power to alter attitudes. A positive atmosphere makes all of the difference when a politician wants to accomplish the impossible. Impression 5 fit into the McKane administration's plans, though it did help that one of my friends, Tom Wilbur, became the mayor's assistant. He too was an unusual man.

After receiving his doctorate and obtaining a responsible job working for the Department of Education, Tom Wilbur decided to drop out. He gave his house, car and all his money to his wife, leaving his family in order to follow in Ken Kesey's footsteps of traveling the world. Off he went, hitchhiking, waiting on tables, washing dishes and even becoming a Muslim for a while in order to participate in the Hajj in Mecca. His life on the road was full of unexpected and varied experiences.

As his daughter aged, Tom's sense of familial responsibility returned and he became determined to earn enough money to put her through college. Back in Lansing, his first stop was Goodwill to purchase a decent suit for job interviews. Tom became immediately employed to wait on tables in a restaurant frequented by politicians. Within a few months he befriended Terry McKane, a lunch time regular, and volunteered to run Terry's campaign for mayor. And so he did . . . and Terry won. Tom was rewarded with a responsible job as the mayor's assistant and with paying employment he could help his daughter attend university. It wasn't long before he met a woman who shared his political soul. They married and the couple very shortly had four sons to raise. Their family along with Dee's became involved in the Paul Goodman School where Gordon, the maker of the bowling ball exhibit, oversaw a free-school environment.

Tom taught me a great deal by his ability to reinvent himself and rebuild his life. He brought confidence to all of his adventures and had the ability to develop alternative approaches whenever there were difficulties. By watching him I learned that a person does not have to be stuck going in one direction. That insight helped me through numerous tight spots in later years.

Dee and I met many interesting characters while prospecting, but one that stands out was the director of the YMCA. With no uncertainty in his voice, the man said to me, "Marilynne, you will never be successful in starting your science museum because in Lansing there are only two things that count: one is sports and the other is sex, and you are not involved in either." His bizarre comment was thoroughly disappointing but provided insight into the local male psyche, something I tucked away securely in the back of my mind to be taken out and studied later. By this time, the few encouraging voices we encountered were offset by many naysayers causing Dee and I to be less confident in our ability to succeed. But still we plowed ahead.

In addition to our promotional work, we looked for an office and storage facility for our burgeoning exhibit collection. My basement was filled to capacity with tables and helter-skelter displays and the children had limited floor space for their play. Maple Elementary in East Lansing came to our aide by providing a desk for administrative work and a place to store our collection in the corner of the school lunchroom. Between the hours of 8:30 and 11:30 a.m. and 1:30 to 3:00 p.m. I was free to use the converted classroom as a display room, make phone calls at school expense, and conduct meetings. Several mornings a week the exhibits would be made available for rotating class visits. Observing students become engrossed in these small science experiments, and the feedback we got from their teachers was an excellent way to test and improve our displays. During the lunch hour all tabletop displays had to be piled high in a corner in order to accommodate hungry children.

Occasionally, students from neighboring schools were invited to spend a morning interacting with the models in our Maple School lunchroom-office. One visiting class was led by Lansing's future mayor, Dave Hollister, who at that time was employed working as a social studies teacher with troubled teens. His small assemblage of high school dropouts occupied themselves cavalierly with science displays that were designed for younger children. Years later Dave served as a representative in the Michigan House of Representatives launching a career that eventually led to his election as mayor. We stayed in close contact. Dave remained supportive and continued to be a spokesperson for Impression 5. United States Senator Debbie Stabenow was also helpful to our fledgling organization. At the time she was in graduate school but got her start in politics on the Ingham County board of commissioners. Debbie became a strong advocate of Impression 5 and helped us greatly as she climbed the political ladder to national prominence.

Working in the East Lansing school had many rewards, and though the next story seems like a digression, I want to take a moment to share what I observed and how it affected me when a black child from a poor neighborhood benefited from positive reinforcement, community support, and a willingness to put himself into an unfamiliar situation.

I got to know of Earvin Johnson's mother, the school's cleaning lady, during a time when Earvin became a local hero. She and her husband were supportive of their talented son and encouraged him to better his basketball chances at all-white Everette High. The transition was difficult. He encountered a great many racial incidents, as he wrote in his autobiography *Life*, but eventually realized that they helped him "understand white people, how to communicate and deal with them."

Earvin was anointed the moniker "Magic" at the age of fifteen when a writer for the local paper recorded a triple-double of 36 points, 18 rebounds, and 16 assists. Earvin had so many fans that the high school had to use Michigan State University's field house for his games. Not giving into pressure to go elsewhere, upon graduation he enrolled locally and we all got to celebrate when MSU's basketball team won the college championship.

A few years later, while Magic was playing for the Los Angeles Lakers, I was invited to attend a birthday party his father organized in Lansing. Having lived most of my life in a white environment, the party was a culturally electric experience. I was one of the 10% of attendees who were white and the event made me realize how little I knew about the black community.

Guests were asked to dress in black or white, and once in the ballroom, the fashion show we beheld was spectacular. Johnson's young female friends were especially dazzling, looking as though they had stepped off of a New York runway while the men, demonstrating their individuality, wore colored spats and bright suspenders under traditional black tuxedos.

At 7 p.m. the doors were locked to late arrivals. I sat down next to a state senator at an all-white table when seven L.A.

Laker giants, accompanied by tall, stunning females, entered amid flashing lights and excited shouting fans. Projecting his well-recognized smile, Magic was in his element when speaking, leaving guests to realize that there was much more ambition in him than simply a basketball player. His favorite band had been flown in from L.A. as a birthday gift from his father. While it played, the black crowd moved and applauded to the sounds while those of us who were white sat stoically in our seats wondering, not understanding.

This party was my first total immersion into a culturally unfamiliar environment. Just as Earvin had to learn about white America, I needed to be exposed to and learn about black culture. I observed many interactions during that evening that made me feel uncomfortable, and I began to wonder how difficult it might be for a minority child to visit a museum where most attendees were white. My eyes were just starting to open.

Before I reaped rewards like being invited to celebrity events, however, I had a lot of bumpy roads to travel. Earlier I mentioned that once established, Dee and I never planned to be running the museum. Shortly after the museum was incorporated Dee returned to work and dropped out of being an active participant. I was in my second graduate year at Michigan State University, studying for a master's degree in psychology and counseling. As part of my training I interned in a community mental health center, listening to very serious emotional problems.

Except for babysitting, I had not been employed outside of my house during my thirty-two years. Though I graduated magna cum laude from Boston University I had never earned a paycheck. I juggled mothering four kids while studying for a master's degree, but I'd never worked in a company or attended a business meeting. Though not a paying job, the mental health center was actually the first time that I was required to work under someone else's direction. The center was never boring, and hearing real-life stories helped me become less naive. The internship spurred me to mature into a more worldly and less shy woman.

As I moved among university classes, my children, the health center and Maple School the museum absorbed an increasing amount of time. Many hours were spent making phone call after phone call in an effort to convince people to serve as a trustee. Slowly volunteers came forth and the board expanded from our original group of three (Dee, myself, and our lawyer) to one of twelve. Thus, the first meeting of the board could be held, and planning it became a great adventure.

"So this is what life is about!" I exclaimed to myself wearing a humongous grin as I entered a posh Lansing restaurant at noon to attend my first board meeting. Happiness could be seen in my step as I energetically climbed the stairs. Dressed in my most alluring attire, I felt ready to tackle the questions I'd be asked during the next hour. In the past, I had always used my appearance to get my way and I assumed my red miniskirt and shirt with plunging neckline would help me succeed. After a decade of vacuuming, making lunches, and kissing away tears, I was starved for excitement, at least a different kind, and glad to join the ranks of eaters of fancy midday meals. This meeting was more momentous to me than simply showing exhibits in schools with my mommy-volunteer friends.

As I reached the top of the stairs I heard the voices of a dozen community leaders settling into the private room I'd reserved. Some of the movers and shakers I most admired had accepted my invitation and were willing to help start the county's first science museum. Yet as I stood in the hallway, self-doubt swarmed over me once more.

Earnings was the word that flew around my head. I toyed with the idea of becoming the paid director. If I did, how would I justify dollars being paid me in exchange for work?

Could I live up to standards that would be demanded, and would I be able to take direction from a board and funders? I couldn't flee the restaurant, so what else could I do but step forward into my future? That fateful noon sojourn into a fancy restaurant involved twelve people ready to make the museum a reality. The food served was delicious and the meeting was effective in clarifying the goals and needs of the institution. An initial piece of advice came at the end of the session when I was pulled aside and advised to send out an agenda before the next meeting. What? Agenda? I never thought of that being necessary since in my world brainstorming was freeform and not linear. Organizing board members to become engaged participants was a skill I had yet to learn.

The second bit of instruction was delivered by a wonderfully sensitive man who knew that I had never managed a budget. My husband paid all of our household bills, and I was given as much money as I needed to purchase food and clothing for the kids. This astute board member invited me to his house where he very firmly, yet tactfully, explained the rudiments of accounting. He told me that keeping accounts is very simple: all you need to know is that one column is for income and another is for debits. That sounded easy enough as I completed my first bookkeeping lesson under his tutelage. Quite frankly I was a bit embarrassed, but I was thankful to have kind teachers and even more relieved when an accomplished accountant volunteered his service as treasurer.

I left the board meeting to return to my Maple School office, where fear of failing kept me on target and naivety about the business world helped me succeed. If I knew when I started how much time it would take and what kind of emotional turmoil my family would have to endure, I am not sure that I would have continued this venture. It was not as easy as I first imagined.

My days focused on organizing a group of mothers to take

displays to various local schools. Cars were filled to bulging, holding tables and interactive exhibits, and off we went to lunchrooms or gymnasiums, inviting classes to march through and play with the displays. I also initiated fee-based after-school classes where inspired teachers developed their own curriculum to instruct children in courses such as The Magic of Science, Math Fun and Games, and How to be a Ventriloquist. Through these programs, Impression 5 built a sizable neighborhood following that expanded our data base. This proved to be advantageous when we were ready to move into our own building.

Marilynne's Lesson #5: It is difficult to do two things well at the same time.

I was not usually in attendance for these classes, trusting the teacher to be there for his/her students. One day, while working at the mental health center, I received a panicked call from the elementary school office. The instructor was not there and children were running wildly through the hallways. I was beside myself about what to do since in ten minutes I was scheduled to lead a counseling session. I telephoned a friend who lived near the school and pleaded with her to stop what she was doing and make arrangements for the children to be picked up and sent home. It turned out that because of an accident the teacher had been stranded in traffic on the highway. In those pre-cell phone days there was no way to notify me of his situation.

This incident became a pivotal point as I realized that it was necessary to be available for inevitable museum emergencies. I couldn't lead two conflicting lives. The decision before me was whether to continue as a mental health professional and study for a PhD or commit to managing a science center. I had been invited to enter the doctoral program at Michigan

State and an answer had to be given soon. The choice was difficult but there were several factors that directed me towards museum work. I found it depressing listening to deeply rooted psychological problems. I imagined that all of my friends and acquaintances lived hidden lives that harbored one or another mental problem. Even strangers became the target of my observations as I wondered what was wrong with them. I prefer to see most people as healthy and was concerned that my worldview would change if I became focused on the mentally ill.

A second and more tragic event sealed my fate. One of my clients was a young football player having a difficult time in his senior year of college because of an injured knee that prohibited him from playing in the NFL. When I first met this student he believed he was being eaten alive and his intestines were disintegrating. I hospitalized and sedated this otherwise healthy-looking linebacker and after many months of counseling I thought he had improved enough to return to college to complete his senior year. The center's health professionals were so overworked that there was never a good time to discuss my cases so I made this decision on my own. I naively thought my skills were better than they were, and though I realized that I was still learning, I was convinced that I could compensate for inexperience by compassion. Love would carry the day. Unfortunately, once the young man returned to his college, he took a pistol out to a vacant field and ended his life. At his funeral his parents thanked me for all I did, yet I blamed myself for his death, for not seeing signs that would lead me to keep him medicated and under closer supervision. This experience was devastating and became another reason for selecting a museum career over mental health.

The greatest argument of all, however, was that there was no one else willing or interested in running Impression 5 with little pay. If the organization was to continue, I was the only one available to make it happen. Because my husband was employed I could afford to build a salary slowly. So, in this way I entered a man's world, following retired Dixie Lee Ray in Seattle, to become only the second woman in the United States to preside over a science center, and I was immediately flung into fundraising.

How do you go about getting funds with no history of accomplishment? Who would be willing to be the initial risk taker, setting the stage for others to follow? Impression 5's first sizable contribution came through a donation from the League of Women Voters, followed shortly by a grant from the Junior League of Lansing. One helpful policy of the Junior League is that monetary donations are accompanied by volunteer help. The League considers itself to be a training ground for young women who will one day assume leadership positions as volunteers in their communities. The organization provides experience through team work in project planning, board service, and raising funds. Today a great many League members hold jobs but in the 1970s most of those involved were at-home moms. Their assistance proved useful, not only in terms of woman power, but because their donation provided needed credibility. It made me able to request funds from potential donors by saying that the two Leagues believed in us, why not you?

— — — — — — — — — — — — — — —

Marilynne's Lesson #6: Bad publicity is sometimes better than no publicity.

— — — — — — — — — — — — — — —

Additional appeals were submitted to community foundations and several wealthy individuals, but responses were not expected for many months. It was tedious and frustrating to sit in my Maple School office and wait for the next affirmative letter. One day, with not much to do, I relaxed in my chair reading a magazine article about how the Playboy Bunnies visited communities to engage in sporting events against local celebrities in order to raise money for charity. My brain started churning and I remembered what the director of the YMCA had said: "Sports and sex would be the secret of success."

The Detroit Playboy Club was close enough to Lansing so I immediately called their manager. Much to my amazement, without hesitation or questions the Bunnies agreed to visit and play basketball against our community businessmen. Days were becoming exciting once more. I began to telephone every well-known chief executive I could think of and asked for his involvement. Not one man declined. The game was on with a who's who of local participants that included the mayor, president of MSU, superintendent of schools, CEOs of various manufacturing companies, real estate developers, the head of Oldsmobile, and state politicians. When the Lansing State Journal learned of the event, we had all the makings of the game to become a feature.

One problem, a big one, reared its ugly head and I was reminded of lesson #1: "Nothing ever occurs as you might imagine." The early 70s heralded in the start of the women's lib movement with books by Gloria Steinem and Betty Friedan circulating and being read by a wide audience. The equal rights amendment was headed to the states for ratification and organizations like Planned Parenthood and NOW were growing in prominence. In East Lansing a group of high school students and university women threatened to picket the Bunny Game. What had started out as a fun crazy event was turning into a political nightmare and we didn't know what to do. Now we had the makings not of a feature but of a gossip column. In fact, the gossip columnist did pick up the controversy with gusto and had a great time splashing the story daily. A number of the men who held public office called to inform me that they were reluctantly compelled to back out of their commitment.

My stomach churned with worry and I started looking for ways to work with the women libbers, finally coming up with the idea of asking Michigan State University's woman's basketball team if they would be willing to hold a practice game against our local celebrities. I hoped that by involving the female team the newspaper would soften the Playboy image and make the game acceptable. Their coach agreed to the practice, and the celebrity men arrived for a grueling session. The women on the basketball team were of course fantastic athletes in perfect condition. Our men, many of whom were potbellied, had to be replaced every three minutes to ensure there were no injuries.

Our celebrity team enjoyed their practice game, but it was not enough to silence the critics. Ticket sales were sparse and we were prepared to fail when a miracle occurred. Thankfully for us (though tragically for a great many) we were rescued by Mother Nature. The night before the game the clouds exploded and it started to rain and rain and rain. The greater Lansing area was deluged with a fifty-year flood and all citizens not concerned with their own water-filled basements were called on to bag the river banks. Jenison Field House at Michigan State, where we were to have played, was swimming in two and a half feet of water, flooding the basketball court. The Playboy Bunny Game had to be canceled. My sigh of relief is still being carried on the winds today. But the upside to the controversy is that the science museum became a known entity and on its way to becoming more than just an office in a public school. By now the entire Lansing community knew what was being planned and though many did not like the Bunny Game they certainly did support our idea for Impression 5.

SEEDS OF PASSION
FOCUS ON MARILYNNE EICHINGER

There are many stories in this book are about people who initiated the contemporary science center movement. In order to understand how hands-on learning centers came to be, it helps to become immersed in the atmosphere and youthful experiences of those involved. It was by accident that I came to manage museums. An East Coast denizen, I went kicking and screaming to Lansing, Michigan, with my professor husband and our four young children. It was there that I entered a vacuum that slowly pulled me into an unexpected life. There was no one else but myself to fall back on.

Born in Philadelphia, I grew up making regular excursions to

Marilynne

the Franklin Institute, the Museum of Art, and the Academy of Natural Sciences. I even took painting classes in the basement of the art museum when I was eleven. At the Franklin Institute I rode the steam locomotive or stared in delicious fear while watching a gigantic spark rise to make a deafening sound as it crackled near the ceiling in the electricity hall. In those days it was safe to wander the streets of Philadelphia and

26

travel alone on the subway. I loved exploring the city. Stepping out on the steps that were made so famous in the movie Rocky, I looked down at the various cultural institutions and sculptures lining the Benjamin Parkway and felt a sense of belonging.

My childhood was a happy one, filled with love, travel and privilege. When seventeen I became engaged to Ron, a tall, witty MIT student whom I had met at the age of fourteen at a Philadelphia summer camp. He was the lifeguard and I a junior-counselor who started each day by assembling 140 lunch bags. When preparing Ron's peanut butter and jelly sandwich I smeared the bread so thick with ingredients that he could hardly open his mouth to devour the sticky mess. Ron was a geek who graduated with honors from Philadelphia's most prestigious high school, and his middle class parents did everything in their power to insure that their son received the education he deserved. That came in the form of MIT.

My parents were old-fashioned and would not let me go to a university near my betrothed. I had the type of grandmother who kept me company whenever I dressed for a date, warning me the entire time of all of the problems that would happen if I lost my virginity before marriage. "My cousin So-and-So lost the respect of her husband when he found out," she would tell me and then go into the sordid details. This advice came from a woman who couldn't say menstruation but asked me if I was "falling off the roof" whenever I got my period.

The year before marriage I spent at Ursinus College, a small strict evangelical school in rural Pennsylvania where I learned about country life from boys who came to class wearing hunting licenses and a roommate who bragged about riding horses with her friends dressed as members of the Ku Klux Klan. After an interminable first year, I was handed over with elaborate ceremony from my father to my new husband.

Boston became my second home. Once the constraints of childhood were lifted, marriage felt like freedom and I reveled in the atmosphere created by thousands of intelligent students. I was delighted to be nameless when walking through the doors of Boston University where I enrolled as an undergraduate. Anonymity was a precious commodity for a young woman who had been surrounded by watching eyes for seventeen years. Every moment of every day of my young married life felt like an adventure. Even studying next to Ron was fascinating as I surreptitiously observed him sitting at his desk, spending ten minutes sharpening about two dozen pencils before tackling an hour or two of formulas and equations. I, with my liberal arts curriculum, had a full plate of reading, memorization and essay writing. He made me feel a bit jealous.

The Boston/Cambridge area is one of the most stimulating places in the country for a teen to experience. It has everything a young student could want—history, theater, museums—and Ron and I took advantage of it all. Weekends were spent driving through quaint New England villages, on walks through Walden Pond to see Henri Thoreau's cabin retreat and visiting museums such as Harvard's Peabody or the Isabella Gardner Museum. Classical concerts were inexpensive so both opera and orchestral recitals attracted our attention and overwhelmed our senses.

As a wide-eyed bride of eighteen years I absorbed new ideas and concepts as fast as they were presented. Learning to cook was an early challenge. Each afternoon, sitting on the floor in our small living room, surrounded by a half dozen cookbooks, I would design the next evening's meal. My family had always employed a cook and I was never invited to make anything more than chocolate chip cookies. My presence in the kitchen was viewed by the help as being "under foot."

Life became a whirl of dinner parties with friends and visits to coffee shops to be entertained by young artists such as Joan Baez, Pete Seeger, and Jim Kweskin's Jug Band. We attended parties along with MIT, Harvard and Boston University students who spent hours interrupting each other's thoughts on the meaning of life, religion, and if LSD was going to raise the consciousness of mankind.

Mind altering drugs had just been popularized by Harvard University's Richard Alpert (Ram Das) and psychologist Timothy Leary. In 1967 I watched Dr. Leary as he debated psychiatrist and neurologist Jerry Lettvin in a WGBH Boston television special about the moral, scientific benefits and dangers of the hallucinogenic drug. It was quite a sight to see the two men walk on the set together: Leary, dressed in white East Indian attire, sat cross-legged at the edge of the stage while his colleague stood erectly in his Western professorial clothes. Leary proposed that marijuana and LSD be used sacramentally, asking that study of the inner world of the mind be put on par with study of the outer, material world. Lettvin argued that use of drugs caused long-term cognitive impairment. On the West Coast, acid became more of the psychedelic phenomenon that was worshiped through song and electric tie-die clothing. Leary's arguments appealed to East Coast college-age students who embraced the idea of using acid to foster religious experiences. My friends wanted to enrich their spiritual lives by using these drugs to open a door into their subconscious selves. Quite a few acquaintances went to the basement of the Boston University chapel to get acid before attending Sunday's sermon. Monday mornings at Boston University always included great gossip.

All of those early experiences were captured in my brain to be uncovered later when needed in my museum career. Chemicals, drugs, and dependency would be good subjects for a future exhibits, and we see that the topic is still relevant today. Museums such as the DEA Museum in Arlington, Virginia and The British Museum in London play an important educational role through exhibitions about legal and illegal substances. They provide places for new research to be presented about the medical uses of drugs like LSD and popular pharmaceuticals. Some of DEA's exhibits travel internationally and are available to science centers.

Living in Cambridge was certainly stimulating, but school mostly meant reading text books and writing term papers. With a husband studying engineering and I engrossed in cultural anthropology, I came to understand Anatole France's phrase that "Even a little dog is the center of his own universe." Each of us sees and evaluates the world through our specific lens that is genetically and environmentally influenced. For years this saying was posted above my desk and to this day it influences my interactions with others.

Ron's lens was different than mine because he had a scientific, mathematical understanding of the universe. He was as immersed in the humanities as I and could talk philosophy and literature with the best of Harvard and MIT intellectuals, yet his thoughts were expressed from a perspective influenced by a knowledge of science that consistently made me curious. He took the time to simplify explanations thereby helping me understand complex principles. Ron was an excellent communicator and later in his professional life received a great many accolades and awards for being an outstanding teacher. My dynamic husband involved me in what he was doing at MIT, even asking for assistance with his master's degree experiment. I proudly held a piece of equipment until he shouted "Drop!" whereupon a device would fall, releasing a bubble that he photographed. Ron tried to capture on film the shape of the bubble as it ascended in the descending tube. I must admit that I still wonder whether the contraption we were using was totally accurate because of the shock wave cause by the drop, but his efforts were approved by his thesis committee and that was what counted. Bottom line: Ron made me want to understand how things work.

Upon receiving his Master of Science degree, Ron applied

for several positions abroad, one for advanced study in England and the second to teach in Nigeria. At the time, I was enrolled in every anthropology course that Boston University had to offer and envisioned my future as being the next Margaret Mead. Lagos became our destination, and I was thrilled that I would be able to accompany him while I pursued my personal research into Africa, with emphasis on Nigeria's rich culture. All things African were interesting to me.

While waiting to get bureaucratic approval we invited Ken, a Ghanaian student, to our house for dinner where we honored him by serving Zaza insects. Black ants mounded in a gooey black molasses-type sauce was his favorite dish but produced looks of disbelief by others at the table who refused even a tiny taste. We learned how marriages were arranged in his home-town when Hannah, his bride-to-be, was sent to Cambridge in order to produce an offspring with him. Ken once asked me, "What does it mean to be in love? Parents know their children best and will make the right decision in selecting a partner. Love is something that will grow over many years." In Ken and Hannah's case, I came to believe that perhaps their parents did do the right thing. They certainly appeared to be compatible and made a handsome couple.

Ken made me aware of a racial idiosyncrasy among black people in the United States. He had light brown skin since he was of Dutch and African ancestry. Ghana was a country he claimed was color blind to shades of brown. In the U.S. he was surprised to find black and white Americans alike practiced a type of caste system that put darker skinned people at the bottom of the scale. This color bias disturbed him greatly. His concern remained with me when I later worked with minority populations of many shades.

You might ask why I relate this story in a book about museums. As a woman growing up in a white neighborhood with black maids I needed to go through a transition in order to be an effective communicator to people of color. Lessons learned are cumulative. As I became more interested in civil rights I developed educational programs in minority areas of town, and became more inclusive in my business and personal life. I give credence to the many small instances that helped me understand people from other backgrounds. There are many rags to riches stories about individuals who overcome their past to succeed in life, but those who grow up in privilege also have to overcome ingrained lessons. Like an onion, the layers of bias and privilege must be peeled back to expose the rawness of life.

In 1960 Ron and I were ready to travel to Nigeria, having passed health exams and a series of psychological interviews in DC that proclaimed we were sane. My father was not quite as sure, for he kept sending articles about every potential disease that might be caught while in Africa. With trunk packed and passport in hand, we expected to leave early on a September morning. But the day before our scheduled flight we received a call from headquarters informing us the trip was delayed because of a civil unrest in Nigeria. We were devastated and most discouraged by the thought of having to return to the Boston area to resume our lives as students. We did not know how long it would take for the civil upheaval to end but what we heard from the State Department was not encouraging so return to our home universities seemed inevitable.

A search for housing had to start immediately since most student rentals were already confirmed. On arrival in Massachusetts we trudged through various neighborhoods with little success. One real estate agent actually had the audacity to ask us to leave her office because we were Jewish. She told us to go to a section of town where all of the Jews lived. Ron was furious and hastily led me away from this insult. Such were the times in the 1960s where we were routinely branded. It wasn't until I lived abroad and was identified as an American first that I realized how often I had been labeled because of my religion. At times it felt like I was wearing a yellow star on my clothes as the Jews did in Nazi Germany.

After a discouraging day of searching, Ron and I took a break from apartment hunting to visit the Boston Museum of Fine Arts. Our hearts were just not into settling into the old college routine. Ron had previously declined a fellowship to study for an advanced degree in engineering at the University of London. As we talked in the halls of the art museum we began to wonder if he could possibly get his grant to England reinstated. It was a long shot but we stopped at a pay phone booth to call Washington. Much to our great astonishment the voice on the other side of the line immediately agreed and a few days later our trunks were redirected to a Hyde Park address. Ron went to study Operations Research at the University of London while I, as my brother crassly put it, baked a baby in my oven.

Operations research applies the scientific method to management and is part of the field of systems engineering. Ron drew me into his London University studies through assignments that we would do together such as, "What is the fastest and most efficient way to make a bed?" The goal was to use the fewest movements possible to complete the task. We counted each step and tuck as we timed our bed-making efficiency. Some of the methods he demonstrated are still embedded in my psyche for whenever setting the table or making a big dinner, I think, "How do I move efficiently to preserve energy?" It is a little game to play in my mind.

Waiting for my April due date to arrive offered me a chance to explore the great city of London—and, of course, to visit all of its museums. My favorite was the Natural History Museum, which was located near our flat. The British Museum and the Tate came in right behind. With an expanding belly, visits to my Harley Street physician increased. It was quite an experience to sit in a tiny waiting room until the butler told me it was my turn to enter the lift, which took me to the doctor's huge antique-filled living room that served as an office. Her small carved desk was off in one corner of the room. I was invited to sit in an elegant upholstered chair to explain how I was feeling before being directed for examination in a more sterile closet-size room. It was almost as if the doctor was apologetic for having to invade my privacy with her prodding fingers.

Our first child was born with English-style care in Queen Charlotte's Hospital in London. With Great Britain's public health system all first-time mothers went to hospital. Those who had previously experienced childbirth were guided by a midwife who came to the couple's home to oversee subsequent births. Approximately one month before the due date, a sterile drum filled with all of the necessary materials would arrive. Once the mother was in labor, a midwife was called to assist and an ambulance notified in case there was a problem. This birth-at-home arrangement meant that labor wards were not overly crowded.

Queen Charlotte's nursery had a policy where nurses and patients alike could wheel the newborns out to mothers for feedings before returning them to a sound-proof room during crying spells. Between contractions during my first long labor I was taken into the nursery as a way of giving me encouragement. Eventually Ryan slithered into the world with a mighty cry emanating from his red old-man face. If you ever noticed the adoring gaze of movie actors portraying new parents, you know what Ron and I looked like as well.

Once home, Ryan traveled in style on his daily walks through Hyde Park, resting in a huge wheeled English perambulator that I proudly pushed through the blossoming spring pathways. I was so proud of the bundle I had produced even though he was covered in a rash that made him look like a pickled tomato. It took some time to realize that my son was allergic to the hand-knit wool sweaters and hats that covered his body.

These idyllic spring and summer days could not last forever and after a year, with teary good-byes, we returned to Cambridge where Ron entered the doctoral program in engineering at MIT and I spent the next two years completing my undergraduate degree. I graduated with honors a year after giving birth to our second child, Kara. Proof of graduation is a cherished photo showing two smiling toddlers pulling my robe as I stand wearing mortar cap and gown.

The environment was turbulent in Cambridge following our return from England. Cuba was in the news and Cold War paranoia was in full swing. I kept hearing about people who were building bomb shelters in their back yards. Unfortunately, I too got caught up in the mass hysteria and was quite afraid, believing that if the United States was attacked, Boston, with so much intellectual power, would be among the first places to be bombed. I begged my husband to move out of the city and into the country.

As though the Cold War was not enough to ignite concern, the civil rights movement entered its infancy. Dr. Martin Luther King Jr. had attended my alma mater, Boston University, between 1951 and 1955. He sought his doctorate under the influence of Howard Thurman dean of the university's Marsh Chapel. Thurman, who had visited Mohandas Gandhi in India. was inspired by his peaceful approach to protest. The teacher shared his thoughts with his student. King's ideals of a non-violent movement were developed over many sessions with Dean Thurman.

Several of my friends were ready to do their part for the civil rights cause by going on Freedom rides into Alabama. They chided my husband and me for not being more involved. But with our young family and study obligations, traveling south to be submitted to violence was not a trip we choose to make, though we certainly supported equal rights for all. In those days, even changing one's language made a statement, and when most people were still calling African Americans Negroes, we were clear in our choice of the word black. The transition, though, was not smooth. When I visited my mother's home and spoke to her maid about the positive changes affecting black communities, instead of being pleased, as I expected, she shouted at me, grabbed my arm to bring me closer to her, and said, "Look at my skin. Is that black?" The confrontation left me confused and not knowing the proper form of address.

Word usage continues to change over time. Taking people of color (another vernacular sometimes used today) to our summer home turned out to be wrought with tension. Grandma was especially horrified that I would bring "Negroes" as she continued to call them, who weren't hired help, into the house. My grandparents were overtly gracious to my visiting companions but behind their backs they directed a stream of derogatory remarks to me for having a racially mixed group of acquaintances. The Sidney Poitier movie *Guess Who's Coming to Dinner* expressed the era well.

Do turbulent changes come in threes? In addition to the Cold War and the civil rights movement, the Vietnam War was just starting to escalate. I came to know it through stateside protests in public parks. Out of curiosity and to show support, one evening Ron and I went to the Boston Commons to participate in a rally that we expected to be filled with the excitement of protest singing and speeches The moment we arrived, however, we were greeted by police vans filled with ferocious-looking dogs. When the animals were released to chase the crowd we were quite terrified and ran with the others as the mob ran for safety. Even today I can feel the terror that gripped me as dogs nipped at my feet and our fear of going to jail grew. Ron was furious with me for having insisted we go to the rally.

The greatest single horror during that time occurred in 1963 when President Kennedy was shot. I did not believe my neighbor when she approached me in the apartment building hallway to relate the news. Certainly she had to be joking. As intellectuals we were against having a TV, so we decided to rent one in order to watch the funeral. For days we were mesmerized by the spectacle, unable to do anything else but watch the event and the reruns of it. A president being shot is devastating to anyone who believes in the tenants of democracy.

And still daily life went on. Within weeks of graduating from college I was given a wonderful opportunity to work at the Boston Children's Museum. It was a dream job with responsibilities for making cultural education kits that would be loaned to schools. Perfect... yes? My response: no. Fear of being judged by my peers seized me during that fateful telephone call when I was offered the job. I was pleased to discover I was employable, yet came up with every excuse I could think of not to work in an intellectual environment. Most of all I was afraid of having a boss. Though constrained by children, my days at home gave me a great deal of independence. That fumble precipitated years of paralysis: though willing to volunteer for all sorts of parent-school and community activities I was unable to join the work force. Once we purchased a mini-van, I became one of the thousands of moms committed solely to driving children to their various events.

Several years later I returned to university for a master's degree in psychology. While a student, a psychologist asked me if I was afraid to succeed and with that question a key to my fears turned. However, in those early years of motherhood, I did not have a lot of time to think about psychology or a career path. Young mothers are always busy, but in the days before disposable diapers they were especially so. During the following seven years, waking moments were filled with baby talk, walks to the park, swings, bedtime stories, and of course visits to museums.

After Ron received his doctorate along with a three-year faculty position at MIT our family moved from Cambridge to Lexington. The small two-story colonial house we purchased for all of $25,000 had an above-ground swimming pool in the backyard. On a hot summer's day I loved watching Ron get a running start to sail over its four-foot wall to dive perfectly into the middle. The house had four bedrooms and a basement playroom that I wallpapered with newspapers and curious tomb stone rubbings that I made while visiting the many old cemeteries of the area. Unbeknownst to me, the uneven walls became my first training ground for a future as an exhibit developer.

While in Lexington, I volunteered to be part of a mental health program designed to help committed patients reenter the world. Because of new medicines controlling psychotic behavior, a group of homemakers spent one day a week learning about psychiatric behaviors in preparation for receiving a patient to reintroduce to society. Entering a locked floor of a state institution was a shocking, eye-opening experience. There was a woman I observed who turned in circles for hours while talking to the walls. A few inmates were tied to chairs while others walked around aimless and glassy eyed. One disturbed patient approached me from behind and put her hands around my neck, attempting to strangle me. It became obvious to the volunteers that most of the clients we were assigned to help had severe problems and did not belong living on their own.

First Nixon and then Reagan promoted a policy of emptying the beds of mental hospitals. They told the public that drugs would free inmates to live a better life. According to an article written in 2013 by Dr. E. Fuller Torrey for American Psychosis, the two presidents associated mental illness with communism. Dr. Torrey, presently at the Stanley Medical Research Institute, is an expert on schizophrenia and bipolar disease, and is now trying to right this wrong by working to eliminate barriers to the mentally ill. The policy our country has been following for the past forty years in treating severe mental illness has led to an increase in homelessness and a great many unfortunate people being wrongly locked in prisons. My experience in the Lexington hospital provided an impetus to return to school for a career in mental health. I now see that this choice also provided excellent training for managing the staffs of my future museums and inspiration for exhibition ideas. Psychology is a subject of great public interest and many museums have well attended exhibitions about the brain, mental health and treatments.

Did I believe that being a volunteer, housewife and raising children was worthwhile? Yes, absolutely and without a doubt I knew that parenting was my most important job. As a child playing with dolls I imagined myself becoming a mother and when that wish became reality I spent a great deal of time reading parenting magazines and books about educating young children. I loved my kids and was determined that their childhood would be stellar. I planned to protect and guide them to the ends of the earth and back . . . forever and ever. However, a part of me also felt like a coward because I had given up on the idea of ever being tested in the workday world. As a high-energy person, I thought it reasonable to be able to encompass both lives. I became driven and wanted to do it all without considering what it would mean in terms of time, stress and emotional balance.

Looking back, it is easy to see that part of the reason I was so ambitious was because of Mom, a smart alluring woman with a great deal of creative energy. She was also a woman's lib wannabe. To my embarrassment, she was the one who attracted whistles from a train full of sailors while we were on a trip to New York to look at wedding dresses for me.

Mom was a reluctant stay-at-home woman who lived in suburbia where a small group of homemakers in her neighborhood had college degrees. Unfortunately, Grandpa had run out of money by the time she graduated high school so college was not an option as it had been for her older sister. Though she read broadly in order to converse intelligently with her friends she felt inadequate and had a burning desire to receive an advanced education. Her cries came to a crescendo as she begged my physician father to let her attend a local college the same year I started my studies in Boston. Dad's response was that a woman belonged at home taking care of her children and husband. Mom had no independent income in this era before women's rights and had no idea of how to proceed with her dream.

Playing mahjong with neighbors and volunteering were fine activities for a doctor's wife so she kept busy with social engagements. Challenging herself, she learned braille and became an aide, copying papers at the Philadelphia School for the Blind. She and my aunt even opened a Christmas store in the basement of our home where monogrammed boxes and lingerie bags were sold to friends, with proceeds going to causes for the blind. Dad was proud of his volunteer wife but I saw Mom as chattel, a mind wasted, a soul in crisis and I became determined not to be stuck and ever wholly dependent on a man. I wanted to make a difference in the world and needed to travel on my own path. No man, I thought, should have that much say over his wife's future and I was more determined than ever to eventually forge my own career. But my first priority was to my family.

Raising well-adjusted children is a powerful contribution to society, and most of my attention in my late twenties and early thirties was to learning how to do this well. I read the latest psychology and education books. I became enthralled with ideas coming from England promoting the free school movement which was developed at a school where children were allowed to set the pace of their own education. *Summerhill*, written by the school's founder A.S. Neill was my first introduction to this open-ended way of teaching and it made a great deal of sense to me.

Montessori also captured my imagination, leading Ron and me to become founders of the Cambridge Montessori School (all five of my children attended Montessori pre-schools). When we moved I was asked to serve on the board of directors at the Lexington Montessori School. In our community Montessori education concluded with kindergarten after which the public school system took over. My children's education did not end when they returned home from school though, for I kept them busy with a litany of projects. Afternoons were often spent visiting museums, taking nature hikes or finger painting in the kitchen. My favorite activity on a sunny day was to give the kids brushes and a bucket of water and instruct them to paint the house. Always on the go, we found each day was a learning adventure.

In the living room of our Lexington home, Ron installed a pole with attached clips to be dubbed the Music Tree. It held instruments that small hands could easily grab, such as recorders, tambourines, maracas, drums and bells. With noise-makers in our hands I led my kids and their friends on parades and dances around the house while they clanged rhythmically to folk, pop and classical recordings. Ron was a long-haired, bearded guitar player as well as a professor who engaged us in word and number games and group singing during evenings at home, around campfires and on long Sunday drives. The two of us were determined to be super-parents and we worked at it. Nightly, we read to our children and as they learned their letters, we listened to them read to us. Our goal was to ensure that each child was an accomplished reader before first grade. Ron and I knew the *Cat in the Hat* and *Hop on Pop* by heart.

Ever since 1964 when Robert Rosenthal, a Harvard professor, did an experiment at a South San Francisco elementary school, there have been studies demonstrating that a teacher's expectations can influence how students perform. An article that drove my ambition as an "education mom" claimed that if your child's first grade teacher recognized he or she as more advanced than other entering classmates, the teacher would treat your child in a way that always called for personal best. The clipping said that given a positive beginning, the label of being intelligent would stay with your child throughout his or her school days, being passed on from grade to grade. Teachers spend more time answering questions, giving feedback and sharing approvals to students they expect to succeed. I wanted to be sure that my kids had that advantage, and were viewed as exceptionally talented from the onset.

Life in Lexington was full of activity, but much changed for me when Ron was notified that MIT would not extend his teaching position. In order to avoid becoming an inbred institution former graduates were rarely given a tenure position. The great hunt for a new job was initiated. Eventually Ron was offered an excellent faculty position at Michigan State University's College of Engineering. I was less than pleased. The Midwest was not my idea of an improvement over my New England lifestyle but I went dutifully, though kicking and screaming all of the way to Okemos, a bedroom community adjacent to East Lansing, Michigan. The move put a crack in our marriage that widened over the years. For the first time I realized that my life was not mine to determine.

There were some redeeming features to our new community that I reluctantly acknowledged. We were able to purchase a much larger house at a more reasonable cost than those for sale in Lexington. Our neighborhood was safe and neighbors were certainly welcoming. My older children had graduated from preschool and could easily walk to the local elementary school. The younger ones were enrolled in Montessori classes not far from home. Strangers actually smiled when passing by on street corners, and automobiles waited patiently for pedestrians to cross. There was quite a bit of socializing in our suburban community of Tacoma Hills, though there was not a bump of a hill in sight. Each Halloween while the mothers stayed home to dole out candy, the fathers would walk in clusters, chatting and nipping from flasks while following their children trick-or-treating house to house. It was that kind of neighborhood.

The community surprised me with its warmth and spirit. University acquaintances were creative academics who appeared satisfied with their Midwest campus lives. They reached out to our family and we developed many close friendships. But it was bitterly cold. I thought Massachusetts had chilly winters, but it did not come near to having the number of below -freezing days of a Michigan winter. On the positive side, it did mean that the subdivision's pond froze over each December, making it an ideal skating rink for local hockey games. On the negative side I saw the Lansing community as a cultural wasteland. Michigan State University's scanty museum and the small historical museum near the state capital were not very exciting places to visit with rowdy children.

Though I had been a regular attendee of museums and visitor centers while living on the East Coast I had never been a creator of one. My young children kept me close to home and I had a growing unease about my lack of intellectual stimulation. It was this sheltered life that thrust me into an adventure that would last until old age. I am not sure that it ever would have happened if I had not perceived a need for my own children.

Finding a Home and Sources of Support

Finding a permanent facility became my paramount concern. Assembling displays in the school lunchroom, removing them over the noon hour, and repositioning them for afternoon visits was not only tedious but damaging to the exhibits. We were going nowhere and I was not sure how to get out of the dismal situation. There was not enough money in our coffers to pay a deposit plus six months' rent, so we began to search for a property owner willing to take a risk on a group of community do-gooders. We also thought it was better to have a short-term lease since, we were not sure about the future. After scouting the streets of Lansing we located a 15,000 square foot warehouse in an industrial park on the edge of the city and asked the landlord if he would work with us. Alan Suits, a civic minded man who was willing to forgo the deposit, charged a reasonable rental fee, and let us occupy the facility on a yearly basis.

In April 1973, our meager exhibits were quickly packed, stuffed into minivans and driven through the warehouse's overhead doors, arriving in what to us was a cavernous building. Barely occupying 1,000 square feet of space with our sparse supplies, we wondered how we were going to turn this expanse into a museum in just five months. Though the task seemed monumental, not a negative word was heard. None of us stopped to consider if what we had planned was possible—for by then we totally believed in our ability to prosper.

Marilynne's Lesson #7: If you are on a roll, go for it and do not look back.

Needing a staff, I applied for funds from CETA (Comprehensive Employment and Training Act), a 1973 jobs program. This Nixon-era program provided workers for public service jobs, helping jumpstart many wonderful community projects. Though CETA came under criticism from conservatives as being a WPA type works program, it did support positions in the arts, and without this intervention Impression 5 would not have had the personnel to manage the fledgling organization. In short time we could boast of an educator, bookkeeper, designer, gift shop manager, and public relations specialist, all hired with CETA funds for a three year period.

Marilynne's Lesson #8: Everyone wants to boss someone else.

I was elated to be getting financial assistance but also astonished when within the first week of employment each new hire privately came into my office to tell of his or her need for an assistant. Each employee carefully explained that the job was much too considerable for one individual to accomplish: therefore an assistant was needed. After managing the museum for over a year without paid help I was absolutely astounded by the audacity of their complaints. I did not know whether to laugh or cry but knew I had to toughen up. It was their job to make the center grow. If they wanted additional assistance they would have to work intensely and manage volunteers as aides until there was greater financial stability. And I told them so.

To avoid bankruptcy we had to meet our five month goal. Building improvements needed to be completed before we could invite the public past the front doors. There were requirements for bathrooms to be updated and made accessible, the electrical system upgraded and a heating system expanded to compliment two lonely space heaters. A large tube was added as the least expensive way to circulate hot air across the warehouse between the noisy heaters. Shop and office area would have to be carved out of the open floor plan. We also needed auditorium and classroom areas constructed and a gift shop with ticket counter installed by the entrance. Many volunteers worked long hours into the evening in order to prepare the facility.

There are numerous ways museums raise money. Local individuals, foundations, and businesses are asked to make contributions for daily operations and larger grant requests are solicited to national corporations and foundations for exhibitions and special projects. A third course, to be discussed later, brings in dollars through community based fundraisers.

Eventually we hired a development director to coordinate local fund-raising, but even with this assistance our educators, designers and expert volunteers had to remain involved in brainstorming and writing national proposals. Though grant-giving organizations were helpful in giving hints about how to increase success rates, I quickly learned that the art of schmoozing also plays a big role. Spending the time to make yourself known, communicating face-to-face with grantors, writing thank-you notes and remembering birthdays are all part of the game. Long phone calls to government agencies in DC, personal visits to foundations, attendance at museum conventions, and participation in grant-writing workshops all helped make us more sophisticated applicants.

Our first major exhibit proposal was to the National Endowment for the Humanities to construct a touch tunnel through time. The idea was for visitors to travel through a darkened passageway that was filled floor to ceiling with objects and textures from various time periods. By feeling with their hands and feet, people would experience history much as a blind person would. We were thrilled to receive word that our grant application was funded, giving staff and volunteers a major installation to construct by opening day. Winston, a hammer-wielding entomology doctoral student, assembled the tunnel. It was a massive undertaking. Molds were made for fiberglass walls which had to be bolted together. Flooring, representative of different time periods, was installed on the walkways allowing visitors to feel cobblestone, brick, wood, and carpet. Winston and I visited antique and junk shops throughout mid-Michigan on a search for historical items that were not valuable since they would be mounted and touched. The Tunnel, when complete, was quite unique in demonstrating how the feel of fabrics, appliances and tools had changed over time.

Within a few months of opening, we received notice that another small request, this time to the National Endowment for the Arts, was funded. The display also involved the sense of touch but with a focus on art instead of history. *Guernica*, a major work by Picasso, would be translated into a three-dimensional acrylic wall hanging. The piece was envisioned as a bas relief, complete with a light bulb warming the spot in Picasso's image where the sun shines. Stepping on a mat would trigger a guided tour around around the masterpiece as it was touched.

The idea for the display had come from Rick, our exhibit designer and one-time medical illustrator. Rick had a talent for helping the blind by translating drawings and family photographs into three-dimensional relief sculptures. His sensitivity led him to volunteer with the local diabetes association where he made relief faces of loved ones for those who recently lost their eyesight. Rick's desire was to enable non-seeing people to understand and gain access to great masterpieces enjoyed by the sighted when visiting art museums. *Guernica* was going to be the first of a series of great masterpiece interpretations. It too was well received when complete but we never did pursue additional funding.

— — — — — — — — — — — — —

Marilynne's Lesson #9: Don't fool yourself, obtaining cash is never easy.

— — — — — — — — — — — — —

Because the first two prestigious grants were obtained so quickly I thought that getting exhibit money would always be easy. I certainly had a lot to learn. Receiving major grants from any of the governmental agencies, most especially from the National Science Foundation or National Institute of Health, take a great deal of research, collaboration, and time. Our entire education and exhibit staff had to become involved in fleshing out ideas and writing proposals for large projects. Crafting timelines, detailing budgets, and outlining the substance of the proposal was just the beginning. There were then compulsory sections describing the need, the proposals uniqueness, personnel requirements, community endorsements, evaluation of community impact, and local funding matches. I was good at starting the process by contributing lots of ideas but was not a great finished writer. Others on staff found it difficult to put the first words on paper but were fantastic at correcting grammar and clarifying thoughts once they saw the outline of the proposal. Team work became finely tuned in our organization. By synergistically sharing ideas, the group accomplishments were greater than what I could have achieved on my own.

Obtaining national support is especially difficult for a small institution. When George Tressel, an NSF program director, visited Lansing I pleaded with him to fund an innovative physics project. He explained that before he could provide money I had to find a way to share our project with a national audience. I quickly realized that to meet this constraint I had to partner with other organizations, allowing the display to travel and be enjoyed by greater numbers. No longer could Impression 5 only think locally. It was important to have the nation in our hearts. I embraced the notion that also released me from feeling trapped in Lansing.

The search for funding is never ending, but openings create a finite deadline for having funds in hand. In the fall of 1973, Impression 5 opened with only three visitors in attendance on that unannounced first public day. A week later we counted three hundred people moving through the doors. It took time to build attendance but eventually we were serving an average of 350 visitors a day. At times we were compelled to turn people away from our small pole-barn museum.

My older children were wonderful assistants, helping when they could by staffing the gift shop or working as guides on the exhibit floor on weekends. This museum enterprise became a family affair, and I felt happy when they were by my side, and pleased that the museum I started for their benefit had become a reality.

DEVELOPING A SCIENCE LITERATE PUBLIC
FOCUS ON GEORGE TRESSEL: THE NATIONAL SCIENCE FOUNDATION

Developing a Science Literate Public—Focus on George Tressel: The National Science Foundation

An individual who greatly influenced developing science centers was a man who survived the Great Depression to eventually direct the Informal Science Education Program at the National Science Foundation (NSF). George Tressel's encouragement and vision was widespread and his ability to fund science programs that made a difference is legendary. The story of why science centers multiplied and prospered would not be complete without sharing his tale. Once more we see the influence of childhood experiences, how World War II led to an interest in science education, and discover how one person can affect an emerging field.

George remembers his two off-beat parents fashioning a unique lifestyle during the Great Depression. Their background and involvement in the arts trained them to think imaginatively of ways to survive. His mother was the daughter of a Portuguese fisherman who migrated to the United States and ended in Newport Rhode Island. As

George

a girl, she coached her father to read and write sufficiently to pass the exam and became captain of a tug boat. She grew up to teach in a one-room schoolhouse near Washington DC and then during WWI became a secretary in the War Department.

When the war ended, she enrolled in a well-known oratory school near Philadelphia, where she met and married a veteran, a Lutheran minister's son who had enrolled in the school to cure his stammer. Together they became actors in Chatauqua, a group traveling from town to town in New York State, performing Shakespeare and reciting classics like "The Face on the Barroom Floor." After their first child, George, was born, the Tressels settled in Fort Wayne, Indiana where they tried to start a small orator school just as the Great Depression struck.

But George's family was lucky. They had just enough money saved to relocate to Chicago, where his father used his college degree to find work as a manual laborer for the Salvation Army. These were tough times. George told me, "Dad was always trying to find a better job, so when one came along sorting and loading mail into the back cockpit of WWI Jennys he took it, helping to inaugurate the start of air mail. At least our family had food on their table," he continued, "when so many did not."

George's Lesson #1: Struggle and living in poverty makes one appreciative of life.

Living creatively through the depression affected George throughout his years, making him sensitive and appreciative to the world around him. George's earliest memories are of the streets near their home being swept by the workers of the Works Progress Administration (WPA), and he has never forgotten the nearby bank, cold and dark, with its big brass handles closed by a chain and lock. The move to Chicago may have given his family a better future than they otherwise would have had: George's father took mail-order math courses from the University of Chicago, and his mother earned a degree from Loyola University while directing theater at Hull House and for various church functions.

The couple made the best of it by staying active. Mother, directing theatricals at Hull House and in the local church, while Father, the minister's son, made elaborate scenery and lighting for her religious pageants. The children were put to work, helping make costumes and scenery to cover the organ and convert the church to a theater.

George describes his parents as being "religious light." Not so his grandparents, who fought over his soul. Though he does not remember his parents ever having anything that would be called a normal social life they savored the communal aspect of the church and their children blossomed in the glow of intense, creative activities. The family managed to save enough to buy a derelict house but couldn't afford to hire anyone to complete the repairs so the kids learned to use tools, electrical wire and plumbing materials. "Being very little," he laughed, "my job was to crawl through the rafters dragging electric cable and connecting the new wiring." George claims that he and his siblings blossomed in the glow of these intense, creative activities and they developed self-reliance and self-entertainment well beyond their years. "In some ways," George said, "it was like living in my own private Exploratorium." He has good reason to draw a connection to San Francisco's science center: George would later work for the National Science Foundation at the time they were developing new and radically improved science curricula. In one of those projects, a young physicist, Frank Oppenheimer, began to develop his ideas about learning through exploring and discovery, insights that he carried along when he went to San Francisco and founded the Exploratorium. George became instrumental in saving the center . . . more on that in a bit.

George did not spend all his time assisting his parents. Perhaps partly because of his mother's teaching experience he was always precocious. He began reading as a toddler and by the time he was old enough for school he was allowed to skip ahead to the second grade though he was so small that at his desk a chalk box was placed under his feet.

He whizzed through classes and at the age of fourteen a teacher suggested that he take a test for entrance into an experimental program at the University of Chicago. The Hutchins program took gifted youngsters after their second year of high school and started them early in classic college courses, reading the Great Books, and learning from debate and discussion. Its highly structured curriculum was designed to provide a grand overview and familiarity with the world's history, literature, philosophy, art and science—an education for a renaissance man. It was a perfect background for understanding museums but socially difficult for a boy who was labeled "a brain."

Completing university in three years with a physics major, George took a job in meteorology research, where he found himself using a transmitter that was on the same frequency as an experimental TV station. George had discovered his direction. These were the very first days of television, and he quickly became hooked with its possibilities, staging programs, developing some of the early equipment, and jumping into a career making commercials and fund-raising films.

— — — — — — — — — — — —

George's Lesson #2: Following your passion and being willing to live in poverty works for a single youth.

— — — — — — — — — — — —

His exciting years as a struggling artist helped him become an independent thinker and inventive individual, but he got the message loud and clear that money was needed to start a family.

After a decade, George was hired to head a new film unit on General Electric's top-secret plane powered by a nuclear reactor. He took the job because he had a child on the way and wanted to make sure he had a steady income. But George was not used to war and guns, or the idea of an airplane being designed for World War III to carry a huge nuclear reactor over the ocean. So he resigned to join the staff of Argonne National Laboratory, and for seven years made films and television programs about peaceful nuclear energy research. In 1964 as co-director of the US film program for the Atoms for Peace Conference in Geneva, Switzerland, he built two multilingual theaters and produced some 25 films. These covered every area of peaceful nuclear research, from medicine and chemistry to power reactors summarizing the state-of-research for an interdisciplinary scientific audience. George wrote most of the scripts as well as developed new procedures for translating and projecting in four languages.

Eventually George moved on to begin a communication research unit at Battelle Memorial Institute. "These seven years were an exciting time to be involved in film and communications," George explained. "During the early days of cable TV the field was developing rapidly." Excitedly he received his first grant from a new Public Understanding of Science emphasis at the National Science Foundation, a program area he would eventually manage. With the goal of educating the average person about science, George produced a TV film, *Science in the Seventies*, that received numerous awards but, being independently made, had only a modest off-hours audience. Coming to grips with the idea that "award-winning" does not necessarily translate to "primetime" and "audience" was a lesson that George learned and remembered well.

— — — — — — — — — — — —

George's Lesson #3: Life is a puzzle to be figured out.

— — — — — — — — — — — —

About that time, H. Guyford "Guy" Stever, the director of the National Science Foundation under Presidents Nixon and Ford, gave a public talk about how uninformed the average person was about science. The public's understanding was primitive at best! Though George did not know Dr. Stever, as a grant recipient he felt comfortable responding to Guy's talk with what he describes as a snotty letter. "I told Dr. Stever that he did not know what he was talking about and that his idea of what the public should know was not the same as the public's notion. To the average person, science means medicine and how my car works, not the third law of thermodynamics!" Dr. Stever is to be commended for not only reading the letter, but by responding and inviting George to Washington to "put his money where his mouth is."

As an outspoken man his first thought was that this job would be a disaster, but when his wife said that she would be just as happy in DC as elsewhere, he accepted the challenge to establish a mission oriented NSF program that would increase the size and understanding of what Jon Miller called the "attentive science public." George decided that he was going to do this by promoting more and better science to a popular mass-audience through museums, broadcast television and publications.

Almost all of the foundation's funds were distributed through grants to universities after a peer review by experts in the particular area of research. This model of funding was fine for research but not at all helpful to a mission-oriented program that called for the production of exhibits, broadcasts and publications. After examining numerous funding models George adapted procedures from the National Institute of Health which established a rubric of standards (for example, all of his programs would be balanced, objective, and accurate) along with an advisory panel to help set policies for the new program, which would then become a standing review panel to sort and evaluate prospective projects for value and impact. This panel would always include eminent representatives from the physical and biological sciences together with outstanding representatives from broadcasting, museums, and publishing. Its members would be selected from an unquestionable elite.

Developing a panel with oversight, and a clear defensible mission were critical to the new program's success because Public Understanding Of Science (PUOS) was subject to intense political scrutiny. Following Sputnik, NSF was charged with designing new and radically improved science curricula for educating the world's best and brightest future scientists. Almost all of these new educational models focused on hands-on experience and discovery learning. They went by a variety of acronyms like PSSC, BSCS, CHEM STUDY. It was in one of these "alphabet soup" projects that a young physicist named Frank Oppenheimer began to absorb and develop his ideas about learning by exploring and discovery, insights that he carried along when he went to San Francisco and began the Exploratorium.

George informed me that "the reason for so much scrutiny was that one of these model curricula was an extrapolation to social science, and it crossed a line of extreme sensitivity. A curriculum called Man: A Course Of Study (MACOS) brought sharp religious criticism and intense political threats to the entire National Science Foundation." The directorate was told that from then on new public understanding programs were going to be watched by Congress, producing more than a little trepidation.

George's first accomplishment with NSF involved the television show NOVA. The foundation had experienced problems with its initial grant awarded to WGBH-Boston that used British producers for a new TV program that largely copied tools and investigative reporting techniques of the British BBC. Highly provocative programs were composed about defoliation in Vietnam and a fire in the Brown's Ferry nuclear power plant. Both the Air Force and the nuclear power industry were outraged, claiming the facts and science were wrong. Without science advisors to back the program developers' claims, the Foundation threatened to cut off funding. The angry producers mumbled about interference with reporting. So when George was hired, his immediate job was to find a way out of the quagmire. He told me that he basically saved *Nova* by persuading the producers that future sustained funding would be greatly dependent on their ability to assure the new PUOS standard of balance, objectivity, and accuracy be met. To do this all of their projects had to undergo the scrutiny of an advisory panel of prestigious scientists. In this way, if there was ever a question about accuracy, there were those who could back up the facts.

A second project that George "inherited" was a program to plan and organize a new Association of Science and Technology Centers (ASTC). This was partly done in response to the American Association of Museums stance that science centers were not museums because they did not have collections. Without ASTC and George's stewardship we would not know the science centers we do today. It was George who suggested that ASTC needed a combination of stable initial funding and a plan for transition to independent support. His guidance worked because since its inception ASTC and the entire science center field have grown to include affiliates throughout the world.

The principal mission of PUOS was always to impact large audiences, so public broadcasting stations and large museums with millions in attendance were most successful grant recipients. However, in order to reach even more people, George made a point of encouraging copies of exhibits to be built for other museums. At one of the early ASTC meetings he ruminated out loud that he couldn't understand why some of the smaller museums didn't get together as a co-op and make an exhibit that would circulate to reach a combined audience. Before long, museums like Impression 5 started submitting just such joint proposals, and ASTC began its traveling exhibit program.

— — — — — — — — — — — — —

George's Lesson #4: Play in the sandbox with wonderful people.

— — — — — — — — — — — — —

George remembers those days as the most demanding and creative of his life, and the people he worked with had talents that were up to the challenges he faced. There were now principles, guidelines and panels of experts in place to review proposals and make recommendations before being fine-tuned by staff who had to submit them to the so called murder board, an adversarial group of representatives from legal, legislative, PR and NSF director offices. If the grant was large the program director had to take the proposal to the National Science Board and defend it yet again. The job was a challenging for a man like George who was mission driven. When there was not enough money in his budget he had to be creative and look for matching funds from a place like the Department of Education or the Environmental Protection Agency. He was always inventive in finding ways to make important things happen.

But once more crisis struck, and this time it was totally devastating to science education. President Ronald Reagan acted decisively in an area where there was little political clout—immediately abolishing the entire Science Education Directorate within NSF. George foresaw this and responded quickly, picking the most central projects and "throwing them a lifebelt" with his last remaining funds. One of these (and among George's favorite projects) was the Exploratorium. As soon as he knew that funding was going to be cut he contacted Frank Oppenheimer to submit a request for a one-year extension of the Exploratorium's grant which the members of the review panel promptly endorsed unanimously by phone. In this way any left over money from the previous year was immediately allocated. George told me, "It was a sad, sad time and a waste of valuable contributions to the nation."

Once Reagan left office, Science Education was reassembled at NSF and George returned to be director of a renamed division known as Materials Development, Research, and Informal Science Education. Though public understanding had come of age, political waggling continued, and much of it was not to his liking. He decided to go back to being a consultant and worked with such notable organizations as the Children's Television Network and the Smithsonian.

George gets quite a kick out of a letter he received several years ago from AAM honoring him with a Centennial award. They no longer fought the notion that science centers were not museums and recognized him as one of the main people who helped build them. He commented, "I suppose if you live long enough, all things change." I speak personally when I say that George W. Tressel is a man worthy of accolades. From the depths of the Great Depression he managed to rise and become a person who had a lasting effect on education and the public's understanding of science. His words of advice to me were: "It is a wonderful life. Be able to look back and recognize just how precious it is."

At the time of this interview, George had reached the age of 88 years. Known as Tango George, he is still actively dancing his way through life. He always knew the importance of mixing mental and physical activities, having ways of reducing stress, and spending time with stimulating friends.

Building Support for the Mission

A major part of the director's job of any nonprofit organization is public speaking. Philanthropic social clubs like the
Lions and Elks, business groups such as Rotary and Kiwanis
and women's organizations would invite me to speak at their
monthly luncheons. I was pleased to be asked but not comfortable in accommodating them. I was a most nervous public
speaker and afraid of fainting at the podium. This fear was
not unfounded, because in fifth grade I did become faint and
nearly dropped to the classroom floor, setting the stage in my
mind for all future speaking engagements. As soon as a few
words left my mouth, I would have a huge adrenaline spike
that sent me dizzily to my seat. I remember someone comforting me by relating that Eleanor Roosevelt had the same
problem when she first started talking before an audience. I
reasoned that if Eleanor could overcome her handicap so could
I, but I didn't know how.

Getting over my fear required a major psychological transformation and I needed help. Luckily I lived during the right
era and was open to attending a workshop on Transcendental
Meditation™, a calming experience that helps control the invol-
untary nervous system. During the 1970s gurus flourished,

especially in university towns like East Lansing. Maharishi Mahesh Yogi (1918-2008) gained popularity by introducing a mantra based meditation technique that was adopted by many celebrities. The most famous converts were the Beatles, who were instrumental in spreading the practice in the United States and Europe.

Before attending a luncheon where I was the guest lecturer I would sit in my car for twenty minutes and meditate. When meditation is practiced regularly it does become possible to control breathing and heart rate. Eventually I was able to take deep meditative breaths up to the moment of my speech even though conversing with others. It would have been impossible for me to have developed Impression 5 if it had not been for the regular practice of TM.

Today I still continue to meditate daily. It proved to be particularly helpful in later life when scheduled for a heart operation to replace a genetically defective aortic valve. Meditation kept me calm and able to go into the operating room stress free. The practice is now widely accepted as a tool for reducing stress. The word "meditation," with its ancient Buddhist roots, carries negative images for some people. It has been renamed as a modern movement called "mindfulness." The study promotes a moment-by-moment awareness of thoughts, feelings, bodily sensations, and surrounding environment. It also involves acceptance encouraging the practitioner to pay attention to thoughts and feelings without judging them.

When I first started public speaking I had to write my speech and read from my notes, but as time went on I was able to improvise and talk more directly to the audience. It actually became an exciting challenge to watch people become engaged with the picture I was verbally painting. Being able to organize, simplify thoughts and communicate them eloquently became a worthy goal not only on the public speaking circuit but with my own staff.

My talks were primarily focused on the "why" of Impression 5. Why did we need to create an interactive institution and why should adults be concerned about education outside of the schoolroom? A great deal of tax money went to schools, so why wasn't that enough to educate our children?

When I began I often started with, "All children are not created equal. Some appear to have an easy time with life while others struggle with hidden demons in a less than tolerant society." I went on to discuss how children were being educated on each side of the economic track, and explained that the reason hands-on museums were necessary was because budget-challenged schools were unable to provide interactive learning experiences. The situation in the early 1970s was not much different than it is today.

Fortunate children benefit from attentive parents. They reside in upscale neighborhoods laced with stellar school systems. These kids are born into luxurious environments, surrounded by friends with similarly educated families. In classrooms and at home they are taught to read, to concentrate, to interpret and implement ideas, creating a skill base that will march them towards successful careers. As a result of so much loving care, these youngsters rarely miss classes, turn in their homework, play instruments in school bands, and participate in sporting events. They and their many friends float with relative ease through their school years. Positive reinforcing feedback develops within each a strong sense of self-worth. When the students do have difficulties, tutors and psychologists are employed to ease their way. Fortunate children live in a win-win situation.

Unfortunately there are less-advantaged youngsters residing in families dealing with serious issues such as alcoholism, drug abuse, poverty, racism and illness. Our country's dominant language, English, may not be theirs or their families'. It is no wonder that so many children do not graduate from high school. Teens who leave before graduation have few legal prospects for work. Opportunities for low level jobs are few and poorly paid, and among certain populations the situation has reached crisis proportions.

Disruptions are an added problem, forcing teachers to focus on the few who misbehave rather than the majority of attentive learners. During the last thirty years there has been an increased epidemic of kids being diagnosed ADD (attention deficit disorder) and ADHD (attention deficit hyperactive disorder). The number of children put on Ritalin or other stimulants remains high.

I often asked myself if an ADD diagnosis is a result of mental deficiency or a fad that gives adults a reason for using drugs to control active children (mostly boys) so they will sit still in the classroom. I wondered if the ability to focus was a matter of physical development that the child will eventually outgrow or was it a life sentence. Are ADD diagnoses increasing because most parents work and are not home as active disciplinarians, or are thirty-five students per classroom simply too many for an elementary teacher to handle? Though many questions remain to be answered, some psychologists question the prevalence of the ADD diagnosis and worry that we are raising a generation of children who will reach for drugs whenever there is a problem.

It certainly bothered me when my first-grade son was labeled as hyperactive and not focused. His wiggles were part of my motivation for developing a museum where children can learn without having to sit still for hours. I was quite concerned that this derogatory label was going to be attached to my son's record for all eternity. Many of the children I got to know with attention deficits were very bright, but their intelligence was not always appreciated because of behavior problems. When my son was administered Ritalin, he became a model classroom student, but he constantly complained that his mind was fuzzy and less clear. He loved the highs and lows of life and did not want to be mellowed out. By fourth grade he was no longer a willing participant, and we took him off the drug. He managed to get through the rest of his school years without using this chemical, though it was not always easy for family or educators.

Overworked teachers want attentive students who can focus and not cause disruptions. Energetic kids often have other ideas. Some children create trouble because it is the only way to get attention in a room of twenty-five to thirty-five students. They may be bored and not willing to do busy work for the sake of classroom order. Since they cause disruption, words of praise are seldom sent in their direction.

— — — — — — — — — — — — —

Marilynne's Lesson #10: Much of success revolves around recognition of self-worth when young.

— — — — — — — — — — — — —

When my son was in fourth grade, teachers were asked to select children to be tested for participation in a Talented and Gifted (TAG) program. My child's teacher did not believe he was bright enough and refused to submit his name. My husband and I insisted that he be tested, and yes, he was deemed intelligent and talented, receiving a top score for creativity and imagination. The teacher, who had been annoyed at having her authority questioned, was quite surprised at his results. We noticed that she treated him differently from then on, which helped our son become a more confident person.

The TAG program turned out to be an excellent alternative to regular classes, and I strongly believe it should have been the norm rather than the exception. Those working in public schools with talented students employ interactive educational approaches. Teachers permit children the wiggle time needed without expressing displeasure. TAG was another influence that strengthened my resolve to develop a museum where similar opportunities would be available for all. TAG programs operate much like hands-on museums that are organized to celebrate creativity and achievement, and I suggest that every child be exposed to this philosophy. Each participant is a winner when positive attributes are the focus of attention, and acknowledgement of accomplishments is often all that is needed to get good academic results.

Schools do exist that accommodate variety rather than homogeny in the classroom, and there are inspired educators who structure learning to reinforce student achievements instead of punishing deficiencies. Attention and behavior difficulties are understood by those like my grandson's third-grade teacher, who purchased big balls for her wiggly students to sit on at their desks. Giving credence to individual learning styles is not rocket science but just plain good practice. Unfortunately schools that are strapped for funds are often forced to teach to the middle. Public school educators do not have the same luxuries as those working with fifteen students in the classrooms of private schools.

What is a parent to do when faced with poor educational options? There is no instant solution or one path to educating children. Augmenting academic training with interactive museums is another way to address learning styles of individual students. Experimental exhibits are a complement to workbooks and computers. They accommodate active children with programs developed to reinforce the child's sense of self-worth. With a variety of experimental approaches, museum educators present invitations to learn. They hope to stimulate the child to want to know more so future study will occur after leaving the facility. When the invitation is accepted, it can lead towards a lifelong journey of discovery.

An OMSI Challenge

Why Science Centers Work

Philosophical Underpinnings of Hands-On Learning

A greeing on a philosophical approach and developing a plan for future growth provides a roadmap for decisions. It sets the core tenets of the organization and helps define the parameters of its operation. Scientific and engineering concepts appear to be complex, yet the world we live in is ruled by technological and scientific breakthroughs. Certainly, we reasoned as we created Impression 5, there should be a way to clarify scientific explanations. Since public schools were masters of textbook learning and distributing worksheets, our organization set out to do the opposite: less reading and more experimentation. I mentioned that Impression 5 started with a glass of wine and a toast to the five senses, but there are several theoretical influences that contributed to the philosophical base of Impression 5, to OMSI, and eventually to my catalog business . . . indeed to the entire science center movement.

Popular books of the 60's included *Summerhill* by A.S. Neill, *How Children Learn* by John Holt, and *Death At An Early Age* by Jonathan Kozol. These publications shook up the educational community. A.S. Neill's Summerhill School was the original alternative free school. It interested so many parents and educators because it offered a revolutionary program where students could be free from adult authority. The book was an instant success in the United States and later spread its democratic ideas to the UK and many other European countries. According to its current website, "The important freedom at Summerhill is the right to play. All lessons are optional. There is no pressure to conform to adult ideas of growing up, though the community itself has expectations of reasonable conduct from all individuals." Neill's teaching greatly influenced schools around the world as well as the hands-on museum movement. There are quite a few people, including me, who think of museums as free schools, where each participant directs his or her own education. This approach works well in conjunction with the more formal structure of the public education system.

Those starting museums during this time period were also influenced by other authors who criticized how our schools educated children. John Holt (1923–1985) became a proponent of homeschooling and a pioneer of youth rights. While teaching in Boston and Colorado he observed that children were "frightened, timid, evasive, and self-protecting." His books *How Children Fail* and *How Children Learn* ignited a firestorm of controversy and spurred other authors to write of their similar experiences. In 1977, disillusioned with working within the school system, Holt started a newsletter called *Growing without Schooling* that advocated homeschooling. He believed that "children who were provided with a rich and stimulating learning environment would learn what they are ready to learn, when they are ready to learn it."

A third and important force was author and social advocator Jonathan Kozol. Growing up in the 1940's in posh Newton, Massachusetts, an area alive with learning, he continued his studies at Harvard and Oxford University. On his return from England he taught fourth grade for the Boston public schools in the African American Roxbury neighborhood. He eventually was fired for teaching the political writing of black poet Langston Hughes. He fortunately was able to continue his insightful educational approach and secure employment as a teacher in his childhood hometown of Newton. During the civil rights movement, Kozol became increasingly involved in social justice issues and dedicated more time to writing. For more than forty years he worked in the field of social psychology with inner-city children. His early experiences were included in his book, *Death at an Early Age: The Destruction of the Hearts and Minds of Negro Children in the Boston Public Schools*, which won the National Book Award in 1967. Kozol believes in integrated public education, is against the voucher system and condemns the inequality in education between rich and poor. Fortunately, today, even though many children still go to schools in segregated communities, their city museums are integrated, with programs open to all.

Maria Montessori was an Italian early childhood educator and physician who in 1907 started a school for children of working parents called Casa dei Bambini. She believed that children develop cognitive understanding in sequence and stressed that they should be encouraged to use all of their senses from an early age, establishing a self-learning process that would be ready to take advantage of the intellect as it matures. She became a close friend of Jean Piaget who shared her interest in children's developmental stages. Most schools today incorporate Montessori type exercises in their early childhood programs.

As a Montessori parent, I was also swayed by the work of Jean Piaget (1906-1980), a Swiss developmental epistemologist who investigated childhood behavior. Epistemology is the study of the origin, nature and limits of human nature and Piaget's research led him to explore a developmental theory that would lead to better methods of educating children. He became director of the International Bureau of Education, and

71

held the strong conviction that education alone was capable of saving society. One of the parents at my son's Montessori pre-school was Seymour Papert, a man ahead of his time who talked about the role of computers in enhancing learning and creativity. For a great many years Papert collaborated with Jean Piaget, who at that time was working at the University of Geneva in Switzerland.

I attended discussions by Dr. Papert who demonstrated Piaget's conclusions to Montessori School parents. He had a marvelous way of vividly explaining theory with the assistance of volunteer children. We watched him direct a child of three and one of six to pour liquid from one pitcher to a second with a different shape. When the younger child was asked to estimate how much liquid it would take to fill the second vessel he could not do it and spilled fluid on the floor. The older child estimated accurately and stopped pouring when the pitcher was nearly full. The two children responded appropriately for their age. In a March 28, 1999, article written by Papert for the *New York Times*, he mentions the fascination people have with "children's primitive laws of physics: that things disappear when they are out of sight; that the moon and the sun follow you around; that big things float and small things sink." Those who understand brain development will not to get upset when a child acts his developmental age rather than with a maturity expected by his/her parents. As Piaget simply puts it, "Children do not act like adults."

A biologist, Piaget spent his life closely observing and recording intellectual activities in infants, children, and adolescents. He noticed that mistakes children made at different ages were quite similar, became interested in their reasoning process, and started observing how a child's mind develops. Piaget postulated that until about the age of fifteen children are not capable of adult reasoning. Though parental expectations often assume otherwise they simply are not able to do so. Through his exploration Piaget searched for a theory of childhood growth that would be understandable to adults.

As a philosopher he was interested in the theory of knowledge and explored an area of epistemological relativism which simply means that there are many ways of knowing, and alternative paths to problem solving. Understanding Piaget's stages of cognitive development helps explain the reasoning used when developing exhibits in science and children's museums. The following paragraphs simplify the distinct childhood stages.

The **sensory motor period** from 0-24 months is when knowledge of the world is limited. During those early months children move rapidly from simple reflex activity such as sucking and grasping to some understanding of symbols and learning simple problem-solving abilities. Language is developing by the end of this stage. Physically children move from crawling, to standing and walking thus experiencing some of the environment around them. Think about it? Imagine the new vistas that open to a toddler who can walk freely. Scribbling with crayons, pointing, turning pages in a book, pushing, pulling, dumping things and rolling balls also become possible. By 24 months the child can feed himself with a spoon, enjoy riding small-wheeled riding toys and thankfully starts to control bowel and bladder. By the age of two a child can choose between two objects, but has trouble sharing, is shy with strangers, and gets angry easily. When I stop to consider the growth from infant in arms to mobile toddler it never ceases to amaze me.

The **pre-operational phase** from 2-4 years initiates a period of increased verbalization. Many parents look forward to this stage, but they have to be ready for the constant question, "Why?" No longer can you ignore your silent child as you go about your daily duties. You will find your child's speech to be quite egocentric and shouldn't be surprised at hearing the word "mine" throughout the day. Motor play becomes more complex between 2 and 4 years. As a child moves into the later part of this phase he or she can throw and kick a ball, draw circles and squares, dress himself and even copy letters. He or she can talk in intelligible sentences, remember and tell parts of a story, cooperate with children and engage in fantasy play. The four-year-old child realizes that there are ways to solve problems.

Between 4-7 years the youngster enters a more **intuitive phase**. Speech becomes developed and language is more social and less egocentric. In the early part of this phase the child has an intuitive grasp of logical concepts though is more likely to focus on one aspect of an object while ignoring others. Ideas and concepts may be formed that are crude and often irreversible. Between ages 4-7 a child finds magic easy to believe in, not grasping reality well. It is the time when a lot of parents try to keep the Santa Claus myth alive as long as possible. Over the three years of this stage, judgment is at first dominated by perceptions, but later the child becomes more adapted to reasoning. A seven year old can tell time, do simple reading and writing, and demonstrate a longer attention span than his younger sibling. Morally the child at first is dependent on adults imposing the dos and don'ts in daily life but slowly over the few years a concept of right and wrong becomes internalized. Cooperation with other children is still not easy though friends are becoming increasingly important. Empathy is growing, which helps in the socialization process. Independence is of great value. Have you heard, "I can do it, Mommy!" in your house? A child at seven loves active play, can do somersaults, learn to swim and is very ashamed of his or her mistakes.

The period of **concrete operations** goes from 7-11 years. It is characterized by more organized and logical thought with the ability to perform a multitude of classification tasks. Objects can be put in a logical sequence, thinking is less egocentric and the child becomes capable of concrete problem-solving.

Unlike objects can be sorted into logical groups, for instance, by color or by shape. Children at this age begin to understand the categories of labels such as color, animal or number. Put all the prime numbers together says the teacher of an eleven year old. As he or she ages, changing hormones begin to affect the child and it is not unusual to discover emotional changes associated with the start of puberty. Eleven-year-olds are very hard on themselves and sensitive to criticism. Popularity and prestige are increasingly important as is faddishness.

The last category in Piaget's theory of cognitive development is the **formal operational stage**, which goes from 14 years to about 25. This is the time when thinking involves abstractions and intelligence is displayed through logical use of symbols. These older children understand more abstract propositions; can formulate hypotheses and have the ability to project various outcomes. As more formal logical systems are acquired, algebraic formulas are understood along with other philosophical abstract ideas. If-then scenarios are analyzed but these youth can also reason contrary to fact. For instance, if given the statement "what would happen if snow were black?" they can respond by developing interesting scenarios.

In designing exhibits and educational programs it is necessary to explore the desired outcome by taking into account the developmental stage of any child. At Impression 5 and OMSI, we implemented this knowledge by designing what we called side-by-side exhibits. If we were exploring a theme like optics, we would build an exhibit that appealed to both a four-year old and fourteen-year-old. In the *Museum Tour Catalog*, we also presented different toys and learning material to appeal to various developmental stages. There was no such thought as one size fits all.

Piaget's theories, though profound, do not tell the entire story of human development incorporated by museums. Another component comes from the work of Harvard educator

Howard Gardner. In his 1983 book *Frames of Mind*, Gardner postulated that there are seven different types of intelligence. His theory suggests that knowledge comes through **linguistics**, the effective use of language and words; **logical-mathematical** ability to calculate, experiment, and solve problems; **visual-spatial** awareness of the surrounding environment; **musical thinking** demonstrating a sensitivity to rhythm and sound; **bodily-kinesthetic** use of the body to solve problems or make things; **interpersonal** understanding of other individuals; and **intrapersonal** understanding of the self. **Naturalistic intelligence** was added later to include those who are ecologically sensitive to the world and its environment.

How does an understanding of Gardner's hypothesis influence education? A visual-spatial individual might be introduced to a subject of study through imagery rather than words. This type of intelligence is used by those who like to draw, read maps and do jigsaw puzzles. The person might daydream, which helps in the creation of videos, paintings and other creative pursuits. Visually evolved people often choose architecture, design or interior decoration as a career choice. A linguistic person differs in that she or he is more likely to think in words and is best taught by reading and speaking with others. These individuals enjoy computers, playing games, going to lectures, and watching multimedia presentations.

Most people are a combination of these eight intelligences but tend to favor one over another. Gardner suggests that learning would be much more successful if students were presented information in a variety of ways. School systems are challenged because it is difficult to accommodate individual learning styles when class sizes are large.

In the early 1990's Gardner wrote an article for *Education Week* titled "Making Schools More Like Museums." In this article, he expanded on thoughts from his book *The Unschooled Mind: How Children Think and How Schools Should Teach.* Gardner said that "schools have become increasingly anachronistic, while museums have retained the potential to engage students, to teach them, to stimulate their understanding, and, most important, to help them assume responsibility for their own future learning." He went on to say that youngsters are living in a time of unparalleled excitement. Even poor children are exposed to a barrage of media and technologies. Science museums and children's museums with their interactive exhibitions and activities are "role models drawn precisely from domains that do engage youngsters." Gardner proposed using the atmosphere and experience of the museum combined with apprenticeship programs that provide more in-depth opportunities to fuse skills and concepts.

Philosophy Becomes Practice

In both OMSI and Impression 5 we took Piaget's ages and stages of development, overlaid Gardner's theory of how people learn and used a Montessori approach to designing a self-learning environment. Displays were made to blend learning approaches that accommodated the various intelligence styles of our visitors. Our merged philosophy created an ongoing challenge because of financial and space constraints, but we incorporated these ideas as best we could. For instance, earlier I mentioned constructing a 3-D representation of Picasso's *Guernica*. In order to present information to an audience broader than just the tactile learner, the display also included a full color picture of *Guernica* and a sound track to explain Picasso's intention.

In addition to understanding philosophical approaches to learning, subject matter has to be shown in a way that will not be confusing. We organized Impression 5 around the senses, starting with the individual and his or her own body which is the way most of us get to know the world, and moving out to encompass invention and technology. The area around the sense of sight, for example, explained basics such as how the eyes and brain work to help us see. A large walk-in pinhole camera demonstrated how the image is inverted on the back wall just as on the retina of our eyes. Take-apart model eyes were put on display tables, dissected cow's eyes were used in demonstrations and visitors could test their own vision by using charts for color blindness and a machine like the ones used for getting your driver's license renewed. Reaching out further from the body, physics exhibits played with light, color, and optics. Magnifying glasses were provided for young children, and telescopes and microscopes included for older visitors. Technology was incorporated in demonstrations with lasers and in displays showing holographic imagery. Use of the senses as an organization scheme gave us a platform with limitless possibilities.

OMSI had a different approach that was more subject matter driven. There were halls for engineering, health, early childhood, natural history, and changing exhibitions. Many labs were installed to give visitors ample opportunity to experiment directly using scientific equipment. Visitors could watch dinosaur bones being excavated from their plaster casts, play with tide water tables, mix chemicals, and work with electricity in various ways. The goal was to eliminate plastic walls that disconnect the participant from the experiment at hand.

SCIENCE THROUGH EXPERIMENTATION
FOCUS ON FRANK OPPENHEIMER: THE EXPLORATORIUM

Science Through Experimentation—Focus on Frank Oppenheimer: The Exploratorium

There is one other philosophy that needs to be explained and now is a good time to do so. A nuclear scientist turned educator greatly influenced the way science centers operated as places that teach science through experimentation. Following is the story of the life and contribution of Frank Oppenheimer, founder of the Exploratorium in San Francisco, California.

Frank Oppenheimer (1912–1985) stands out as the individual who, in my opinion, has had the greatest influence on the modern science center movement. I encourage you to read *Something Incredibly Wonderful Happens: Frank Oppenheimer and the World He Made Up* by K.C.Cole for a full description of Oppenheimer's life. Here I present a synopsis of the life of this man who went from atomic physicist and communist sympathizer to innovative educator to museum founder.

Frank with Older Brother Robert

I first met Frank Oppenheimer during the summer of 1972, shortly after he opened the Exploratorium, when my husband and I, along with four of our children, went to Stanford University, my husband to work at the university and I to study more science centers. Impression 5 had been incorporated earlier that spring and I was interested in visiting as many science museums as possible. My cofounder, Dee, happened to be in California that same summer so we arranged to meet with Oppenheimer. During our first face-to-face conversation he squatted on a chair focused intensely on Dee and me standing in front of him. He resembled a frog on a lily pad the way he was gingerly perched in order to converse at eye level. The three of us animatedly discussed our two fledgling science museums and I shared how difficult it was to proceed because I had no credibility. He told me that he, on the other hand, had lots of credibility but it was still hard raising money for his unusual venture.

As a well-known scientist and educator he certainly excelled intellectually, but I was thankful that he also had practical know-how because when leaving the building, I saw that my keys were locked inside the car. Frank gallantly came to the rescue to release the lock so that two women with five children could return home.

Frank Oppenheimer grew up in New York City the son of wealthy parents, and as a child studied painting and also flute to the point where he considered making a career as a flautist. He had many other interests and would often be found taking apart motors, alarm clocks and other "junk" that his older brother Robert was fond of giving him. Enrolled in New York's Ethical Culture School, Frank was greatly influenced by his seventh grade science teacher; soon science started to tip the balance away from music.

As a child of privilege he spent summers on Long Island at the family's waterfront estate, and was exposed to Oppenheimer dinner parties, lively affairs with animated discussions about the arts and politics. Several trips to Europe rounded out his education, but also exposed him to some of the horrors of an occupying army. At that time French troops were still occupying the German Rhineland.

Between 1930 and 1933, a great deal was happening in physics, and after receiving his bachelor's degree in nuclear physics from Johns Hopkins, Frank decided not to go directly to graduate school but instead accepted a position in the Cavendish Laboratory in Cambridge England. This appointment gave him access to many of the important scientists of the day. By 1935 the young scientist was working with nuclear particle counters at the Institute of Arcetri in Florence. Not content only to work, he spent many of his European days exploring the great art galleries of Italy and France. His integration of art and science would remain throughout his life.

Feeling the growing menace of war throughout Europe, Frank decided to return to the United States to complete his PhD at the California Institute of Technology. Political unrest was at its height when he met Jackie, his future wife, and also a member of the Young Communist League. Soon after they married in 1936, Frank decided that his sentiments were similar to hers and he too joined the Communist Party. At the time it seemed like the right thing for any socially concerned, idealistic young person to do, although his brother Robert urged him otherwise. It wasn't long before Frank realized that he was not going to make a good communist, so he and his wife resigned from the party in 1940.

In 1941, he obtained a position as a particle physicist at the University of California Radiation Laboratory under the direction of Ernest Lawrence, inventor of the cyclotron. Much of the work was dangerous, dealing with radioactive particles. Shortly after he started at the lab Japan attacked Pearl Harbor and Roosevelt initiated the Manhattan project, giving Frank's brother Robert, who would rise to fame as a renowned physicist, the challenge of secretly devising a nuclear weapon. Frank meanwhile moved to Oak Ridge, Tennessee to participate in a project dedicated to separating uranium isotopes. Later, both brothers would land at Los Alamos, where they observed the test for the first atomic bomb. According to K. C. Cole, they toasted the bomb's success saying, "No more wars!"

After the war Frank returned to Berkeley to help develop the linear accelerator. He left in 1947 for the University of Minnesota to engage in research leading to the discovery of heavy cosmic ray nuclei. As time passed, Frank continued to be politically engaged and along with other scientists became increasingly fearful of atomic physics being controlled by the military. He worried about secrecy and control of information by a war machine that could be dangerous.

Frank's career hit a sudden obstacle when he and Jackie were brought before the House Un-American Activities Committee. The McCarthy hearings resulted in his being blackballed from the work he loved. Asked to leave his university position he fortunately had enough family money to escape to Colorado where he bought a cattle ranch. Days on the ranch were lonely and long for the couple and their children, Michael and Judy. Life was not easy, and the family learned a lot about how farmers struggle at the level of subsistence. Though the children attended a one room school house they were pulled into a great many engineering and biological projects just by working the ranch. During the ten years that Frank and Jackie spent in Colorado raising cattle, Frank's emotions were explosive. To make ends meet he had to sell off one of his Van Gogh paintings, a difficult loss. To make matters worse his relationship with his brother Robert became strained, and his great friendship with Ernest Lawrence ended.

Frank was liked by his neighbors because of his work ethic and willingness to become involved in local farming issues.

He volunteered to teach kids at a 4 H club, and when there was a vacancy at Pagosa Springs High School, after taking distance courses to get teaching credentials, he was permitted to teach general sciences. To keep his students' attention he had to come up with creative experiments to overcome classroom apathy. He discovered that if he could get his students involved in construction and experimentation their inquisitiveness would increase exponentially. Suddenly the students at the school began winning science fairs and an increasing number of them went on to college. It was during his time teaching high school that Frank started developing what would eventually be the driving philosophy of the Exploratorium, one that encouraged active exploration and tinkering.

In 1957 when the red scare lessened and his success as an educator was noted, Frank was given a position as a professor at the University of Colorado in Boulder. Still, his communist background interfered with his obtaining tenure. It was not until 1961 that he was made a full professor at the university where he became increasingly interested in pedagogical improvements to science education.

The Soviet launch of Sputnik in 1957 was a wake-up call for the nation, and science education became a national priority. The National Science Foundation actively promoted new science curricula and gave Frank the resources to expand on the experimental curriculum he had developed at Boulder. The result was a Library of Experiments comprising nearly one hundred activities that could be used when teaching high school and college science classes. A Guggenheim fellowship brought Frank back to Europe in 1965, giving him an opportunity to study the history of physics in Europe. It was during this stay that Frank was introduced to European science museums and was inspired to develop a museum in the United States. Upon returning home he gave a speech at a Smithsonian sponsored conference where he promoted the need for science museums throughout the United States that would encourage people to actively experiment with phenomena and not just focus on historical objects. Having verbalized his philosophy, Frank became willing to change his career and begin anew.

It was 1969 when Frank Oppenheimer decided to move to San Francisco to establish the Exploratorium, where he served as director until his death in 1985. He articulated the rationale for the place in an early document that drew parallels between science and art through the workings of human perception. Frank wanted his center to be accessible to everyone, a place where visitors could experiment, experience failure, and be given the opportunity to try once more. What Frank developed became the most influential model for science and children's museums throughout the world.

What I saw during my first visit to the Exploratorium in 1972 was a cavernous building left over from the Panama-Pacific Exposition. It was a far less comfortable facility than the engrossing museum now located on the Embarcadero. Half of the building contained a mobile home that had been converted into an office plus a series of mostly small, often table top displays; the back part of the cold, drab facility was filled with airplanes. Lighting was poor, with carpenters noisily producing displays while the public watched with fascination. It felt like some inventor's hobby shop. Frank developed displays that were engaging and novel even when they were inexpensive. Thirty years later, a friend of mine told me he still remembered one of those early displays: a heavy-duty spring was poised solidly on top of a barrel with a sign saying "Touch the spring." My friend was surprised when his hand went right through the ghost-like piece of metal. A parabolic mirror had been positioned so that the spring beneath the barrel's top appeared sitting above it. A newer version of the display is still on the Exploratorium exhibit floor.

Very early on, the Exploratorium became a training center

for teachers and science museum personnel from around the world. One January I spent several weeks at one of the training workshops run by Sally Duensing, who was in charge of professional development programs at the Exploratorium. It was my privilege to hear her introduce the Exploratorium's philosophy our small group. Frank was most interested in what motivates people to learn and the exhibits and programs reflected his theories. At the time I was almost eight months pregnant with my fifth child and starting to look like a barrel myself. As I was actively producing a next-generation museum goer, it was very exciting to share ideas with colleagues while enjoying the energy and creativity of the Exploratorium staff.

During that workshop we were shown many installations and proposals developed by artists for a residency program the Exploratorium had established. One such display stands out in my memory: it was a card-table-sized screen that had been pierced with thousands of pins, suspended vertically, points down. When you pushed your hand or an object up into the points and raised the pins there was no pain. On top of the screen, the pin heads took the shape of the object and formed a shiny, raised pattern. Ward Fleming was the artist who designed the piece, but it was eventually copied by an entrepreneur who made small pin boxes that were sold through the toy and gift shop market. Neither the Exploratorium nor the artist ever received any money from the first commercial sale of that display. Eventually Mr. Fleming won an injunction against the interloper and started manufacturing and marketing a higher quality version of the pin box.

The toy gave parents and children an opportunity while at home to share an art/science activity that defined the Exploratorium. Frank saw art and science as having common elements. Both artists and scientists recognize patterns in the natural world but have different goals for expressing them. He believed that by integrating the two, we have a greater ability to understand the whole of nature.

In 2013 over the winter holidays my children, grandchildren and I visited the new home of the Exploratorium located in a wharf on the Embarcadero. Nineteen of us entered the facility for a day of play. The building was filled to capacity with families at every station deeply involved in trying to conduct experiments and solve problems. One of my grandsons traveled slowly and methodically through the exhibitions while another moved more quickly around the cavernous building. The third and youngest child was on the run, not wanting to miss anything. The Exploratorium reminded me once more of the free school movement where children could learn in their own way, pacing themselves as they did so. There was something to hold the attention of each visitor, young and old alike. Frank would have been delighted at the different discoveries that my family members make. And, he would have been pleased to see people all around the world following suit.

Frank was generous with colleagues, seeking to share ideas for specific exhibits as well as his educational philosophy as a whole. For decades people in many institutions bought the Exploratorium "cookbooks" (for cooking up exhibit ideas) and fashioned their own versions of the canonical displays on light, sight, sound, and hearing. Frank's personality and his background as an experimental, hands-on physicist, rather than a theoretician like his brother, strongly influenced the generation of science museum leaders to follow. A third generation of museum leaders who never met Frank Oppenheimer are now still guided and inspired by his work.

The Importance of Touch

In 2012, a young social work student at the University of Rochester was featured in national publications as a most unusual entrepreneur. While studying brain and cognitive sciences as an undergraduate, Jacqueline Samuel became aware of the negative effects of living in a culture that does not sanction touch for its own sake. Throughout the world people are more willing to hold hands and hug friends and family than in the United States.

Adverse consequences of tactile isolation are known to be agitation, anxiety and aggression. Jacqueline decided that she would ameliorate the situation by opening a cuddle parlor she named the Snuggery. Her focus centered on bringing the healing power of touch to those who are tactilely isolated. The rules she and her employees devised were strict; staying clean, keeping clothing on and not engaging in any "funny business." Her non-sexual touch emporium was singularly based on the platonic need for physical closeness. Business boomed, spurring copy-cat cuddle parlors throughout the country. One even opened where I live in Portland, Oregon.

You might wonder what type of person needs to pay $60 for an hour hug? Clients come for a variety of reasons and include those on graveyard shifts returning home to empty beds, the physically handicapped, and the chronically depressed. There are thousands of people, many elderly, others single or with a physical disability who are never touched, held, or hugged. Having a friend to talk to and being cuddled is important for overall emotional well-being.

Jacqueline's insight is backed by volumes of research showing how touch reduces cortisol, the stress hormone that suppresses the immune system. The Touch Research Institute at the University of Miami is a center that concurs with Jacqueline's concerns. They recently completed a study showing that teens who lack hugging are more likely to be aggressive than their peers who are regularly hugged. Elderly people who are touched are healthier and less likely to develop dementia. Premature babies who are stroked gain weight faster than those who are not and infants who lack adequate physical and emotional attention are more likely to have behavioral, emotional and social problems as they age. And now we see that tactile learning can also be highly effective.

Hands-on museums are cognizant of sensory research, and tactile solutions especially form the basis of many of their activities. Not only do people need physical contact with others but they also have a need to touch and play with objects. A friend of mine shared an insight that it was not just his auditory sense that made him enjoy playing the piano, but his tactile contact with the keys.

My work in the museum field was influenced by an exercise I had to complete as a graduate student in psychology. One of my assignments was to write a paper imagining what it would be like to lose each of my senses. I was also directed to explore my feelings about loss of sexual sensitivity. To start the exercise I would sit for an hour in an easy chair imagining myself as a blind or deaf person. As I delved into the assignment, I was surprised to realize that losing my hands would be one of the most horrendous handicaps I could have. The hour spent with handless imagery was torturous, leaving me scared, almost frozen. What if I could not touch a door knob or wave my hands while talking? How horrible it would be to not be able to tousle my child's hair. Touch was not the only sensation that affected me deeply. I quickly realized that losing my sight would be just as awful. As a visual and tactile person I am so fortunate to have both of these faculties.

By the time I ranked my sensory preferences, I better understood the choices I made when selecting a profession and choosing hobbies. Sight and touch were prime motivators for most of my activities. For instance, the visual arts are important to me, and I integrate them into much of my leisure time. In choosing life partners and friends, I was drawn toward those who work with their hands as painters, sculptors, or builders. Museums and galleries are my eye candy. When not working at a paid job, I can be found creating textured paintings in my studio or pounding clay in pottery classes. Putting hands in clay to kneed, build, and shape a final product offers the greatest relaxation imaginable, and hours pass effortlessly when so engaged.

After moving to Portland to accept the all-encompassing job of managing OMSI, my Michigan days as a novice potter ended. For twenty-five years my fingers craved the feel of clay and though I substituted painting for pottery, within a month of retirement, I signed up to take a pottery class. When visiting art fairs, as I linger at the pottery booths, I am compelled to place my hands inside each pot to feel its texture and thickness and the skill of the potter. Our living room is filled with a collection of over fifty pots from Native American artists whom I greatly admire. My hands are always in action, moving when I talk, at times knocking into things as they dance. Hugs and cuddles with children and grandchildren are an important way for me to communicate love and caring. Educator Howard Gardner would conclude that my strengths are with visual and kinesthetic intelligences as opposed to auditory (musical) or olfactory (smell).

Each of us is compelled by biological predilections and we are most happy when we allow daily activities to be guided by these predispositions. In observing my second husband, sculptor Martin Eichinger, I saw how his fingers moved magically over clay to express movement and emotion. He started working with this medium as a child and is now nationally considered a master bronze sculptor who is collected and exhibited throughout the world. But his experience as an artist started young, when his parents and teachers enabled his visual and tactile abilities to grow and flourish.

Ray Losey, my partner for the past two decades, employs touch similarly in his work through his medium of carving. He too learned his craft as a child by assisting his father carve and paint totem poles and planks for various installations. Both of these individuals were fortunate to have parents who were in tune with their kinesthetic intelligence.

Hands-on in museum lingo is an invitation to use one or more of the senses to obtain information. Get involved, experiment, make mistakes, feel and draw your own conclusions. These are all messages evoked through the displays. Once engaged, the participant starts to comprehend his or her own learning mode. An alert parent can observe the manner in which his or her child is drawn into the many eclectic offerings, whether through sound, visual cues or tactile challenges.

Understanding a child's sensory preference helps parents and teachers design appropriate educational programs. The visual learner may love reading books, but there are many children who are hesitant readers and need to be drawn into the learning process through an alternative sensory route. A history teacher might design a curriculum for tactile learners by challenging them to make dioramas. The process still requires the children to read in order to know what to include in their 3-D pictures, but their interest in the project will be internally motivated.

Surgeons, experimental biologists, dentists, landscapers,

and carpenters are among those who use tactile abilities to gain professional standing. Strength in this area may be why so many designers love working on displays in museums. Parents, grandparents, friends and teachers please think twice before you tell a child not to touch. Your curious child might just need a little guidance to encourage safe and constructive activities that take advantage of his or her way of communicating. Remember, a broken glass can be dangerous but there are safe ways to turn broken glass into a mosaic—touch me, touch me not.

While at OMSI I was asked to consult with a small Ohio historical museum. The museum had twelve old-fashioned wood-burning stoves that had been manufactured in a local, now defunct, factory. The staff's idea was to assemble the stoves behind a rope barrier so visitors could view them while reading informative signs as they marched by. The thought bored me as much as it did the foundation ready to give the museum money for an overhaul. Not only would the exhibit be uninteresting to children, who would never read the signs or pay attention to details of stove design, I can guarantee that no adult would ever visit the display twice. The story of the industry that built the town would be lost to the younger generation. The Ohio community was proud of the manufacturing business that had employed so many residents over the years, and the museum wanted to make others aware of the town's industrial heritage, an idea I applauded. The challenge was how to present the stoves in an interesting way.

One obvious observation was that the stoves were practically indestructible. There was no real reason why children could not touch them, so why start with a barrier? Of greater interest than the stoves were stories about those who originally worked in the factory, stamping and molding metal and applying decorative patterns. After much discussion we developed final plans that included a compilation of audio stories presented by old-timers. The exhibit had a mock assembly line that invited children to put together toy stoves. Those with an artistic flair put their talents to work in a drawing area by designing stove-front logos. Displays explained health issues resulting from inadequate ventilation. Small parts of the fireplaces were available for handling so visitors could feel the heavy weight of material used for their construction. Science displays compared conductivity of different types of metal that might be considered in engineering a fireplace. Educators developed a section to discuss environmental issues such as pollution caused from burning wood, the advantages and disadvantages of coal and wood, and the heating efficiency of various fireplace designs. Challenging games and puzzles tested knowledge and intuition. The display was much more to the foundation's liking, and the museum was awarded a grant to proceed.

Understanding sensory exploration and use of the scientific method form the basis of science center communication. Men like Galileo, Newton and Edison used their senses of touch, sound and sight to devise experiments that have led to mankind's basic understanding of the laws of nature. Their observations and experiments found answers to questions we take for granted today. What does a bell sound like when it rings in a vacuum? What falls faster in a vacuum: a feather or a ball? What about outside the vacuum? Why do gyroscopes keep ships moving in a straight line? Why can two people hear each other whisper when standing inside parabolic reflectors placed at opposite ends of a hall? How does a telephone transmit sound? An airplane fly? A rocket propel itself in space?

Science centers are filled with exhibits that are scaleddown versions of laboratory tests that were done in the past to prove various principles of nature. They permit visitors to replicate the aha moments of understanding that come from messing around. However, learning the facts about a scientific breakthrough is not the end of the story, for we need to know just how an insight, discovery or invention affects our lives.

Most of us will not become scientists, yet we are regularly asked to make complex social decisions based on science to develop political policies. A dramatic example occurred in March, 2014 when a one mile long mud-slide buried highway vehicles, homes, and residents in the town of Oso, Washington. An excessive amount of rain caused dirt and trees to bury roads and hillside as deep as forty feet. Part of the Stillaguamish River had become dammed. Geologists had warned Oso residents that there were unstable areas that had experienced mud slides in years past, but builders, city officials and home owners did not take their cautionary words seriously. As a result many people got hurt. Why didn't they pay attention and how can we prevent such events from happening again?

Perhaps if Oso's city planners had introduced an exhibit that included an erosion table explaining why the ground was unstable, residents might have given more credence to the dire geological warnings. Displays, filled with rocks, branches, and houses allow visitors to create their own mud slides, change the course of flow and observe what happens when a dam breaks. Hands-on experiences are dramatic and tend to stay buried for years in the mind, ready to reemerge when needed.

The State of Oregon is at risk of a major earthquake. The last big one was about 315 years ago and Oregon State University's paleoseismologist, Chris Goldfinger, predicts that within 50 years there will be a major quake between 8.7 and 9.2 accompanied by a Tsunami. OMSI has been involved in preparedness programs for at least thirty years. A shaker room gives visitors a dramatic experience of what it is like to be in an earthquake. Lectures, geologic exhibits and a variety of static and interactive displays make the public aware of why and how they should prepare for the event. Now others are getting involved. Over these many years I have seen the city adopt more stringent building requirements, tsunami prepared-ness, and home readiness programs. Recently the state put out a notice stating the need for more volunteers to be trained to work in an emergency situation. Attention to these dire geo-logic predictions is not fully appreciated by the state's residents. Science museums are excellent conduits to educate millions of people through both exhibitions and educational programs.

SERVING THE UNDERDOG
FOCUS ON BOB RUSSELL:
OMAHA CHILDREN'S MUSEUM

Serving the Underdog—Focus on Bob Russell: Omaha Children's Museum

The following story is about a youth who was given a great deal of freedom to explore and experiment and as a result became an advocate for interactive learning. Bob Russell provides insight into what it was like to operate a small emerging children's museum before accepting the challenges of a larger science center. Early in his career he embraced an interactive approach to learning. He later served several stints as a program officer at the National Science Foundation, ran a non-profit serving the Latino community, and became a consultant for museums nationally. Bob is part of the reason that there is a hands-on science center in most states.

Bob

Dr. Robert Russell is dear to me because he became director of Impression 5 about three years after I resigned. He probably knows more about the good and bad parts of my leadership than anyone else. We always have a lot of memories to share when we get together to gossip about past staff and board members. He was a good choice as director because of his knowledge and understanding of the psychology that led to informal learning in museums.

Born in a small farm town outside of Omaha, Nebraska, Robert Russell was the middle child between an older brother and a younger sister. His family life was very lively with a father who owned a lumberyard and building supply-company giving the children all of the materials they needed for imaginative construction projects and summer jobs. Mom was a stay-at-home woman who set the stage for learning through classical music, books, and frequent use of a well-worn encyclopedia. She too was active and remained committed to work as a community volunteer.

While a young boy Bob was never pressured to learn, but rather absorbed education with ease in his small town school. With his mother's encouragement he mastered the piano and was left with a skill that still gives him a great deal of pleasure. At the age of nine Bob started ordering science kits from the *Science News* weekly magazine, taking great pride in putting together crystal radios and electromagnets among others. A larger chemistry set also encouraged the budding scientist to become an explorer though his mother complained when he tried to make portable stink bombs in his "lab," which was also the laundry room.

Bob grew up in an era when children were able to play with their peers outside of an adult agenda. He and his neighborhood friends experimented with ways to improve the projects in the science kits that came by mail for one dollar. They went on bicycle rides to collect interesting rocks and butterflies. Some of their explorations were risky. They could have electrocuted themselves or blown up the house. But they learned how to work independently and collaboratively. Bob told me that he is concerned about today's "overprotective adults who do not let their children explore and create on their own." Because of parents' fears over a host of issues—unsafe internet exploration, being hit by a car on increasingly busy streets, and addiction to computer games, children's activities are now more heavily programmed with rare opportunities to experiment unsupervised in nature or with scientific apparatus.

Bob's grandparents played a significant role in his development by taking him to various museum sponsored lectures and to the art museum. His granddad took him fishing, influencing his enjoyment of the outdoors. The young boy was a product, as were all of our museum directors, of being raised by education-oriented adults. One or more remarkable teachers impacted each of the people I interviewed, and Bob was no exception. Because of class requirements developed by his high school civics teacher, as a teen, Bob wound up tutoring weekly at a community center in an African American neighborhood. Seeing the response to what he was doing, he was inspired to go beyond being the center's sole tutor to start a broader based program to help people learn to read.

As a small town child he was given more freedom than most big city kids, and was not booked up with lessons and sports. He read continuously and was influenced, even though only in high school, by writers discussing "free schools" and free choice in education.

Armed with the ideas of social activists such as A. S. Neil, John Holt, George Dennis, and Jonathan Kozol, he went off to the University of Nebraska, and more specifically to a curriculum within the university called Centennial College, where approximately two hundred students were invited to live together and participate in a predominantly independent-study program. Bob told me that, "The program was invigorating because I could pursue my own interests which included reading the works of Freud, Marcuse, Utopian type thinkers, Wittgenstein, German poets, and French novelists. My minor in French, major in psychology, interest in science, and involvement in social action put me in good stead for my unanticipated museum career, one that blended psychology, philosophy, social awareness and science."

After obtaining his undergraduate degree Bob decided to take a year off before plunging into the rigors of graduate school. He returned home to work in his dad's lumberyard and reinstated his high school tutoring program, eventually developing and running five centers in low-income areas. His mother continued operating the centers after he went off to Cornell to study for an advanced degree. Bob's interest in cognitive development led him to do research into how kids develop math skills. He was particularly interested in those with disabilities, and compared their problems within the educational context that defined present-day school experiences. His expectation upon graduation was that he would spend his life teaching and doing research in academia.

"For a while after graduation I taught at Georgetown University and worked for the Senate Committee on Labor and Human Resources," he said during an interview. "Eventually I acquired full-time work with an educational evaluation company." He describes this work with one word: boring. "I wanted out." When his brother told him of an opportunity near his birth place, he applied and was offered the director's job at the Omaha Children's Museum, a tiny institution with 4,000 square feet of exhibit halls and an equal amount of space for offices and classrooms, which employed a staff of seven. He plunged into the frenetic pace of building new programs, changing exhibitions, and traveling broadly to visit the new style of interactive displays being developed at the Exploratorium, the Ontario Science Center and the Indianapolis Children's Museum. Over the next 3 years his children's museum attendance and programs grew to the point where a larger facility was needed. In his museum, board seats were filled with mid-level business people who were the sons and daughters of the heavy hitters more likely to be found at the Art Museum. They were fearful of raising the two to three million dollars necessary for a new building. "I had no support for my vision of growth so I decided to leave a dead-end situation. When my conservative board said no to all of my reasoning," Bob related, "I looked for a different job."

— — — — — — — — — — — — —

Bob's Lesson #1: Plan ahead to make the board yours. It takes time to get everyone on board and willing to take the risks inherent in operating a museum.

— — — — — — — — — — — — —

"Know what you are getting into and ask yourself if you can manage," Bob told me. "After the Omaha Children's Museum, Impression 5 seemed large and I was naïve about how to step in and obtain the authority needed to operate successfully." Newly employed museum directors often inherit a board of trustees who are not 100% behind the new executive. In hindsight Bob thought he should have gotten to work immediately on developing a strategic plan that the board and the entire community could endorse. "Armed with this new vision," he went on to say, "I then should have gotten involved in the board selection process to insure that those asked to join would support the plan's goals." As a newcomer to Lansing he never fully gained control of the board, and as so many directors realize, without obtaining their trust and showing strength, the job can become quite difficult. He needed allies to help him achieve his ends. Instead he was undermined by people who told him one thing and then would do another.

Where he excelled was coming up with creative ideas for new programs, and writing and receiving the grants to support them. The more mundane but necessary part of fundraising, obtaining operating donations, was less to his liking. At first Bob was viewed as a hero because he increased attendance from 80,000 to 140,000 by expanding the traveling exhibit program. He participated in the Exhibits Research Collaborative with eight national museums, operated a new Dow

Chemical Chemistry lab, developed distance learning centers in low income areas, and initiated a great many educational programs. Bob said that "Impression 5 was a good lesson in how to operate a museum. My experiences also gave me a broad base of connections within the science center community."

Bob's Lesson #2: Before accepting a job, review the organization's finances.

When Bob arrived at Impression 5 the museum was in an 80,000 square foot facility operated by a staff of twenty-five people. Money was always tight and by the time Bob arrived, three directors after I left, a recession was in full swing making obtaining operating dollars more difficult. Staff had to be trimmed but it was done in a way that was not Bob's first choice. His desire was to lay off a few of the less-productive higher paid employees and keep program staff. The board felt otherwise, which led to closing down a program area that let five less well-paid people go. Unfortunately, these were just the type of employees who had the potential to increase revenues in the long run through their innovative programs. Money . . . money . . . money; it is a challenge, and often a reason to say good-bye to a director. Impression 5's board members were not active fundraisers and put the burden of fundraising on Bob. Though he went to cocktail parties and political events, he was not successful. He operated in a city without a philanthropic spirit, one that had few wealthy residents or corporations. At the end of three years he left his position and turned his attention to establishing the Nokomis Native American Learning Center in Okemos, MI.

Bob later traveled back to Washington, DC to accept a position as a program officer at the National Science Foundation, working under George Tressel in the Division of

Elementary and Secondary Education. This became his chance to have a major impact on the country.

— — — — — — — — — — — —

Bob's Lesson #3: Keep an open mind.

— — — — — — — — — — — —

"There is a big world out there," Bob said, "and when you start looking for a job, apply for opportunities outside of what you might have thought of consciously. Take in new experiences and don't be constrained. You might find that there is something that would be better for you than you thought." For Bob, ultimately, the National Science Foundation had the right stuff. He moved from becoming a writer of grants and a developer of programs to overseeing funding of informal education projects at a time when NSF had become quite concerned with science literacy. His sphere of influence broadened as he promoted grants that influenced the way science was taught. He enjoyed working with the rapidly growing field of informal science education by encouraging projects that engaged minorities in science, supported newly developed science centers, and addressed society's increasing digital divide.

In 1972, NSF started to support the fledgling organization known as the Association of Science and Technology Centers (ASTC). Their goal was to put science in the hands of the average person, and NSF wanted to make it easy for people to find nearby centers. As interest in these hands-on institutions grew over the next few years, NSF funded the Institute for New Science Centers, a five-day training program covering everything needed to operate a science center, from board development and finance management to marketing and how to build exhibits. By the time ASTC received their second grant, Bob had started work at NSF and was assigned as program officer for the next institute, allowing an additional forty directors from various small museums to receive a crash course in Science Museum 101. "Those who attended this training were often naïve. They had passion but knew nothing about how to operate the organization they so much wanted to develop." Bob mentioned proudly that the program was a tremendous help to the profession.

He also oversaw several grants to the Pacific Science Center to develop Science Carnival, a tent show that was taken around to country to communities that wanted to start a science center. Several colorful tents displayed exhibits and held demonstrations and classes. The small admission fee enabled most interested people to experience what a science center was like. A second round of grants provided ten museums with a set of interactive exhibits along with professional development for teaching staff and exhibit developers. It was quite a practical orientation that went a long way to further the national trend to build science centers.

According to Bob, NSF was there to help get things rolling. The foundation was challenged to stimulate development of products and services in museums, spur informal curriculum and teacher training, and promote the media to develop educational science programs such as *Nova*. Bob helped fund and oversaw another expansionist program. This time COSI (Columbus Ohio Science and Industry) received money in the early 1990s to aid twenty emerging science centers. The Exploratorium also received continuous grants to help new institutions by providing exhibit starter sets. Other groups were given plans for exhibits and invited for residential experiences. This story of growth and expansion continued for nearly twenty years.

NSF tends to hire staff on a three-year rotational contract, so it was inevitable that Bob would once more return to work as a consultant and grant writer for informal science and health education projects in museums, youth programs, for radio, and IMAX films. His enjoyment in helping others led him from advisor to director of a Latino non-profit that developed media and community outreach in science.

Returning in 2013 for a second stint at NSF he found that the directorate had changed. The heyday of burgeoning government funds to develop small and middle size centers had ended with new focus given to education research and development.

In looking for a pattern in Dr. Robert Russell's life, one that consistently stands out is his interest in serving the underdog. He is a compassionate person who shares a great deal of himself in order to help others achieve their potential.

THE DIGITAL WORLD:
CHALLENGE OR BOON?

A few years ago during a technology luncheon I was seated next to a distinguished-looking, well-traveled Australian oil man. We easily struck up a conversation and animatedly discussed our respective work environments. The gentleman complained that many of the young men working for him were talented computer geeks, but when asked to spend time in the field they fell apart. Afraid of living in the wild with the possibility of meeting a snake or kangaroo, they were ill equipped to solve practical problems of an environmental or engineering nature. These techies had never been exposed to field work requiring them to integrate mechanical and electrical equipment with software development. Instead of relishing the adventure of a trip to the outback, these digital wizards could hardly wait to get back to the safe applications they were designing in their comfortable heat-controlled offices. The oil executive told me that he wished schools taught by using more practical hands-on approaches with not as much emphasis on textbook and technology-based learning.

An article written in December 2013 by Linda McAlert for *University Business* cites research by the Melior Grove conducted with fifty hiring managers and top executives. Their results concluded that employers believe that problem solving and critical thinking skills are missing from most educational curriculums. In addition to competency with the three Rs, management wants creative, innovative problem solvers with do-it-yourself skills. Companies look for those who act collaboratively, take an interdisciplinary approach and understand the resources available to them. They want people who "get out of silos and see the big picture," and they want to hire those with real-world experience with diverse populations in various business settings.

Interactive problem solving experiences have limited space in contemporary curricula leaving students with half-understandings of important issues. Instead areas of study that rely heavily on computer aided instruction have become the norm. We have only to look at local and state legislators to observe burgeoning societal problems coming from lack of first-hand experience. How many senators and representatives involved in environmental policies hike in the woods to witness the state of wildlife populations and see changes in flora and fauna? Few have had educational training to enable them to evaluate scientific documentation in support for or against specific legislation. Lobbyists with vested interests are likely to have their attention instead of scientists.

The *Washington Post* wrote on September 28, 2014, about the emotional toll military drone operators face. These young people, mostly men, who were hired for their computer gaming skills are asked to make life-and-death decisions from the safety of offices located halfway around the world from their targets. They are not exposed to the cries and screams of people who have happened to step in harm's way. Slowly they realize that the job that appeared to be "just a video game" is far from that, and it begins to affect their mental health. Post-traumatic stress disorder is on the rise among drone operators who begin to understand that what were previously gaming icons are now innocent people.

On October 23, 2013, the American Academy of Pediatrics offered guidance on managing children's use of media. These recommendations grew out of a 2010 medical report that surveyed children between the ages of 8 and 18, finding that more than seven hours a day were being spent on digital media devices. Parents are instructed to "limit kids' tweeting, texting and to keep smartphones, laptops out of bedrooms." Dr. Victor Strasburger, a lead author of the American Academy of Pediatrics policy on media exposure and children, says that "unrestricted media use can have serious consequences linked with violence, cyber bullying, school woes, obesity, lack of sleep and a host of other problems." His recommendation is to limit entertaining screen time to viewing no more than two hours a day.

As schools and adults nationwide purchase tablets or smart phones for every child, daily usage of electronic devices will only continue to grow. Indeed, a recent Pew survey found that teens are now averaging nine hours a day on social media platforms. When still publishing the *Museum Tour Catalog* in 2011, I observed a dramatic change in buying habits. Very young children were being given tablets and smartphones. Parents who had previously helped their children assemble science and art kits were content with the situation because it did keep their youngsters quiet. Even those who worry about excessive computer time give in to pressure when their kids lobby to own the latest electronic gadget used by their friends.

Conflict over electronic devices is not new. In my generation discussions centered on how much time should be allocated to watching TV. Then, as now, establishing rules and boundaries create quite a challenge. Initially my husband and I solved the problem for our family by not having a television in the house. My mother-in-law, however, was quite vocal and railed against our decision. She believed her grandchildren were missing out on programs like *Sesame Street,* and we were missing the news. She took matters into her own hands by giving us a TV as a gift, insisting that we use it. To keep peace in the family we accepted it but set limits on its use.

Limits are possible. One beautiful September evening I observed a child sitting around a fire pit interact with her father at a family gathering. The child's phone binged and she immediately stopped participating in the general conversation and responded to the text message. Dad told her to put the phone away, explaining that it was not polite to use it in social situations. The daughter ignored her father's words and continued to text. After a second warning he popped out of his seat and with lightning speed grabbed her phone, saying that it was being taken away for a week. Though my guess is that her punishment did not last that long, it still served as a lesson in good manners, and demonstrates that parents can be in control by taking responsibility for socializing their children.

"But my kids are so quiet when they are on the computer or watching television and I am given this wonderful gift of time to get my own work completed," I have heard a mother say. My advice to parents—don't go there. Instead, seek out alternative activities that develop creative and imaginative thinking. Keep those young muscles and minds moving and interacting with others.

Family outings and excursions are in daily competition with the instant gratification that comes from using hand-held devices. Yet there are exciting alternatives in the real rather than simulated world. Providing such opportunities takes thoughtful planning, but a child's smiling face is all that is needed as a reward. Electronics can be turned off, the plug pulled or the battery removed. It is good to get children out in nature and to increase tactile problem solving opportunities.

Yet innovators are constantly introducing new technology

to which we have to adapt. Or do we? Who in the world comes up with such strange new ideas? The November 25, 2013, issue of *Time* magazine was a special edition devoted to the top 25 inventions of the year. The one that got my attention was the Edible Password Pill which I could surely use as I acquire more and more hard-to-remember passwords. Motorola's Edible Password Pill is made to be swallowed daily. The tiny chip reacts with the acid in your stomach for it to activate and start emitting an 18 BIT - EKG - like signal that can be picked up on your phone or computer. What the pill does is turn your body into a password. Hard to believe but it did get FDA approvals, though as of October 2014 the pill was not yet on the market. By 2015 the internet was full of comments by bloggers on sites such as Bitcoin. They were mostly negative, but some people still think these personal pills are part of our future. This invention is most certainly a creative one and you might imagine the mind of the ingenious designer. Motorola is owned by Google, which has plans to make swallowing a pill ease the way you sign into Gmail.

Parent-Child Interactions in the Museum

In designing alternative experiences, museums not only provide fresh perspectives but also set the stage for family members to form closer bonds. Observing adult-child dynamics aided me in understanding how to overcome barriers to learning. I often watched parents enter exhibit halls with timidity, preferring to read signs rather than to play with displays. Their children, on the other hand, were reluctant readers but had no fear about plunging in even if they did not know what they were doing. It never took long before parent and child were involved in a symbiotic relationship, interacting with each other to play with the displays. Parents read, and kids do. Kids try and parents help. Parents demonstrate and kids create. Finally most adults overcome their embarrassment and tackle the problems and challenges before them. In short order the entire family becomes involved with touching, smelling, feeling, hearing, and seeing. Without realizing it, both adults and children start to take control of their own learning experience and are on their way to become more active problem solvers.

This chapter never would have been written in the early twentieth century. Today's city dwellers rarely learn to fix cars, bake bread or sew their own clothes. As these traditional crafts continue to wane, it is important to replace them with meaningful alternatives. Well-rounded, critically thinking kids still need to overcome obstacles. As I mentioned earlier, many businesses need employees who think dimensionally and use all of their senses in dealing with complicated issues.

My earlier work with patients in the mental health center taught me what happens when people lose the ability to think holistically to solve problems. One instance that stands out in my mind occurred during the Vietnam War. I was working at night in a deserted office wing of a Lansing hospital when a strong, haunted looking marine entered, shut the door and said, "I feel like killing someone." The office had two doors, one to an adjacent bedroom where the evening counselor could rest between clients and the other to a dimly lit hallway. There was no way anyone could be contacted if the situation became violent, so my adrenalin immediately spiked. When I calmed down I learned that the young man, whom I will call Scared, had gone AWOL and had become paranoid walking on city streets in anticipation of being caught. With every step this upset fugitive expected someone to grab him and take him to jail. He was confused about what to do, hating the idea of returning to the marines where he might have to shoot an enemy combatant. Scared was not a warrior and could not conscientiously stay in service as a fighter.

I admitted Scared to the hospital for a few days. He

needed sleep if he was going to be able to make rational decisions affecting his future. Luckily, during these tumultuous Vietnam days, Dee was working for a law firm that helped military personnel in trouble. A lawyer in her firm was able to negotiate his release as long as he was willing to return to his unit for a short time. His other choice would be years of jail time before receiving a dishonorable discharge. My patient agreed to return to his unit, though he told me he would be beaten once back on base. Unfortunately, that is exactly what happened. Scared received a severe bashing, resulting in quite a few broken bones and was put in solitary confinement before his eventual release. Despite this, he was pleased with the outcome for his release was with honor.

How did I help Scared solve his problem? Counselors are simply teachers or coaches who foster a degree of self-awareness. Many mental crises are complex and require a multi-pronged response, one of which is regaining confidence in critical thinking. Once a patient fully understands their situation and can analyze it, then options can be discussed and a plan of action developed. Basically, while in counseling, a person learns to recognize the facts and then form a hypothesis about the situation. The counselor then helps the client develop a way to test the hypothesis. When the results are back, the client has a new factual basis for planning, and the process starts over again. This is life. This is the scientific method. This is science education.

Experiential learning in museums is similar to counseling. Staff use the same type of reasoning when designing exhibits that encourage visitors to solve problems. The approach starts by posing a question. Then background information is given and tools supplied for solving the puzzle. This is a style of learning based on inquiry. The visitor is presented with the facts, asked to form a hypothesis, and provided a way to test the hypothesis through experiment or game.

This student-centered approach requires strategies originating with the participant's guess, and because it is self-directed learning, it has an ancillary benefit of being self-motivating. Museums repeatedly employ inquiry-based models to help children organize their reasoning. By acting as scientists, families can enrich their enjoyment in the museum of the whole wide world.

CREATIVITY: CAN IT BE TAUGHT?

Museum educators continuously look for technologies such as the Password Pill in order to help the public understand technology as well as its social implications. They also use such examples to explore the creative process itself. Is creativity something that can be taught or are a lucky few just born with amazing talent? Are there genes that make some people more imaginative than others? Which is it, nature or nurture? Though there are many geneticists and psychologists on both sides of the issue, a definitive answer still eludes them.

Creativity is the bread and butter of most cultural institutions and a great deal of attention is given to the subject. It is expected that exhibitions, classes, marketing and fundraising events will all be executed with pizazz. Many traditional museums do not trust visitors to understand an artist through their own observations, so they employ guides to explain the art and why the person is considered inventive. Science centers, with the aide of explainers, are a bit different for they encourage attendees to expand their own creative abilities and test their hypotheses. They set up displays that are self-teaching devices and look for ways for visitors to enhance their own creative expression. Innovative thinking processes and open ended challenges allow the participant to experience that aha moment.

In my thirties I took a class in creativity. It was designed to open minds and increase problem-solving abilities. The instructor came to each session with exercises aimed at freeing our playful core. One day, he brought in an old L'eggs stockings container. It was shaped like an egg, though hollow and split in the middle, the kind that you often see in Easter baskets. The students were instructed to close their eyes and imagine walking up and down the aisles of a supermarket looking at the imaginary shelves. The task was to develop new uses for the egg. We approached this with enthusiasm, as a group generating more than eighty ideas. Suggestions ran from using the container as a plant starter to inserting dried peas to make a rattle. Known as image streaming, this approach to problem solving works well for me and I turn to it whenever I am at a loss of how to proceed.

The instructor stressed that to come up with creative ideas, it is necessary to have a thorough knowledge of facts and information about your subject before letting your mind wander in a search for solutions. He emphasized how important relaxation is as a part of the process. A university friend reinforced this insight by sharing that when he gets stuck with a research problem he stops what he has been doing and goes out for a big lunch before returning to his office to nap. He claims that upon awakening, ideas flow, most of the time helping him get over a hurdle. This period of relaxed attention is why so many people have their aha experiences while driving a car or standing in the shower.

I am convinced that creative thinking processes can be learned or, at the very least, enhanced. Finding the right tricks is all that is needed to stimulate thinking outside of the box. My personal formula has several steps. The first involves becoming immersed in the subject to ensure that I completely understand all aspects of the situation. I then conduct experiments, research, or simply talk to people to get different points of view. Once I have acquired a base of knowledge I spend alert time in totally unrelated activities. Eventually my mind starts to combine many unrelated observations with the problem I am trying to solve. Sometimes I even wake up at night with the solution popping into my head. For some unknown reason I find that my relaxed problem-solving sessions tend to be enhanced while pacing the floor or driving a car. Employees at OMSI had to get used to seeing me wandering randomly around the building. From their comments, some thought I was being nosy, but the truth was that I was not paying much attention to them at all. I was thinking of the problem at hand.

The 2014 movie *The Internship* presents an excellent example of people discovering a new idea through relaxed attention. The story takes place at Google headquarters where a team of mixed age interns is given the task of developing a new app. Their creativity will be judged by staff who will decide whether to offer them a job at the end of the internship program. Rather than staying at headquarters in a non-productive brainstorming session, at the urging of two older and less computer savvy interns (played by Vince Vaughn and Owen Wilson), the group goes out for a raucous night on the town. While lounging in the early morning, an inebriated young team member wants to send a gross and foolish text to a girl he just met. It is then that the horrified group comes up with the idea for an app that asks partygoers to respond correctly to a list of questions before making fools of themselves by sending inappropriate emails. In the movie the app turned out to be a great success and the two aging applicants wind up getting the job. The story demonstrates how old fashioned problem solving techniques can be effective even in a society immersed in computer technology.

Image streaming involves looking inward to develop the ability to recognize and describe mental images imagined while on a mind-walk. I learned the following exercise in a museum class, but it can be done at home as a party game with friends. Everyone is asked to close their eyes and imagine walking on hot coals. Once images appear the participants are instructed to describe the experience, especially the sensory part. The leader then suggests that each act out what it is like to walk on hot coals. A piece of paper can be distributed for those who wish to write or draw the experience.

This practice helps fine-tune the ability to see and express what is in your mind's eye. When shopping, most of us walk through a supermarket and purchase food without ever thinking about new uses for these items. Creative cooks, however, are always on the alert when they travel the same aisles. They visualize how to combine unusual items in imaginative ways and might even be able to fantasize about the enticing odors resulting from their concoction.

Image streaming and other problem solving techniques give me a sense of power. Knowing that I have an arsenal of tricks to use when I need to stimulate creative juices is very comforting and keeps me from worrying that I might run out of ideas.

Museum classrooms can be a place to learn creativity exercises, but home is where the practice should occur. Another amusing party game places random objects in front of a group, challenging each, in turn, to describe new ideas for their use. It asks the participants to ignore the original purpose and develop alternatives that can be silly and ridiculous, as well as practical. Anything goes when brainstorming. Children are often better at this exercise than adults who are more practiced at following rules and instructions. The game teaches the mind to first of all be observant and second to be flexible and think in new ways.

My younger son meets annually with a group of friends who dress as Santa, joining hundreds of others in a pub-hopping event known as Santa's Night Out. One year a number of his Santa friends met for a craft night in preparation. Each person arrived with old toys and spare parts to be refashioned. By sewing, gluing and welding items together in outlandish ways they designed new products. On Santa Night their bags were bulging with items to be given away. Making crazy contraptions was a social activity that simultaneously stimulated their creative juices.

Events such as Burning Man and Maker Fairs as well as science centers are part of a burgeoning technology-craft-art movement. Burning Man is a giant exhibition dedicated to the arts and sciences. The event, which occurs annually in Black Rock Desert in northern Nevada, now attracts 70,000 people gathered in a celebration of creative expression. Music, drama, costumes, technological and traditional art wonders are featured within a gift giving rather than money economy. Attendees are artists, scientists, computer geeks and engineers who enjoy working together during the year to develop spectacular visionary pieces. Burning Man promotions claim the event encourages "the individual to discover, exercise and rely on his or her inner resources." The gathering is communal, respects the environment and insists on civic responsibility.

Another rapidly growing craft trend is the maker movement. Conceived by Maker Media, hundreds of thousands of people attend annual Maker Faires that bring together curious people who love learning and sharing talents. Sponsors come from well-known businesses such as Disney and Intel. In Portland, the Oregon Museum of Science and Industry holds a mini-maker event and has refashioned its exhibit halls to accommodate "maker"-type tinkering.

The maker movement developed because the web has made it easy for people to share ideas, which in turn has inspired acquaintances to become involved in weekly Do-It-Yourself (DIY) projects. General Electric supports "GE Garages," spaces where makers assemble to learn modern ways of prototyping and manufacturing new devices. 3D printers, laser cutters, welding tools and open-source electronics platforms have fed into the growth of these techie arts and crafts gatherings. Traditional crafts also benefit by this DIY movement. I went to one maker gathering with an acrylic painting to complete. While there, I observed a woman crafting jewelry, a man designing something on his computer, two men discussing formulas for making a liqueur, several people welding and a woman knitting from a design previously fashioned on her computer. A large number of other friends were involved in a communal art project that featured computer driven electronics. The movement is getting an added boost from Quirky and Kickstarter, two web-based companies that help makers find financial resources to turn their ideas into real life products.

Though young adults increasingly embrace the concept of creative expression, our school systems have been lagging. When the recession started in 2007, boards of education did a great disservice by eliminating art and music programs from the curriculum. Children increasingly were taught to think linearly rather than creatively. I am pleased that the National Science Foundation realizes how important it is to use the arts as a stepping stone to technology and science. They developed new grant guidelines to promote art/science/technology projects.

Weekends and vacations provide an opportunity for parents to develop creative thinking skills by promoting open ended non-linear activities. Not only is right brain thinking expansive—it is practical. Employment opportunities increase for individuals who have a flexible approach to thinking and solving problems.

I previously mentioned the reason for selecting the word Impression for my first science museum. We wanted our center to make an impression on the public just as we hoped the visitor would make an impression on staff. This goal is shared by most contemporary science centers and children's museums.

Marilynne's Lesson #11: Ideas come from unexpected places and people.

Visitors as well as museum staff are a great source of ideas for exhibits and programs. At OMSI, it was the gift shop manager who came up with the idea for a Star Trek exhibit. Though he talked about it for years, until I arrived, no one would listen to him. Once he was taken seriously, his suggestion became the basis of one of OMSI's most successful displays. Another time a museum trustee arrived in my office with reams of information about new research being conducted on the brain. His enthusiasm was contagious. His visit stimulated a series of programs that still continue in conjunction with the Oregon Health Science University. Being open to the original ideas of others means finding a way to bring them into your busy day. Blogs are great because there is often a trail of comments and responses that acknowledge innovative thinking.

Those involved in brainstorming sessions may invite unusual participants to contribute to the conversation. The goal is to shake things up a bit by involving thinkers outside the comfort box. Exploratory meetings that include a diversity of opinions and approaches bring in ideas that make everyone more sharp. Sharing perspectives is electrifying and especially useful when planning a new museum, creating a program, planning an exhibit, or, for that matter, starting your own business. Visitors who have something to contribute to a museum should never be afraid to volunteer their expertise and ideas. It is a great way to make new friends and contacts with people who share common interests.

By inviting members of the community to conceptualize the future of a museum, you offer them the opportunity to become part of the creative process, simultaneously forging a strong connection to the organization. When OMSI decided to move its facility, a series of very intense brainstorming sessions were held during which 150 invitees were sub-divided into fifteen-person focus groups. The goal was to redefine our mission, better understand community needs, and learn which cutting edge scientific discoveries should be featured in the new museum. These gatherings produced many ideas and gave us a base of knowledgeable individuals to use as our programs expanded.

— — — — — — — — — — — —

Marilynne's Lesson #12: A broad spectrum of creative people can synergistically produce an outcome with an end result greater than that of a single individual.

— — — — — — — — — — — —

Values learned from my early days of lounging at Synergy in East Lansing are reconfirmed each time I participate in a group idea meeting. People continue to amaze me with their inventive aptitudes. When I eventually did start my own commercial business the lessons I learned in museum brainstorming sessions accompanied me. Family, friends, and even the general public were quite willing to help with ideas and suggestions even though it was for a private venture. I communicated with over 200 people before finding the right title for this book.

It is also important to listen to your customers. Their criticisms can be the source of your next important idea. I have always tried to avoid the pitfall of asking for input and not really meaning it. A short time ago I called a cosmetic company to complain about a poor design for their blush compact. The telephone operator was very polite but would not tell me how to make a written suggestion. Instead, I was given a coupon to make me happy and go away. The coupon was not the purpose of my call. I seriously wanted to explain why their design was poor and how the compact broke each of the past five times I bought it. It did not take long to realize that no one cared to hear my message. I stopped purchasing that brand. Their headquarters has no way of receiving a small suggestion that could create a solution to improve sales.

THE HAPPINESS BUSINESS:
PLAYFUL LEARNING IS GOOD

What is the secret of life? This question is an easy one for me to answer: happiness, of course. I am not talking about giddy-happy like you might feel if you won the lottery but rather calm-happy producing a general sense of well-being. The Greeks described happiness as the joy we feel moving towards our potential. It is a process and not an end in itself.

Museum professionals are in the happiness business, parents too are in the happiness business, and managing your own life is immersed in the happiness business. In an August 2013 article in the *Huffington Post,* Carolyn Gregoire reported on a seventy-five-year-old Harvard study that explored the secrets to a fulfilling life. What the researchers learned was that for most people, love rates highest, with happiness second. What creates this sense of satisfaction? Joy, the study went on to say, is created by connections and challenges because new perspectives can make you happier. Dealing with challenge through creative expression produces a feeling of well-being. What the researchers learned may seem obvious, but as a *Huffington Post* article said, "It doesn't make it less true." Philosophers as ancient as Aristotle, as contemporary as the Dalai Lama, and as scientific as University of California professor and researcher Sonja Lyubomirsk, who in 2007 authored *The How of Happiness: A Scientific Approach to Getting the Life You Want,* agree that happiness and contentment are goals that give meaning to life.

Providing opportunities for children to play freely is an important part of parenting. When my children were young, dress-up was a big part of their playtime. I salvaged a large cardboard box and filled it with old nightgowns, prom dresses, suits, ties, scarves, swords, hats and crowns, stethoscopes, homemade armor and makeup. Many days, between five and eight youngsters could be found parading around the neighborhood dressed like royalty, Hollywood sirens, or superheroes. This opportunity to develop their own creative expressions gave them a great deal of pleasure.

Their imagination ran the gamut as they put together dramas in our garage or on the back lawn. It often surprised me to hear the actors parroting adult conversations or activities that they witnessed in our home or at school. These children practiced the life they thought they would be living when they became grownups. They analyzed the world as they knew it and presented it back for all to see. Negotiating sessions for parts in their dramas were intense before they let their imaginations run wild with the day's spectacle. Often the kids became teachers or students and organized a school complete with reading and math activities. Younger children definitely benefited by the very strict instruction they received at the hands of an older brother or sister. If a paid teacher ever acted so rigidly, I am sure she would have angry parents knocking at her door. In contrast, I rarely heard a complaint from their play activity even if the selected teacher put a child in the corner with a dunce hat on his head. When in preschool, my grandson was fortunate because his two older sisters decided to give him daily English and math lessons. All three children became totally involved in their play-school activity.

My grandson flourished with the attention of his siblings and absorbed as much of their teachings as he could comprehend. This youngster was well prepared for kindergarten and looked forward to going to school.

These children were happy and committed when they were playing and practicing at being part of adult society. In later life, when I met clients in the mental health center I could not help but wonder if they had ever experienced spontaneity and a sense of wonderment when they were young. Unfortunately, the adults I saw in counseling sessions had lost an essential and playful part of themselves. I worked diligently to discover if they had ever experienced what it felt like to be free spirits in control of their future. Those patients coming from a restricted childhood had a more difficult time finding a path towards their own well-being. They needed to be taught how to laugh, shout, and fly.

My husband and I encouraged this type of imaginative play in a variety of ways. On long hikes or car rides, we would start telling a story, stopping when the action got complex, then turning the story over to the next person to complete. One never knew how the plot would develop and who would get the hero or heroine out of his or her current dilemma. Our crazy stories made us laugh, and the children remained content during these excursions.

As our children entered their middle and high school years, they stayed involved with whimsical play in different ways. My youngest son became addicted to computer games. This was at a time before laptops and internet connections, so in order for their children to network with friends, parents would load up heavy monitors and keyboards to take to one house or another. The children would eat, play games and sleep at the host house for upward of three days with pizza boxes piling up on the dining room table. One evening, I watched the teenage game players take a break from their networked computers by running through the woods behind our house waving home-made wooden swords. They had transformed themselves into the knights and villains of their computer game while getting rid of a lot of excess energy.

Melinda Wenner in 2009 wrote in *Scientific American* that "free, imaginative play is crucial for normal social, emotional and cognitive development. It makes us better adjusted, smarter and less stressed." The article went on to discuss the work of Stuart Brown at Baylor College of Medicine in Houston, who investigated twenty-six convicted Texas murderers. He discovered that there were two things the killers shared in common: they came from abusive families and they never played imaginatively as kids.

In our current society children play soccer, computer games, go to music lessons, and join structured play-groups, leaving little time for free play. Anthony Pellegrini, psychologist at University of Minnesota agrees that structured game rules are a good wholesome source of social learning and group coherence, but he also warns that, "play, on the other hand, does not have a priori rules, so it affords more creative responses. This freedom challenges the developing brain much more that following predetermined rules."

Free play helps develop strong social skills. Children learn these proficiencies by interacting with their peers, practicing fairness, and sharing. Because their own imaginations spark their fantasies, they wind up with improved negotiating skills and learning to be persistent without giving way to frustration. To keep any childhood game flowing, communication skills are required of the players. Research shows that children use more sophisticated language when playing with peers than they do when talking to adults. In other words, childhood games play an important role in improving language skills.

Play, also a stress relieving activity, is critical for emotional health, according to one study in the *Journal of Child Psychology and Psychiatry*. Another classic study published in *Developmental Psychology* reported that free play actually makes kids smarter. Even play fighting has been found to improve problem-solving skills. In general, play is practice for the unexpected.

Marilynne's Lesson #13: Playful learning creates happiness at all ages.

So—why not loosen up? Free time, play time is good time, important time. As adults we can feel guilt-free in not scheduling every minute of the day with activities that have rules. Children thrive when they are allowed to just be children and have fun with their own fantastic visions.

Children's museums focus on imaginative play activities more than museums for older adults but that does not mean that this basic need for imaginative comedy and drama should ever be forgotten within any museum environment. Adults also thrive when they integrate frolic into their lives. Museums of all types are entertainment centers first, so most museum staff members keep that fact in mind. They know that if people do not have fun they will not want to return. Epcot Center is a good example of a destination playground that was developed by combining science, education, and entertainment. Many contemporary museums have learned a great deal by participating in workshops that explain Disney operations. The word "edutainment" says it all.

FOREVER YOUNG

Just as children fantasize so do adults need outlets that let their imaginations run wild. I watched a group of designers, contractors, and architectural firms participate in a museum sponsored sandcastle contest with teams of company employees competing to make the most creative structure. The groups had a great deal of fun imagining possibilities with the added benefit of knowing that they were assisting a worthy charity. The most important part of this activity was that it gave the adult participants an opportunity to be as whimsical as they were when they were children. There was a secondary benefit to those watching on the outside, for they were able to observe the creative process at work.

In my early Portland days I brought Otto Piene (1928-1914) from Boston to lead a workshop with exhibit staff and educators from OMSI and the Portland Art Museum. Otto at that time was director of MIT's Center for Advance Visual Studies and celebrated internationally and recognized for his paintings as well as his involvement in technology-inspired art. Otto especially enjoyed working with concepts of light, form, and movement. Among other things, he assembled a stadium size rainbow out of plastic that he called *Sky Art*, flying it over the Olympic Stadium in Munich, Germany in the summer of 1972.

In directing our workshop, Otto taught us how to make and inflate huge plastic bags to be turned into kinetic sculptures with the use of fans. Integrating science and art museum staff enabled us to have a delightful experience and fertile exchange of ideas. We were divided into small groups that were each given the task of developing a novel outcome with the colored plastic bags. While we demonstrated our ingenious pieces, laughter could be heard contagiously moving from person to person making it a wonderful and positive experience. Cross-institutional bonds were developed through playtime that led to the two institutions working together on other projects. As a joint effort, we were able to share the costs of bringing such a well-known figure to Portland. During the day the workshop was conducted at OMSI and in the evening the Art Museum held a public presentation, giving Otto a platform for his rich portfolio of art.

Workshops are helpful in letting people pause from daily chores in order to promote thinking outside of the box. When I owned the *Museum Tour Catalog*, I always designed ways of keeping staff playful and imaginative. It is easy to become immersed in the details of operations and forget the vision and excitement that propelled the original venture. Lightheartedness is a precious commodity that needs to be continuously nourished. The world is at your disposal to use as your playground.

MAKING LEARNING FUN
FOCUS ON DAVID UCKO: SCIENCE CITY

Making Learning Fun—Focus on David Ucko Science City

Very early in his career David Ucko was hired by Victor Danilov, president of the Chicago Museum of Science and Industry, in response to a white paper blasting the institution for being an advertisement for industry. Since that auspicious beginning he not only turned the museum around but moved on to Kansas City to develop one of the most innovative approaches to museum exhibitions I have seen. By immersing visitors in the workings of the city, Dave opened new pathway for playfully exploring the world we live in. His work shows ingenious understanding of the happiness factor in museums.

While on the phone interviewing David, my husband whispered in my ear asking me who I was talking to. When

David

I answered, "David Ucko," he responded by saying, "I remember David. He is one of the nicest men on the planet." This was offered by a man who rarely gives compliments. Quiet, thoughtful and with an unassuming manner David Ucko moves through his life as an education change agent. In each of his endeavors he has been able to swim through political and social mine fields in order to implement science programs that capture the imagination and emotions of participants.

127

His most impressive and difficult undertaking, as president of the Kansas City's Science City at Union Station, demonstrates what the combination of intelligence, education, and perseverance can do to accomplish a task that appears to be impossible. Dave's story also speaks of the personal sacrifices that are made when tackling a 24/7 enterprise. Redevelopment of Union Station from a dilapidated train station into a mixed-use educational attraction based on a themed immersion experience cost over $250 million. That is a lot of money for a nonprofit organization to raise and it was not an easy task to accomplish.

David's idea of promoting recreational learning was unique to science centers. He drew on what he saw in theme parks, interactive museums, Hollywood, and the media and mixed them in a synergistic manner to create a unique concept. Ideas do not happen in a vacuum but are the result of an inspired combination of past experience and study. To be able to implement a concept is partly dependent on timing but is even more reliant on one individual who has "the right stuff." What made David able to be this visionary and what strengths did he have in order to accomplish the tasks that define his life?

David Ucko grew up in New York City's Washington Heights neighborhood as the second son of immigrant parents. He was fortunate to be born into a family where education was a top priority. He happened to live across the street from a local celebrity who was on the *Mr. Wizard* television show and became an important acquaintance to this budding scientist. As a youngster Dave sailed through school, skipping third grade, reading constantly, and getting academic rewards. He loved chemistry and used to putter around the house mixing all sorts of chemicals and kitchen products to see what would happen. He must have had a very tolerant mother.

Mom provided a warm supportive environment while Dad's interactions were strict in the belief that children should be seen but not heard. It is easy to understand why David with his quiet demeanor and excellent posture, is perceived as reserved but somehow his warmth also comes through. All one has to do is look at his eyes. You know the people who age with little smile wrinkles? Dave has them.

Teachers are important influences in a child's development, and David managed to find several gurus who encouraged his interest in chemistry. At the Bronx High School of Science, he assisted his chemistry teacher in the prep lab and also edited the *Physical Science* journal. Then it was off to Columbia University where he was employed as a work-study student and given an opportunity that influenced much of his future. Steve Lippard, then a new assistant professor fresh from MIT, needed an assistant, and for three years Dave worked alongside him, leading to the joint publication of several papers in the field of inorganic chemistry. MIT was the perfect institution to attend for graduate school and within three years, in 1972, Dave received his doctorate in chemistry.

Dave's years in postsecondary school were also years of great political upheaval. He remembers when Students for a Democratic Society (SDS) took over the campus at Columbia University. Though not politically active himself, he did acquire the belief that having an educated public was important for the nation's future. He started looking for jobs in higher education, eventually accepting a position at Hostos Community College in the South Bronx. There David saw many students struggling with chemistry. To help he distilled the basics into a series of self-teaching modules using slides programmed with audiotapes to help students learn the content.

After presenting these modules at an American Chemical Society conference, he was contacted by an editor from Academic Press, which eventually led David to write textbooks translating complex science in ways understandable by those with limited knowledge. He completed *Living Chemistry* for health students followed by *Preparatory Chemistry* for freshmen with deficient backgrounds. Crisis struck after four years of teaching at Hostos. The City of New York was bankrupt and all faculty were furloughed with no pay. It was his first time joining the unemployment line.

It wasn't long before Dave was offered a position at Antioch College. A city boy who grew up in apartments, he became enamored by his first home in Yellow Springs, Ohio that had a garden view. Dave remembers looking out the window and commenting to his wife Barbara how beautiful the yellow flowers were only to be told that they were dandelions. (Teachers . . . if you are reading this book and work in the city, you might want to introduce wildflowers into your biology classes.)

Antioch is a fun place for an educator to be employed. Classes are small, teaching informal and students smart and engaging. Since it operates with a co-op program, the undergraduates take five years to complete their degrees, working while studying. The college has three major themes: commitment to excellence in scholarship; commitment to full-time cooperative work programs that support a link between theory and practice; and commitment to active engagement in the community and to social justice. The science center movement parallels Antioch's perspective in many ways. Interactive museums maintain an interest in scholarship, connections between theory and practice, and social and community involvement. David spent time living in the midst of people who embraced these concepts until once more bankruptcy struck. Shortly after he became an associate professor, in 1979 Antioch ran out of money and had to furlough faculty. Applying for unemployment for a second time did not feel good.

Dave's trust in the solvency of educational institutions was low and he listened when his wife Barbara suggested looking for a position in a science museum. It did not take long for this experienced young man to be hired the day he was interviewed by Vic Danilov of Chicago's Museum of Science and Industry (CMSI). This move began Dave's career as a change agent.

In the late 1970's a white paper by the Center for Science in the Public Interest had blasted CMSI's policy of letting corporations control the content of displays. The blast made quite an impression on the science center community. CMSI had lived by the golden rule: "Whoever has the gold makes the rules." Founded using the model of World's Fair, CMSI relied on corporations more familiar with marketing than sponsoring educational displays with a scientific perspective. Among CMSI's exhibits was a U.S. Army sponsored display featuring a helicopter that invited the visitor to practice shoot at the Viet Cong. Another exhibit, built by the local electric utility, attracted protesters wearing gas masks who handed out anti-nuclear literature.

David's first job as research coordinator was to develop concepts and content for exhibits. He was charged with transitioning to an educational rather than a promotional perspective. To further that transformation, David and his staff applied for and received National Science Foundation (NSF) and National Endowment for the Humanities (NEH) grants. The change enabled the museum's staff to manage the educational content and exhibit design. Another aspect of Dave's position was to develop new rules for working with sponsoring organizations which permitted the museum to develop the exhibit's science story before being presented to a corporation for review. Working with companies that had previously used the museum as an advertising platform and making them feel good about promoting science education was an early lesson in diplomacy. There were cases, as with General Motors, that Dr. Ucko's skills in advocacy and diplomacy were well tested. Yet David succeeded. What the museum might have feared—that corporations would pull their support—did not happen.

Change is not easily accepted, and David also had the

difficult task of cajoling and converting the fifty people who reported to him to the new policies. It was his task to ensure that everyone work together to meet their target. At Antioch, David was the kingpin, responsible for his classes. In Chicago, he had to manage a creative and opinionated group of individuals. Consensus building was the model he learned how to use.

— — — — — — — — — — — —

David's Lesson #1: Talk to people face to face. Avoid trying to resolve issues in written form.

— — — — — — — — — — — —

David gained insight by watching Vic Danilov hold his famous luncheons at his V-shaped conference table (a relic of the Century of Progress World's Fair), observing a master communicator at work. His own test came when he had to confront an ultra-religious staff member who was quite unhappy with an NEH awarded grant for a humanist-in-residence. The man was a creationist who thought that humanists were spreading a message contrary to God's teachings. Creationism is rarely discussed in museums dedicated to teaching the latest scientific developments. As he continued implementing the museum's mission, David tactfully managed to maintain a comfortable working relationship with this colleague through respectful face-to-face interaction.

— — — — — — — — — — — —

David's Lesson #2: Tell the whole story. Do not sugar coat the truth.

— — — — — — — — — — — —

For CMSY's 50th anniversary celebration in 1983, the Museum developed a major exhibition called *Technology: Chance or Choice?* that highlighted the most important developments of the past half-century. For the first time, the exhibits discussed both positive and unanticipated negative aspects of technology, presenting it as a double edged sward. Personal computers were quite innovative during that era, but a donation from Texas Instruments enabled stations to be installed that gave visitors a chance to share thoughts about the various new technologies. This exhibition had a major influence on the way museums integrated technology within their displays. Presentations became more balanced and were laced with interaction and feedback modules.

David continued to produce innovative exhibitions such as *My Daughter, the Scientist*; *Inquiry (On the Process of Science)*; and *Everyday Chemistry*. However, once Vic Danilov announced his retirement, David chose to move to the California Museum of Science and Industry in Los Angeles where he was offered the deputy director position by Museum President Jeff Rudolph. David told me he learned a great deal working with Jeff at the California museum because, "I was exposed to management challenges that immersed me in the political process for the first time. There was internal conflict between our state financed museum and its nonprofit foundation. They were two interrelated parts but run as completely different organizations. I also accompanied Jeff on visits to Sacramento, where I learned how to work with state legislators and administrators," he related. "I also became more involved in raising funds to support general operations and capital expansion."

All of these experiences proved to be extremely beneficial as he moved into the next change in his career. In 1989 Dave was approached by a Kansas City Museum trustee and asked to head their institution. Ready for a new adventure, he and his family pulled up their coastal roots so he could run a small science and history museum located in the middle of the country in a historic neighborhood that was renewing itself through preservation. It was located in a large old mansion that was inadequate for the bustling metropolis of Kansas City, Missouri. Neighbors loved the museum, but not the traffic created in front of their homes. Though many times the board of trustees had tried to expand the facility, they always failed. This time they wanted to succeed.

Upon arrival David was taken by his board chairman to lunch to meet Bill Hall, head of the Hall Family Foundation (funded by the family of the founder of Hallmark). David heard his trustee boldly ask Mr. Hall to donate five million dollars towards the start of a new science center. After Mr. Hall stopped laughing, the philanthropist told David that it would take ten years to get the center off the ground. His prediction proved remarkably prescient. As plans progressed the Hall Family Foundation along with the Ewing Marion Kaufman Foundation, and Sprint Corporation became involved as major donors.

David understood what many museum entrepreneurs are slow to realize: they need to have community awareness and buy-in to succeed. His first task was to create exciting exhibitions that were placed in rented spaces in a downtown shopping mall. The museum's own space was much too small to be able to display gigantic robotic dinosaurs and other large traveling exhibitions. David then raised $800,000, the largest amount of money the museum had ever obtained, to build a Challenger Learning Center as the "launch pad" for the new facility. By generating successful programs and getting the necessary funds, the staff was perceived as doing something good for the community, raising the museum's profile, and enhancing the validity of their long range plans. He was also able to leverage community backing into political support in Washington D.C., including a $10 million increase in funding to NSF's Informal Science Education program while chair of ASTC's Advocacy Committee. David was later appointed by President Clinton, with confirmation by the Senate, to the National Museum Services Board.

— — — — — — — — — — — —

David's Lesson #3: Build relationships and earn credibility.

— — — — — — — — — — — —

It took three years to increase the museum's visibility and credibility before reaching the "trustworthy" stage. During that time the museum also was working on a new concept for a relocated facility. What exactly should the center be? Duplicating the Exploratorium, the solution selected by many new science centers? Something similar to Chicago and California's museums of science and industry? Or a new concept?

David realized that he needed to communicate a philosophical viewpoint that everyone could understand and embrace had to be developed in order to achieve public buy-in and involvement. This became a unique concept called Science City.

David's Lesson #4: Keep your mind open, visit many places, and mix (it's the chemist in him) the best of what you see in your mind's eye to create something new.

"Who sees further a dwarf or a giant? Surely a giant for his eyes are situated at a higher level than those of the dwarf. But if the dwarf is placed on the shoulders of the giant who sees further? . . . So too we are dwarfs astride the shoulders of giants. We master their wisdom and move beyond it. Due to their wisdom we grow wise and are able to say all that we say, but not because we are greater than they." –Isaiah de Trani, Jewish Tosafist who lived from 1180–1250

Already familiar with immersion experiences by trips into a coal mine at the Chicago museum, David became even more intrigued by this approach after visiting *Cité Cine*, a temporary exhibit in a new Parisian science center. *Cité Cine* consisted of a text-free set of environments including a roof top, a garage, and a jail cell. Visitors watched famous movie scenes that had been filmed in those settings while listening to audio with headphones. Of the experience, Dave said, "It felt as though I was placed in the movie, experiencing the different environments, and it made me start to consider another way of presenting science." This idea was further strengthened when Dave visited the First Division Museum, a small museum in Wheaton, Illinois, that presented the military history through immersion experiences. For example, one display put the visitor in a small PT boat to watch a film of the landing at Dover Beach. At the end of the film, the screen lifted up, and the participant stepped out of the vessel on the simulated beach. Such displays are experiential and leave participants with a lasting impression. David was a strong fan of visitor immersion, believing that learning is enhanced when it is an emotional as well as intellectual experience.

The gears started turning in David's head as he envisioned an entire museum where theme parks, theater, and science center blended, allowing visitors to became involved in a series of themed environments (e.g., crime lab, high-rise under construction, science-themed golf course, weather station). Immersion would be reinforced by graphics and props appropriate to each setting along with costumed "interactors" who "lived" and "worked" in the city. There would be no exhibits in the usual sense in this new kind of science center. Signage would be kept minimal.

To gain feedback and build support, David spent a lot of time on the speaking circuit. The creation of the Science City Volunteer Council, dubbed the "Militant Mothers" and led by past Junior League leaders, played an important role. Everything appeared to come together when a prominent downtown site was donated. But when David and the board chair met with the city's mayor to share the good news, they were greeted with a big surprise. "You guys are giving me a headache," the mayor said. He did not like their proposed location because he wanted the museum to be the anchor of an empty and dilapidated, center-city train station. While that would lead to many benefits beyond the museum's scope, it also came with many new challenges: the fund-raising goal was to raise nearly two hundred million dollars, and voter and government approval was required. "At the time the decision was made, architects estimated significantly increased costs, but nowhere near the actual figure once work began on the deteriorated structure," Dave related. Two separate organizations, the Kansas City Museum and the Union Station Assistance Corporation (USAC), managed the project. Because the museum's emphasis was Science City and the USAC priority was historic renovation, disagreements were inevitable. Each organization had its own board, linked through a smaller joint coordinating committee. Science City alone required three design firms, and both organizations had to agree on those as well as overall architecture and construction teams. The media loves controversy and readily gave press to those who were obstructionist. Some wanted the Station to be used once more for transportation, while others did not want change made to historic architectural features.

Fundraising was a mammoth effort but ultimately more than one hundred million dollars was raised privately, including a forty million dollar endowment to support ongoing operations. That was a start. For me it might have been a finish, but not so for David. His next effort was political. A bi-state cultural district was formed to get public funds. The goal became one of convincing voters in five counties adjoining the Missouri-Kansas state line. Four counties eventually passed the measure and taxpayers contributed another one hundred and thirteen million dollars.

There were a great many problems from the beginning. Headache became the word David used to describe the opening months. The two organizations, the Kansas City Museum and the Union Station Assistance Corporation (USAC) linked through a joint coordinating committee to a third board of political representatives, formed to oversee expenditure of bi-state tax funds, added further to the complexity of governance. Project managers hired by the Museum and USAC were a joint-venture, as were the architects and the construction team. The size of Science City, nearly 70,000 square feet of exhibit space was a huge enterprise for the three design companies. It was an extraordinary complicated undertaking that involved nearly 1,000,000 square feet of existing structure and new construction.

By opening date contractors were still not finished. Though most people who visited were very pleased with Science City, spending over three hours on average, there were also those who said they would have preferred a more traditional science center.

David's Lesson #5: Be skeptical of contractors and consultants who tell you what you want to hear.

One of the biggest challenges resulted from a world renowned consulting firm hired to project attendance. Projections turned out to be over-optimistic, and actual revenue proved lower with costs higher than projected. The Station's electric bill alone was over $1 million a year. The project had numerous start-up issues, including escalator breakdowns, large-format film projector problems, and ticketing system discrepancies.

(In this respect, David suggests that it might not be a bad idea to hire two consultants to independently make projections. This advice rings true for many museum expansions. My own experience also suggests that consultants tend to give information to reaffirm what board and staff want to hear, and reports are often overly optimistic. I heard this story over and over again as I interviewed museum directors.)

It took many years before Union Station finally became the multi-use urban center that it was intended to be. Science City, the anchor attraction, offered more than fifty learning adventures. Flying bats abound as spelunkers visit the Hidden Treasure Cave, while giant ants hide underground at the Community Nature Center. There is a Crime Lab complete with detective who is asking for assistance in solving a case. I remember being impressed with the Medical Center where I participated in open heart surgery projected on a mannequin. It felt like I was in a real operating theater. My favorite display was Pop Wheelie's Delivery Service, a high wire bicycle that carries fearless participants over thirty feet in the air between two parts of the City.

Kansas City now has an interactive museum that residents point to with pride, but it took a man like David Ucko working around the clock for ten years. It meant sacrifice not only by him but his family as he attended social events for work instead of participating more in at-home time. It involved an understanding of science and of how people learn, and being able to creatively develop his own palette of ideas from which to paint his masterpiece.

The story does not end here, however. The next stop on David's journey was with another start-up museum. He was hired to launch a new museum for the National Academy of Sciences (NAS) in DC. Funding was not a problem because one man, Dan Koshland, a professor at Berkeley, donated $20 million dollars to the Academy for the purpose of building a small museum. The public and community were not involved in philosophical discussions because the museum was to be internally organized to represent NAS's mission. Composed of a distinguished society of scholars, the academy had been established by an Act of Congress under President Abraham Lincoln to provide "independent, objective advice to the nation on matters related to science and technology."

Different project, different set of problems. The donor wanted to have a say in every decision. Dr. Koshland saw the undertaking as his private museum. He fell into a common trap of the person gifting money who believes that he or she has the right to call the shots. Legally that is not so when donating to a 501(c)3 organization that offers the philanthropist tax benefits. When a donation is made, unless terms are specified in writing and agreed to in advance, the organization is not bound by the ongoing direction of the donor. Unfortunately, the benefactor may look at the donation as a swan song, designed to keep his or her mind active in retirement. Under such circumstances the museum's director has to be especially sensitive.

Dan wanted the new museum to be organized around the theme of light and Maxwell's equations. David saw Dan's vision as limiting, and once he understood what was important to the Academy, he developed a broader plan for serving their mission to educate the public. The displays were to be targeted at teens and adults who would be invited to interact with scientific issues of the day.

Working with Dr. Koshland continued to be dicey though. Dan called daily, insisting to be involved in all aspects of development and operation. At the end of a year David resigned, but his imprint remained and today the overall theme he developed remained in place.

— — — — — — — — — — — — —

David's Lesson #5: Presidents and directors of museums must be experienced professionals.

— — — — — — — — — — — — —

David was in a special position to observe and influence further professionalization of science centers through his next employment at the National Science Foundation. Working in a small government agency with many features of a university, he associated with academics who valued research, and with federal officials who valued accountability. Always an innovator, he established and managed a five year, $20 million grant with two rounds of funding that had a great impact on the field.

The Nanoscale Informal Science Education Network (NISE NET) was created to help the public learn about the emerging field of nanotechnology. Rather than have individual science centers develop their own exhibits and programs as is usually the case, the network allowed collaborative, open-source development and sharing of all resources. It was initiated by three museums: Boston's Museum of Science, Science Museum of Minnesota and the Exploratorium which created a national infrastructure of regional hubs connecting nanotechnology researchers with informal science educators. The network has grown organically and now involves well over a hundred museums and universities. Each spring, they organize weeklong NanoDays activities across the U.S. as well as internationally. This turned out to be a great new model with far reaching consequences.

David also encouraged and funded a study by the National Research Council (NRC) of the National Academies that resulted in the "Learning Science in Informal Environments" report. This seminal document gives external validity to the field by synthesizing the research and evaluation that supports informal science learning.

David continues to work as a consultant, most recently going back to his chemistry roots as co-chair of the NRC committee preparing a report on Communicating Chemistry in Informal Settings. He founded Museum and More LLC as an avenue to focus his creative energy to be focused on assisting informal learning organizations to develop innovative plans and solutions.

WHY RETURN? I'VE BEEN THERE!

O nce you have visited a museum, why would you ever return? The museums and science centers I enjoy best are those that continually stay fresh, providing changing exhibitions and rotating displays. Knowing that there are sights and sounds not to be missed means I sign up for mailing lists of many local institutions, and I pay attention to media promotions, gathering friends or family to join me to explore their enticing new displays. Membership growth is greatly impacted by unique exhibitions, so creating an expectation for constant change is always in a museum's best interest. When there is a lot of activity, people are willing to receive newsletters, class schedules, and announcements and even attend fundraising events.

— — — — — — — — — — — — —

Marilynne's Lesson #14: Consider everything that might go wrong and then some.

— — — — — — — — — — — — —

With a temporary attraction in mind, holding an art contest was one of the early projects we embarked on at Impression 5. We asked artists to submit two sample pieces, and a guest art evaluator selected six artists to be featured in a month long show. We had quite a few entries and the screening process was very difficult, but finally choices were made, the show date selected, and the artists informed of how many pieces they could display and installation details. Set up was on a Friday with an opening reception scheduled for the following evening.

As the artists arrived with their paintings and sculptures, we watched with horror as one woman carried in a series of pieces that were far-fetched variations of her previewed work. She called her dimensional art "vaginal pools" and invited visitors to splash their hands around the sculptures, which she filled with a small amount of water. Staff was absolutely shocked and did not know what to do with these potentially offensive art objects. We prided ourselves on being an open-minded museum and believed in unhampered expression of ideas. Should her work be censored or allowed as free artistic expression? We worried about children returning from a visit and telling their parents, imagining a public outcry.

Since no one liked the censorship option, we decided to go ahead and hang the show. Fortunately, most people did not deduce the artist's interpretation, and we choose not to explain it. During the following month we avoided taking school children through the art exhibit, filling their time with other engaging displays instead. Staff managed to sidestep public outcry but were unable to fully enjoy having this art display in the museum. Most of the pieces by the six artists were of note and worthy of discussion, but the vaginal pools did not belong in a museum that catered to children.

The experience became another learning moment. I spoke to the directors of area art museums to inquire how they would have handled the situation and learned that we should have had clearer instructions for the solicitation phase that described what type of art was deemed appropriate and inappropriate for a museum that catered to children. Once selected, the artist should be asked to sign a contract outlining the museum's obligations as well as retention of rights to reject any submission.

Finding interesting, affordable exhibitions is always a challenge. Those who work in exhibit departments are like archeologists looking for a hidden gem that will attract not only visitors but donors to underwrite rental, installation, and marketing costs. A friend recently asked me why museums are so expensive. "They should be free," she said. I agree with her. It would be wonderful if our citizens valued the arts so highly that they would be willing to pay through tax subsidies. Until that epiphany strikes the general public though, admission prices are bound to remain high even though they only reflect a portion of true operating costs. Building or renting a temporary exhibition is quite expensive. Maintaining interactive displays is even more of a burden because, as anyone who works with machines knows, they break and need repair. Exhibits such as *King Tut from Egypt*, *Body Worlds*, which contains slices of human anatomy, or a display of Van Gogh's original paintings carry multimillion dollar installation price tags even after the mega bucks of renting the exhibit itself is paid. An inexpensive exhibit is also more costly than imagined. Consider the time to freshly paint walls, clean floors, install the exhibit aesthetically, safely, and securely; to develop signage, pay for shipping and insurance, prepare educational posters and brochures, develop marketing materials, train guides, and arrange for related lectures and classes.

Large-scale spectacles can create havoc with a museum's budget. The public may flock to see an installation of note, but when it is over, there usually is an attendance dip, the unfortunate aftermath of a good thing. Though money may flow into coffers during the three-month display period, the following season sometimes means laying off staff, so planning for these fluctuations has to be considered when bringing blockbusters to town.

New exhibitions are not always easy to discover, so competitive directors travel and network at conferences in order to meet promoters. There are times when ideas for exhibits come from vacationing visitors who return with suggestions about a fantastic must-have display that they have just seen. Exhibits, planetarium shows, and films are like factory furnaces that need to be stoked all of the time.

Our small Lansing museum with its fledgling staff was quite competitive and jealous of the "big kids." We not only wanted to be considered a venue spot for new exhibitions but we aspired to create our own exhibit and have it circulate nationally. A group of eight of the country's largest museums had gotten together to create an exhibit collaborative in which each institution agreed to make a display that would circulate to the other member sites. In addition to having fresh offerings to liven up the museum, it also created an advantage for obtaining funds. Granting bodies such as the National Science Foundation (NSF), The National Endowments for the Arts and the Humanities, and other private foundations want their money to serve a broad audience. If a museum demonstrates that an exhibition being assembled will circulate to a minimum of eight committed sites, the audience is dramatically increased and the likelihood of funding improves.

Because of space constraints, Impression 5 could not accommodate a large exhibit, so we decided to form our own collaborative of eight smaller institutions with facilities ranging from 70,000 to 90,000 square feet. Of this, only about a third of this space goes to exhibit floors, with the remainder accommodating offices, theaters, classrooms, gift shops, and public spaces. The area for changing exhibitions is even smaller, in most cases little more than 5,000 square feet

The staff of these smaller institutions have an equal amount of creative energy as those who work in the biggies but operate with the constraint of a smaller budget. They also have a lot of ambition. The group that I assembled was known as the Small Exhibits Collaborative. It launched successfully by following the contractual lead of the large museums. Member institutions met at conferences to discuss plans and back proposals for national funding. The increased opportunities we had were motivating, and once more reinforced the benefit that comes from working together synergistically. The shop area in Impression 5's warehouse noisily hummed all day as staff and volunteers honed their carpentry, metal working, and electrical skills to complete displays for a growing exhibit agenda. Because of national recognition, we felt more important and had lots of fun being able to take an idea to completion.

The Oregon Museum of Science and Industry (OMSI) was part of the Small Exhibits Collaborative. Years later I accepted a position as president of OMSI which enabled me to continue to work with Impression 5. When OMSI moved to its new expanded building, it was invited to join the larger exhibit collaborative known as SMEC (Science Museum Exhibit Collaborative).

Permanent acquisitions came to Impression 5 from a variety of fronts. One Impression 5 procurement was a gift from a group of oddball artists involved in something called The Popular Arts Workshop. Their members developed public art projects and painted murals around town. One of their projects was to have a major impact on my personal life because it introduced me to my future husband. Ukor was a giant paper-mâché puppet built for Lansing's Day with the Arts. The animated ten-foot sculpture that resembled both dragon and dinosaur, and stole the hearts of those attending the show. With three people inside to manipulate his arms and head, and another hidden in the crowd surveying the audience, the puppeteers were able to conduct personal conversations with the captivated crowd. When Ukor occasionally ate a small child much to the squeals of the audience, the crowd would remain in the vicinity for quite some time after the show, waiting to see if the child would reemerge.

Ukor needed a permanent home once the art day ended, and I was asked if Impression 5 wanted the puppet. How could I say no to this fantastic smiling behemoth? Once installed, Ukor became Impression 5's mascot, entertaining visitors with his wisdom and tales. He was able to explain the difference between dragons and dinosaurs, and tell people why the dinosaurs became extinct.

An important exhibit area of most science centers focuses on the human condition, including anatomy, exercise, psychology, and health. At Impression 5, we installed an exhibit sponsored by The American Medical Association called *Life Begins*. It showed stages of development of the human embryo during the nine months preceding birth and included several real fetuses along with diagrams explaining the interaction of egg and sperm. When preparing to introduce a new sibling to the family, pregnant parents used the exhibit as a prop to describe embryonic growth to their children. We noticed that very young children were not at all interested in the exhibit, preferring to spend most of their time watching the "Egg to Chick" display a short distance away. Children self-select information about sex and conception, paying attention only when they are psychologically ready to do so. We did observe, however, that some parents pushed the subject before that appropriate developmental moment while others avoided the topic altogether. Many religious schools in Michigan arranged field trips to the museum, and several of the more conservative groups asked if we would cover the display with drapes before their visit. The answer was always a polite no and in some cases the class cancelled their visit.

Controversy was not confined to human growth and development. In one instance a fundamentalist group visiting OMSI asked for a lecture about evolution to be presented to their students. We accommodated their request, but as soon as the talk was over the children were asked by their teachers to remain in the auditorium for further discussion. Their principal then proceeded to tell the children that what we were saying was contrary to the Bible and therefore wrong. His way of using our museum was a low point in my career, and it made me quite concerned about academic ignorance promoted by certain spheres of society. Impression 5 ran a science center, not a church, and those visiting should be open to learning what science has to say about the world.

There were many high points to compensate for these few bad experiences. One such occurrence initially scared me as I worked quietly in my Lansing office. Outside the door I heard a commotion and saw two people shouting while running across the floor to find me. I immediately imagined that there had been a terrible injury. Instead a teacher and young mother were excited because an autistic child had talked for the first time in front of an oscilloscope set up to demonstrate voice patterns. The child was on a class visit with other handicapped children who were permitted to roam freely throughout our small museum. With no one paying attention to the young girl she wandered over to the oscilloscope and started vocalizing through a microphone, becoming fascinated with her moving voice pattern.

Several weeks passed before mother and teacher returned with child in tow, hoping to repeat the event. This time the adults walked the child up to the oscilloscope, pushing her in front of it and telling her to talk into the microphone. The child did what might be expected under pressure, and rebelled by remaining silent. This occurrence reinforced our philosophy of museums as free schools, places with well-planned space that invite children to move without constraints following their personal time frames. Giving children freedom to explore without hovering over them is the best way to encourage those aha experiences.

It is easy to abuse a good thing, and there are limits to what a museum can provide. One homeschool group of parents and children visited weekly, convinced that they were giving their children a science education by letting them run wild through the building. Our small facility in Lansing was packed with displays but not rich enough to provide the in-depth teaching that is part of a school curriculum. The museum hoped to inspire and trigger enough curiosity that a child will want to learn more after leaving the building. Those attending on a weekly basis without supervision became bored, ran from display to display pounding buttons and behaving in an unruly manner. Homeschooling mothers who brought their children were content to sit and chat in a corner, oblivious to the chaos.

Staff finally got wise to what was going on and decided to develop educational workshops that would satisfy the science needs of these home-educated kids. Families were asked to pay a small fee for in-museum classes, and it turned out that they were pleased to do so. In later years we devised additional methods of working with homeschoolers. When I worked at OMSI, a group of children with their parents were invited to learn chemistry in return for volunteering their time as explainers for those walk-in visitors who wanted to experiment in the chemistry lab. These students became knowledgeable, enthusiastic demonstrators who paid close attention to the needs of our visitors. The lab experience remains to this day a happy blending of the museum's desire for volunteers and the homeschooled student's need to learn chemistry. OMSI, as do many museums, continues to involve homeschoolers and volunteers in operating science labs and exhibit halls.

A few words about homeschooling. Over many years I have interacted with a great many children taught at home. My son and several grandchildren spent years at home being schooled by me or my daughter. By having participated in homeschooling and observing home schooled children in the museum, I formed an assessment about the movement that is quite mixed. Benefits gained have a direct correlation to the intelligence, educational background, and commitment of the parents. Half of the children I interacted with did well by following a rigorous curriculum that supported their individual learning style. The other half came from families that were less academically inclined, rarely participating in support programs, and often reluctant to have their children tested by the public school system. Unfortunately these children grew up unprepared for their future careers.

Those who do decide to teach their children at home quickly realize that it is impossible to be an expert in every subject so they make supplementary arrangements, often involving tutors or a museum's education staff.

Ukor the Dragon

An Electrifying Experience

SECTION III
LEADING THE CHARGE

Management and Board Shenanigans

Good management is part of operating any nonprofit institution. In the early days of Impression 5, I was invited
to a meeting organized by IBM along with other community
groups. The moderator started the session by welcoming the
"non-business" organizations to the meeting. I was horrified.
This man's belief was that if you were in a nonprofit organization you were not operating a *real* business. From his corporate
vantage point, work done by such groups was playtime. He
held a belief common among commercial business leaders that
has taken many years to shake.

In 1978, when I attended my first Association of Science
and Technology Center (ASTC) conference in Iowa, there were
64 people in attendance representing twenty institutions. All
of us were passionate about educating through interactive
methods, paying less attention to operations than we did to
philosophy. Times have changed since then and a museum
president can no longer be inexperienced about operating this
type of business. Big money is involved.

ASTC now has approximately six hundred member
museums with over two thousand registrants from around the
world attending conferences. There are ninety-eight million

people visiting affiliated institutions in the United States alone. In the 1990s, as international interest grew the European Network of Science Centers and Museums, ECSITE, was founded. It presently links museums in over fifty nations. Red-POP was then initiated to serve Latin American centers and ASPAC was created for the Asian-Pacific area. As ECSITE so aptly says on its website, "Visits to science centres and museums contribute to changing attitudes towards science and technology, increasing young people's motivation to choose science as a career." India, China and Saudi Arabia are building dozens of centers in rural and urban settings in order to help their citizens stay abreast of changes in science and technology. Managing nonprofit businesses requires a trained, networked staff. Science centers can no longer be managed by winging it, but rather requires and demands sophistication. Many directors have business degrees and all attend informative conference workshops.

Today you would never hear an IBM executive call a meeting of all the "non-business organizations" in the community as they did in the 1970s. Museums with their multimillion dollar budgets employ accountants, lawyers, development officers, personnel directors, and business school graduates. My staff at OMSI back in 1995 was composed of approximately 350 employees as long ago as 1995, and if we did not operate with sound business practices, the museum certainly would not have survived. Our budget in 1995 was over 18 million dollars and it has greatly escalated since then.

Learning how to manage volunteers is a critical part of management training. These generous people donate their time, and are the life blood of most charitable organizations, helping to keep them afloat. A volunteer coordinator was one of the first people I hired in Lansing. People offered their assistance for many reasons that ranged from being retired with a desire to do something new to wanting to share their skills

by giving back to the community. One volunteer in particular, a tall gangly fellow, arrived daily with Band-Aids on his
face. It took me a while to realize that he was preparing for
a sex-change operation and needed a safe place to be while
undergoing his transformation from he to she. In the early
'70s, it was unusual to have a girl electronics genius, so we
were pleased to have this transforming person's assistance
since we could brag of a female electronics assistant.

Most of what I learned at Impression 5 was on the job,
but as time went on I did take advantage of a great many
cutting-edge workshops and training programs. My master's
degree (doctorate would have been better) helped by providing
the acceptance needed to represent an academic institution.
By the time I was asked to manage OMSI, I had over 13 years
of practical experience, had served on the Board of Directors
of the Association of Science and Technology Centers, was
involved in community committees often with a board position, and was ready for a bigger challenge.

A Question of Power

In 1972 most businesses, public institutions and museums were
run by men. Even today the number of women running businesses or sitting on major corporate boards is low. According
to a January 2015 report from Catalyst's Census of Women on
Boards (conducted in 2014), only 19.2 percent of board positions
in Fortune 500 companies are filled by women as compared to
Norway where women occupy 35.5 percent of the seats. Our
country falls behind Norway, Sweden, Finland, France, United
Kingdom, Denmark, South Africa, and the Netherlands.

Women in the work place in 1972 tended to have jobs as
secretaries, teachers, or as clerks in retail outlets. Men in the
early '70s did not know how to react to a woman in a position
of power and women were somewhat unsure of their role as

well. Not being the main breadwinner in my family, my salary was not a high-agenda item. I was particularly innocent since I had never worked, outside of baby sitting and teaching ballet to neighborhood children in my basement. By the time Impression 5 was in its own building and my co-founder Dee had stopped participating, I was flying solo, learning along the way. I did give myself a salary of $12,000 the first year, but since the museum could not afford it, only took half of it home. My goal was to eventually take a full salary, which was the only way to insure that the organization would survive without me.

Charm and friendliness were two attributes I developed over the years, and I learned to manipulate them for the benefit of Impression 5. Like Margaret Thatcher, I wasn't above a little flirtation. I paid quite a bit of attention to my wardrobe, with outfits that showed my figure off to advantage. Plus, being in style with the times meant low necklines and high hems.

Because of the chauvinist era, I thought it funny, yet outrageous that during my first meeting with one newly-elected board chairman he assumed that sex went along with the job. He was nervous during our initial conference when he brought up the subject and seemed quite relieved when I told him that because he was board chair, let alone because of our respective marriages, we especially could not sleep together. The two of us went on to have a wonderful relationship, and together we accomplished a great deal. I wish this confrontation about sex had been the only one.

I have a secret and it is not a pretty one. One of my board chairs raped me. There is a lot more that goes on behind the walls of a museum than most visitors imagine. This man, of all people, should have treated me with respect. After all, he was an executive of an organization that served the poor and downtrodden. What a hypocrite he was as he went about his days projecting his broad smile and glow of benevolence. It is only now that I am writing this book that I have the courage to share what happened. For over forty years I put the truth in an envelope kept in the back file of my mind. The nightmare was never given words so it festered unnamed until today. My husband, children, and psychiatrist never heard about the occurrence, and I still have knots wondering what they will think when they read these words. As my life enters its final chapter I find myself wanting to talk about this rape as well as many other compromises unknown to the public.

A new board chair, a man whom I had greatly admired, called an evening meeting to discuss an agenda item for the next board meeting. After a half-hour discussion he began to fidget and told me he wanted to show me something, a surprise that was a short car ride away. It was getting late and I was anxious to return home to my family, but since he was so insistent, I went in his car to be taken to the unforeseen location. This man was a respected member of the community and serving our organization as a volunteer, and I felt beholden to him for the time he was giving. I assumed he had something to show me that would benefit the museum.

Our destination turned out to be an isolated motel with a room he had procured earlier that day. He pulled me frozen out of the car and into the empty room. I was scared, shocked and eventually abused and did not know how to handle the situation. If I went to the police, his reputation would be questioned but, given the times, mine might be destroyed. My husband and children would be pulled in nasty directions by the press and court system if I pursued the matter. In those days, women did not talk about rape and, if we did, we rarely won a court case. It was not until 40 years had passed and the man had died that I mentioned the experience.

Though this chairman continued his efforts to get me into compromising positions, I managed to put a stop to his expectations in a way that let us keep a working relationship. However, there will never be an excuse for what he did. I tried not to be angry, but with each passing year I became more upset. You might wonder why I share this incident after so much time has elapsed. It is because those in leadership positions must realize that at some point their integrity might be compromised if they don't think about the possibility in advance and considered how to respond. Naivety about sex and power is not a good excuse.

I have had numerous discussions with executive women about the role sexual encounters have played in their work lives. Unfortunately forty years after my experience, the power play continues. It is still very difficult for those at the top to deal with a powerful man asking for favors. A young woman I spoke to recently told me that when she did not succumb to an important colleague's charm, she became subject to disparaging remarks that undermined her position in her field as a consultant. Some women are in a position to prosecute, but many cannot for fear of losing their jobs, reputation or even their careers.

Men are vulnerable too. A friend of mine was in the development department of a well-known east coast university. Part of his responsibility was visiting potential donors to convince them to leave a sizable endowment to the institution. He told me of a situation with a wealthy older woman who was appreciative of the charms of this young man and invited him into her bed with promises of a major donation. He had to very gracefully decline so as not to lose the gift. A good sense of humor helped him.

Sex is not the only compromising imposition placed on directors. At the height of the "Praise the Lord" movement, one of my board members became a follower of TV evangelist Jim Bakker. Every time the directors sat down to a meeting, this religious zealot stopped the proceedings and started to pray. Whenever he heard a positive staff report, this otherwise quiet gentleman would shout out, "Praise the Lord!" One day he accompanied me on a fund-raising call. As we exited the driveway, he asked me to stop a moment and pull the car over in order to pray for a successful outcome. I was quite offended but reluctant to create a division with this otherwise very generous executive who was donating his time to raise funds. Finally, after months of listening to his outbursts, another board member told him that his behavior was inappropriate. Not long after that Jim Bakker was taken to court for rape and embezzlement. He was convicted in 1988 of mail fraud, wire fraud and conspiracy.

Marilynne's Lesson #15: Handshakes are not enough.

When there are few paid bodies to do the work of an organization, board members are often asked to pitch in. They handle legal needs, publicity, and fund-raising, locate facilities, review architectural plans, oversee financial management... and most everything else, including washing dishes after an event. These good Samaritans are committed to the cause and willing to spend hours to see it succeed.

As the Oregon Museum of Science and Industry (OMSI) grew, a different type of trustee was needed. Wealth, power, and contacts become more important than muscle power. Board members are expected to give not only time but money to the organization. Contributions need to be discussed with those asked to serve. Those with more limited resources may give a smaller amount of cash but more of their time and talents. I remember one board member who never attended meetings, yet he was instrumental to the museum's development due to his personal financial contribution and to his reputation. Once the community knew that the individual was involved, this trendsetter was effective in getting others to donate. He helped legitimize what we were trying to accomplish.

At times it was difficult to say goodbye in a way that

would not hurt the feelings of those founding members who slowly needed to be eased out of their positions. I found it particularly difficult because over the years some of these people had become close friends. Though changing the board makeup periodically may be good for the organization, it may not be good for the individual who is being replaced. That person may lose friendships and will definitely lose access to inside information and certain social opportunities.

Looking back at the makeup of various boards, I noticed that the ones that worked best were composed of people who enjoyed being with each other. Quite a few business and social alliances develop as a result of participation, and trustees are more likely to attend meetings and to work on various projects together when they see mutual benefit. Our board members were quite proud to be associated with a prestigious institution.

Trustees and volunteers often have expectations and economic realities that are unknown to the organization. In the initial phase of moving into Impression 5's small warehouse a board architect volunteered to help with the planning without a fee. When there was a recession, his company had difficulties and filed for protection under chapter 11, resulting in our museum unexpectedly receiving a sizable bill. One of the most uncomfortable situations I ever encountered was to face this board member in court. The museum did win the case, but quite a few feelings were hurt. I still feel distressed about the incident, and the damage done to this very generous man who experienced hard times.

There were occasions when board members arrived with their own agenda. This was particularly true when I began to undertake OMSI's large building project. A few of our trustees lobbied for construction and architectural contracts for friends. City planners also had their own vision for a new development, wanting the museum to raise money to showcase the waterfront, alter road access, and pay for a public bike trail. When we received a donated submarine we were required to put in a public dock that could be used by water taxis, for fishermen, and as a launching site for jet boats in addition to a pedestrian river walk. These requirements added a great burden to the museum's fundraising committee.

In my years of managing museums there were many things I did to improve board morale. As President I met privately with individual board members at least once a year. My husband and I also did a lot of entertaining at home. In the relaxed atmosphere around the dinner table, we turned strangers into friends.

I was able to give individualized attention because the number of trustees was not overly cumbersome. I know of some organizations that have over one hundred people serving as trustees. I was always fearful of large boards because they take up so much time. One of my colleagues told me that he spends 40 percent of his day dealing with board issues. Large boards are often unwieldy and the members feel disenfranchised if contact is not maintained. Some organizations have large boards as a display of power and as a way of getting money. In those cases a smaller executive committee is the group that meets on a more regular basis to guide the organization. My preference was to have quarterly board meetings with monthly executive committee meetings. This arrangement gave time for members to serve on various committees without being too overburdened.

Was board management a creative part of my job? The answer is certainly yes. I repeatedly pulled people together for brainstorming sessions that resulted in synergistic outcomes. Developing strategies for using volunteer help calls as much on creative problem solving as it does in most areas of human interaction.

A Good Board Member
Focus on Jean Auel: Author and Philanthropist

A Good Board Member—Focus on Jean Auel, Author and Philanthropist

What type of person becomes a board member? They are usually successful, recognized in their field, and have a strong affinity for the organization. Author Jean Auel was one such person who, with the help of her husband, used her knowledge, contacts and influence to help many non-profit organizations and museums. Starting with *The Clan of The Cave Bear* she has authored six books and is represented throughout the world with an estimated 60 million books in print. For me she represents exactly the type of person we all hope to attract to serving on the board.

"How does one find their passion?" I asked Jean Auel, noted author of the Earth's Children Series.™ "One doesn't" Jean replied. "It finds you, and when it does you have to be willing to hold it tight and follow where it leads." Jean did just that.

Jean

She grabbed the reins and for the past thirty years has taken the ride of her life.

Born in 1936 to dairy-farmer parents of Finnish descent, she along with her four siblings were exposed to a rich and varied childhood that included exploring nature each summer on the family's farm in rural Michigan's Upper Peninsula. In contrast, the school year found the children traipsing through museums within reach of their downtown Chicago home.

164

At home, "Mom was an inspiring cook who could bake a cake without following a recipe. Somehow she seemed to know how much flour or sugar to put into the mixing bowl and by taste and feel would add ingredients necessary to produce a masterpiece." Jean sat transfixed by the counter observing her mother's talent, and as she grew, she discovered that she also loved to cook. She had ample opportunity to develop her skills in later life as a mother with a burgeoning family.

Jean's father, a union painter, introduced her to the importance of being part of a brotherhood . . . a community of workmen who took pride in their work. Union radio talk shows were regularly heard at home and the entire family became part of the fellowship through events such as the annual Labor Day picnic. "Dad was also the neighborhood's 'fix-it-up chap,' the person people would go to whenever there was a problem." The traits of independence, community and social responsibility were absorbed by the young woman simply by being a part of this particular household.

With school located across the street and city attractions within walking distance, Jean experienced independence at an early age. She was always curious and interested in learning about most everything and especially wanted to read. Unfortunately her first day of kindergarten was upsetting. "I started crying when I was told that I would not be taught how to read until first grade." In those days everyone in class progressed at the same speed, and precocious children were not exposed to Talented and Gifted (TAG) programs as they might be today. But as soon as she did master her letters her path was set. She became an avid reader and, to this day, continues to have a love affair with fictional books and science magazines.

School was easy for Jean and she quickly became engrossed in math and science, subjects she enjoyed above all others. Her inquisitive mind was always questioning in an effort to interpret her surroundings. "I especially remember my sixth-grade teacher, Mrs. Chamberlain, because she read stories to the class." A Norwegian fairy tale, "East of the Sun and West of the Moon," made a lasting impression in that it featured a woman as the protagonist creating the happy ending. The idea that a woman could have power captivated young Jean, and she tucked this liberated notion into the recesses of her brain. Later, Jean would create a powerful woman in Ayla, heroine of her book *The Clan of the Cave Bear.*

Chicago has many amenities and because Jean's family lived within walking distance of major institutions, Jean could swim in Lake Michigan, walk to the zoo and museums of Lincoln Park, attend the Hayden Planetarium, stare at fish in the Shedd Aquarium and be awed by mummies at the Natural History Museum. The Art Institute was nearby and it, along with the Science and Industry Museum impacted the mind of this impressionable child. If ever there is an example of how cultural institutions can shape one's outlook on life, Jean's rich wanderings point the way.

She was married shortly after high school to sweetheart Ray who was enlisted in the air force during the Korean War, where he worked as a hydraulics engineer on in-flight refueling systems. He brought his eighteen year old bride to the airbase in Roswell, New Mexico, where the couple quickly fulfilled one of their dreams, that of parenthood. Jean gave birth to RaeAnn, the first noise maker in their blossoming family. After military service the couple decided to settle in Portland, Oregon to be near Ray's aging father. Pregnant with her second child, Jean looked forward to a western experience. I have known Jean and Ray for thirty-five of their sixty years of marriage, and have never met two people who seem more in tune with each other. They shared jobs, career aspirations and the raising of five active children in their bustling Portland household.

Though child care became the most important job for Jean as a young adult, it was not enough to keep her active mind content. Craving adult companionship after her husband started working at Tektronix, she thought it would be a good idea for her to have a job as well. With strengths in math and logic, she was able to land a position in the accounting department of Tektronix, eventually becoming a credit manager. Jean always was on the hunt for opportunities to better herself. When she discovered that the company would fund college educations for managers, the twenty-eight-year-old talked her manager into sending her to Portland State University even though she would be starting as an undergraduate. It took a great deal of persuasion since she was a low-level employee. After attaining her bachelor's degree she succeeded in getting approval to continue on for an advanced degree.

Raising children, working full time, and taking night classes would be discouraging to most couples but it was invigorating to the Auels. With perseverance and cooperation, Jean and Ray eventually marched down the aisle in tandem, each to receive a Master's Degree in Business Administration.

— — — — — — — — — — — —

Jean's Lesson #1: When you find your passion, embrace it. You don't have to look for it, but when you recognize it, hold on tight.

— — — — — — — — — — — —

Opportunity knocks at unexpected moments as it did when an argument with Jean's boss resulted in her resignation. For the first time in years she had time on her hands. Her children were growing up and did not need constant attention, so she started to play with the idea for a story, a tale of a girl living with people who were different. One night, as her idea evolved, she began writing a short story, and has not stopped writing since. Jean Auel had found her calling and that meant she just had to write. Nothing could get in her way. Jean became absorbed, committed and with her husband's support was able to finish her tale rather than return to work.

Jean's Lesson #2: Passion is only the beginning.
Hard work and follow-through is the pathway to
success.

In her early writing career, Jean did not think of herself as
a writer, but simply as someone having fun putting thoughts
on paper. After a time she realized that imagination was not
enough. A great deal of research was necessary before she
would be able to complete her story. So . . . off she went to
the library, returning with a huge pile of books. Jean had the
mind of researcher, the curiosity of an anthropologist and the
heart of a psychologist, and used all of these interests to weave
her tale. She was looking for two conflicting cultures living
near each other that had major differences in knowledge and
life style. Jean noted, "I could have written a story set in the
future as well as one in the past."

The years spent as a child in science and natural history
museums opened her eyes to the idea that there are many
mysteries in the natural world. She was fascinated with the
Alaskan Eskimos and curious about archeological finds in
Europe and Africa. She sought out practical experiences in
archeology and survival skills and was willing to get her hands
dirty. During her investigations, Jean discovered that there
were two ancient cultures living simultaneously in Europe—
Neanderthals and modern humans—and wondered if they
ever interacted. Most anthropologists at the time thought that
the two species lived separate and independent lives, but a
questioning Jean was always asking, "What if?" As she learned
more, her questions and ideas expanded exponentially, slowly
evolving into a story to be told in the six novels of her Earth's
Children series.

Jean's interest in museums continues to this day. The
Auel's made sure that when their children were young they

had exposure to the same cultural opportunities Jean had as a youth. Jean loved art and was a frequent visitor to art museums, having even received a scholarship when young to the Art Institute of Chicago. The Auel's home is adorned with a magnificent art collection, and many artists are invited visitors. The family became active members of the Oregon Museum of Science and Industry (OMSI) which Jean describes as "my children's best babysitter. On Saturdays the children would walk from home in order to hangout in classes or on the exhibit floor." OMSI had developed several science kits and Jean dutifully brought them home, often finding herself the one assembling the apparatus and conducting the experiments. Jean never stopped learning, and enrolled in OMSI's adult classes, learning such things as how to survive if stranded in the snow and what is involved in building a snow cave. Her curiosity about wilderness survival grew so strong that she enrolled in eastern Oregon's Malheur Field station in order to learn such things as how to make fire without matches, the secret of tanning leather and ways of knapping to create stone tools. These participatory experiences added authenticity to her writings about primitive people.

As a successful writer, she established relationships with international scholars who contributed to the richness of her work. She became especially close friends with anthropologists at the Natural History Museums in London and New York. "Wherever I travelled," she related "I found people who were pleased to help." As doors opened she gained access to prehistoric ruins, visited caves that were closed to the public containing primitive rock art, and was shown artifacts and relics found in closed stacks in museums and universities. I remember one time she told me that she was going on a diet in order to be able to fit through the tiny opening of a newly discovered cave. These places that were beyond the reach of the general public became breeding grounds for new ideas, and lively discussions with scholars challenging existing hypotheses about evolution were interwoven in her tales.

Dr. Chris Stringer of the London Natural History Museum originally disagreed with Jean's assumptions about the intermingling of Neanderthals with Homo Sapiens. Years later, when she was a celebrated author, Dr. Stringer invited her to London as a guest speaker. During his introduction he apologized to Jean for disrespecting her ideas. New research had come to life supporting her hypothesis about sexual intermingling between Neanderthals and Homo Sapiens. Jean was a woman ahead of her time who used intuition to surmise what anthropologists have since confirmed.

— — — — — — — — — — — — —

Jean's Lesson #3: If you have success, you need to give back to the community.

— — — — — — — — — — — — —

Once Jean became an acclaimed writer she and her husband became community philanthropists, donating to museums and nonprofit organizations throughout the country. What she and her husband absorbed from their farm parents, the notion that one helps one's neighbors, was translated into a life of assisting others through their donations. Even while a young working woman, Jean held an internal dialogue that said, "If I can afford to send my kid to music lessons, then I can afford to help someone else."

The Auels are especially supportive of science education and have benefited from many programs and exhibitions at OMSI. Jean accepted a position on OMSI's board of directors and worked with me for three years. She told me that the reason she decided to participate was in part curiosity. "I wanted to understand the inner workings of a board and was surprised to discover how many decisions were politically motivated." She was amazed at how much money it takes to run a museum and observed with disquiet the maneuverings for power that take place behind closed doors. Her knowledge of science and education provided a firm contrast in board meetings to the singularly financial-minded individuals in the group. There were many times when her voice rang out in support of an controversial though scientifically relevant educational endeavor.

— — — — — — — — — — — —
Jean's Lesson #4: Learning is fun.
— — — — — — — — — — — —

When asked, "What do you do for fun?" she responded, "I educate myself. It makes a more interesting life. You get to know more interesting people. It doesn't matter what your area of interest is, learn all about it. Cultural organizations are important because they are learning institutions. It is fun to grow intellectually all of your life." Ray and Jean continue to experience life fully through travel, reading and community involvement. They believe they are lucky and readily share their good fortune with family and friends. Both husband and wife enjoy new experiences and are committed to never stop learning.

What Makes a Great Leader?

Have you heard these phrases? *Opportunity only knocks once. When one door closes—another door opens. When you see a chance, grab it. Every day is a new beginning.* Do you believe that you should lay back and just keep an eye out for your chance or are you the type of person who is ready to push the barricade open a crack and slide through? My favorite quote by Rita Coolidge is, *Too often, the opportunity knocks, but by the time you push back the chain, unhook the two locks and shut off the burglar alarm, it's too late.*

Advice to seize the opportunity was given to me by another entrepreneur when I started Impression 5. It was during a time when I wondered if I would ever get the museum off the ground because of all the nay-sayers unwilling to provide money. My luncheon partner was emphatic when he said, "People make their own opportunities. Don't listen to anyone else. Do what you have to do and just go for it." Opportunity is a crack in the material that has to be pried open. Each promising occasion has to be acknowledged and molded. Whether you are advancing a career, initiating a business or starting a non-profit organization, it is important to be ever on the lookout for threads of connection that advance your cause. Once begun, there is no looking back, and that act in itself creates pressure to take the bold steps needed to move your agenda forward. Consider what it means to be successful and rise to the top.

You may wonder if there are guides that can help insure that your child becomes a successful leader. Actually, there are many, but do they work? Some prep schools assert that they are training the leaders of tomorrow. The Junior League claims to be coaching women to be community volunteer captains. I noticed that many achievements are a result of rubbing the right elbows. Upper-class friends make it much easier to launch certain types of careers, get into country clubs, and participate in politics.

Though class standing may make life smoother, it does not account for all or even most of the attributes needed for leadership. Biographies of museum leaders included in this book point to people who grew up in an era that permitted a great amount of independence. They were not all wealthy but had the freedom to roam their neighborhoods for hours at a time traveling by bike or subway. They lived in environments that were not only safe but were socially rich. Many had parents who introduced them to the wider world through travel, cultural activities, and acquaintances. Armed with curiosity, these men and women were encouraged as children to engage in their own passionate pursuits. Games they played and projects they embarked on molded them into adaptable, resilient, self-confident people. Their friendships provided practice in team building and helped them develop leadership abilities.

Psychologist and Harvard faculty professor Jeff Brow and assistant professor, Mark Fenske, of the University of Guelph in Ontario, used cutting-edge neuroscience to study attributes of successful people. In the *Winner's Brain* (Da Capo Press, 2010) they described eight distinct win-factors that include:

- Self-awareness—Know how you relate to others and how others relate to you

- Motivation—Want it even when the rewards are uncertain
- Focus—Concentrate 100 percent on the goal
- Emotional Balance—Manage emotions without denying them
- Memory—Use past experiences to predict the future and exercise the mind
- Resilience—Don't worry about failures; learn from them and bounce back
- Adaptability—Train your brain: brains adjust to new circumstances
- Brain Care—Take proper care of the brain which is, after all, a part of the body; this means a good diet, stimulation, exercise, and sleep.

Brown and Fenske shattered common myths stating that success in life depends on inherent intelligence, fortunate circumstances, financial backing, or just plain good luck. Instead, they implied that a critical success factor lies in having a failure-resistant brain. Though some people are born with a disposition to be averse to failure, the authors assured us that everyone possesses the foundational material for creating a brain that is failure-resistant.

Rising to the top of a field is not simply a matter of luck. Surprisingly, upward movement does not depend on the position in which you might presently find yourself. Research shows that the brain is constantly being shaped and reshaped by thoughts, behavior, experience, and emotion. It continues to evolve for as long as you live. So . . . you do have choices, and you can act to improve your lot, whatever your age. Whether it is a museum or a business enterprise of your own choosing, anything is possible. It is a matter of seeing opportunity, reaching for the unknown, persevering, learning from mistakes, and trying again. It involves looking inward and calling forth your own commander qualities.

Years ago, I read a study about women who rise to the top. I have since lost the source, but remember that some of the findings were quite unexpected. The most significant difference between women who became presidents of major corporations compared with those at the level below was emotional balance. All of the women studied were competent, experienced, and motivated. But surprisingly, in their late thirties to early forties, the top achievers changed the way they socialized and interacted with others. This transformation occurred over a relatively short period of time. Some got married, others developed a significant love relationship, and quite a few decided to have children. They all softened the way they dressed, and even took more time-off from work for their own pleasures. Not quite as driven as they were previously, they became more relaxed and improved their relationships with co-workers, inquiring about their personal lives rather than only communicating through business speak. As the women became better listeners, they also became more effective leaders. It was these compassionate people who broke through the glass ceiling and made it into CEO positions.

The eight psychological factors for leadership are not part of the common curriculum goals, so to acquire them strategies are needed to supplement teacher designed lessons. Development of well-educated, confident, and creative executives starts at home and not at school. Good nutrition, safe living conditions, healthy bodies, money for basic needs, adults who are willing to listen, and challenging opportunities form the basis for intellectual growth. Teachers cannot continue to be blamed for poor test scores when the problem may be inadequate parenting, so we must find opportunities outside of the classroom must be found to help those who lack the essential ingredients for success. It is when basic needs are met that a person has the possibility of developing into a socially responsible leader.

Informal learning experiences provided by museums help by supplying intellectual stimulation for inquiring brains. Gift shops purchases can extend the experience, providing fuel to be used at home. There are a great many energizing activities parents can do with children that develop observation skills and curiosity. Collecting rocks or seashells is inexpensive and builds categorization and organization abilities. Promoting group-play activities provides a practice forum for leadership and team building. By learning to be observant of the surrounding environment, a child starts seeing opportunities. I know an African American father who challenged his children to discover why some trampled chewing gum on the sidewalk was shiny and clean looking while other pieces were dull and dirty. Their research started an investigation that led to gum trees in Africa and the black scientists who transformed pitch into a chewable product. For these children, that lesson ended up supporting the school's curriculum while building their own leadership abilities. To develop daily habits that incorporate the eight factors of success, your local habitat has all of the needed props.

ON GIVING BACK
FOCUS ON CYRUS KATZEN: THE KATZEN ART CENTER

One of the most playful men I have ever known is Dr. Cyrus Katzen. His sense of humor, eye toward opportunity, compassion and willingness to take risks is legendary. The following biography is the story of a self-made man who saw a need, provided the funds, and oversaw development of an Art Center and Museum in Washington, DC. He is included in this book because he sheds light on what happens when a philanthropist wants to manage how his donation is spent.

Leaving behind the pogroms of western Russian, the Katzen family arrived in the United States in the early 1900s making their way to Philadelphia. "Your father was the eighth in a family of nine children growing up in a ghetto area of the city," my cousin Cyrus Katzen (1918-2009) told me. Cyrus and his brother Bernie were the sons of my father's oldest brother, but being nearly the same age as my dad the boys formed a cousin-like . . . really, a brother-like bond that lasted a lifetime.

Even though Cy's family moved to Washington, Cyrus remembered "frequent visits to Philly to see the old folks where we cousins always

Cyrus

played together. We were close, the three of us, even joining the service together during World War II. In fact, when I heard that your father was ill and near death, I rushed to England to make sure he was getting the best treatment."

Always a good student, upon graduation from Central High in DC, Cy enrolled at Georgetown University to become a dental surgeon. It was not long before Cy had a star- studded practice that included many of the nation's congressmen and Supreme Court justices. Business blossomed, and his practice grew, allowing Cy the freedom to use his inventive mind in new ways. In the early 1950s he identified a need for a high-speed automatic x-ray developing machine and designed one of the first in the country. "Those were exciting times." Cy smiled. "My first patent was followed by a second, you know. The military asked me to make an adaptation so it could be used on submarines to monitor exposure from radiation." As a child, I listened to him share tales of coast-to-coast travel to install and repair his devices. Through the wonder of my childhood lens, Cyrus was an exotic man who was always jolly. I looked forward to his visits.

Dentistry was not enough for this mountain of energy who realized early that he had a head for business. Both real estate development and banking intrigued him enough to spearhead three separate financial institutions and many important construction projects. "When I started out," he said, "Washington was a small city surrounded by farm land. I just knew that the city had to grow." Recognizing the potential for burgeoning suburbs he took risks, used intuition, contacts and innate intelligence to became a major player. In DC he built such places as the landmark Embassy Row Hotel on Massachusetts Avenue NW and a shopping center at Baileys Crossroads to name a few of his seventy worldwide developments. He helped broker the contracts that created the Tysons shopping mall complexes, Crystal City and Rosslyn. Dr. Cyrus Katzen was a shrewd entrepreneur, a competent dentist and an inventor who knew his way through the political and social fabric of DC. He exemplified the American dream of a self-made man who moved from poverty to riches.

Cyrus's sense of humor and gift of joyful living was renowned among his acquaintances. He thrived on happiness and making people laugh. His collection of brightly colored antique tin wind-up toys spun and popped with animation, never ceasing to amuse him. Monkey Playing Cymbals was as prized as any of the fine art he later purchased. I remember watching Cy pay a restaurant bill by "accidentally" pulling out a one hundred dollar note printed with his grinning face instead of Benjamin Franklin's. When the startled cashier got the joke, instead of sputtering with the shock of receiving a counterfeit, she joined in Cy's infectious belly laugh.

Though he lost his wife Sylvia, the love of his early life, he found a wonderful companion with whom to share his later exploits. His second wife, Myrtle, had artistic talents that were recognized in her youth. When only eleven, Myrtle's art teacher suggested she study seriously, so she enrolled at Abbott Art School. As an adult, Myrtle worked as a graphic and commercial artist before receiving a diploma from American University's Art Department in fine art painting. She described her training at the university with fondness, saying that the faculty was stellar. Myrtle was joined by fellow artists who continued to meet with faculty member Luciano Penay in weekly critique meetings.

As Cy's wallet grew, so did his interest in purchasing art. His taste tended toward brightly colored, feel-good pieces that matched his personality as a jokester. At first his collection was naïve and not considered worthy by art aficionados. Myrtle attempted to stimulate and refine his critical eye but did not have an easy job. Cy remained quite headstrong about his purchases, convinced he understood art, but was a person who appreciated masterpieces and circus toys with the same gusto. He was pigheaded in his belief that his eye was the only one that mattered, so when he first started collecting, he purchased works by both unknown and known artists that passed his personal appreciation test. It took years before he became a bit more sophisticated and assembled a diverse selection of glass, paintings, and sculpture that would be considered assets to any art collector's portfolio.

When Cyrus was in his seventies, with the help of the deputy director of the Hirshhorn Museum and Sculpture Gallery of the Smithsonian, Steve Wiel, I arranged to have the president of the Hirshhorn brought to the Katzens' condo to evaluate their collection. After the visit Steve called and suggested, "Cy's collection is all over the place. He needs to take a course we offer in how to collect." The two experts advised Cyrus that he should become more knowledgeable before purchasing investment-grade art. Their words had no meaning to Cy, who would never consider taking such a class, since all that mattered was that he like what he bought. It many ways Cy was right to think this way, since it was his money and he was living surrounded by the works he loved and purchased. It is just that the rarified world of curators and art collectors have different criteria that include pieces maintaining monetary value over time. The principals of the Hirshhorn Gallery were not ready to kow-tow to Cy's whims though, if they had courted him, it might have resulted in a sizable donation to the Hirshhorn.

I loved to visit Washington DC and stay in the Katzens' spare bedroom which stored many of his paintings. Cyrus and I had a lot of interests in common, I with my tales of starting and managing science and technology museums and he with his early exploits with x-ray machines and his later foray into collecting. We were kindred souls who loved both the arts and sciences, enjoying visits to museums and galleries where we shared our likes and dislikes. He even went with me when I approached the American Association of Museums (now Alliance for Museums) for assistance with Shop for Museums, one of my commercial ventures designed to benefit museums through financial contributions.

Though Cy continued to purchase artwork with his heart, the advice he consistently received did have an impact. He did start to pay a bit more attention to artists of note. Gallery owners up and down the East Coast contacted him regularly to promote their hot artist of the moment. The most expensive piece purchased was a Dubuffet valued at well over $1 million. He knew and purchased works of Gene Davis, of the Washington Color School, known for his canvases of vertical stripes. An original small foundry copy of *The Kiss* by Rodin was collected as were works by Paul-Emile Pissarro, the son of the French Impressionist. Cy's assemblage grew to the point that in his 6,000 square foot double-condo, paintings were arranged floor to ceiling on every wall in every room, including the bathroom. Sculptures dotted the floors, the dining room table, side boards and end tables making it almost impossible to walk through the rooms. There was hardly a place to set a glass of water down. When staying overnight, I would get up early in the morning to wander his halls alone. I was especially drawn to a group of whimsical glass sculptures.

Dr. Katzen was philanthropic and caring, believing that it was important to give back to the community that had nurtured his successes. He made sizable donations to a great many health, cultural, and educational organizations. Among other gifts of significance he gave $10 million dollars toward the Dr. Cyrus and Myrtle Katzen Cancer Research Center at George Washington University Medical Center to honor his first wife, Sylvia, who died from cancer.

When he and Myrtle considered what would happen to their, by then, very eclectic art collection, Cy became excited by the idea of building a museum to house it. He had grand plans, at first talking of purchasing a mansion in the heart of DC to turn into a private museum. He took me on a car ride once to pass a magnificent old house he was considering.

Under Myrtle's influence he changed direction in 2005 from considering a private museum to making a more public one. Because of her attachment to American University, the Katzens' wound up donating $15 million toward building expenses and $5 million in art, to launch a 130,000 square foot art center and museum that would bear the Katzen name. Concerned for how AU would maintain the facility the couple designated a commercial building as part of the gift in order to provide office space with rental income that could be used for collection upkeep.

Cy's leadership skills were needed to get through the city's red tape. Receiving construction permits was difficult because of the prominent location for the proposed center. Over a ten-year period, American University had tried to put a law school on the same site, but the neighborhood outcry was against the move. It did not seem likely that an art center and museum would be acceptable either. Cyrus had informed the university that only after the zoning issues were overcome would he carry through with his donation. The land AU desired was located at Ward Circle, at the intersection of Nebraska and Massachusetts Avenues, near many foreign embassies and clearly visible to all.

Because of Cyrus's considerable knowledge of zoning rules, his political acumen, and his skills gained over many years in real estate ventures, the impasse between university and surrounding neighborhood was quickly resolved. He used his personal contact with Congressman Tom Davis of Virginia to put pressure on Washington's mayor in order to obtain needed permits. He threatened the mayor with losing the art museum to Virginia if zoning was not approved. The mayor capitulated.

Once the building was on track, Cyrus stayed involved in all aspects of the project, from architectural planning to selection of the first director. Jack Rasmussen, the current director of the Katzen Art Center said of that time, "Cy was the six-hundred-pound gorilla in the room."

Now complete, the Katzen Art Center sits proudly atop Embassy Row in Washington, DC, one of the highest points in the nation's capital, and represents a real coup for the university. However, in getting to that point Cy faced personal disappointments. He originally wanted the museum to be the building's major focus. Over time, university officials convinced him that there was need for classroom and theater space as well. Space for the lovely three-story fine art museum kept getting smaller as the teaching areas grew. This, in turn, created an ever growing problem as to where to house his own collection. Cy's original plan to donate $5 million in paintings came with the expectation that they would be kept on permanent display. But the museum director was concerned about showing good as well as mediocre pieces, as well as the larger concern that displaying all of Cy's collection would have taken over the entire gallery. In order to entice visitors to return, there needed to be rotating exhibitions. Though Cy's pieces could be displayed periodically, for a good portion of the year, they had to be stored to accommodate an ever-changing show schedule. Cyrus was not very happy about the more than three hundred paintings and sculptures he was ready to donate taking a backseat. Some of the more important art and glass sculptures included pieces by Pablo Picasso, Marc Chagall, Robert Rauschenberg, Milton Avery, William DeKooning, Jean Dubuffet, Red Grooms, Amedeo Modigliani, Alexander Calder, Jasper Johns, Andy Warhol, Nancy Graves, Roy Lichtenstein, Larry Rivers and Frank Stella. I was personally fascinated by the canvas of Jacquelyn Kennedy by Chuck Close and glass art by Dale Chihuly. Though the museum today does have a few of these promised pieces, the majority of the art bequest was never granted to the university because of this misunderstanding.

Selecting the first museum director for the gallery was fraught with much difficulty. The original selection, Barbara Rose, had very different ideas for the layout of the museum from Cyrus and the university. She wanted the project put on hold and redesigned. She also was not excited by Dr. Katzen's mixed collection, and started pushing him to purchase works of well-known artists like Claus Oldenburg, many of whom were her friends. Cyrus liked pop art, while she preferred the modern works of contemporary masters such as Frank Stella, Barbara's ex-husband. Though she was a very talented and dynamic woman, Barbara did not last long in her position.

The second director, Jack Rasmussen, was more tactful and able to inform Cyrus, without turning him into an enemy, that his collection could not be on display 100 percent of the time. Jack had known Dr. Katzen from the project's inception when he worked in the development office assigned to raising funds for a new art center. Once the Katzen Art Center opened, Jack brought the gallery great acclaim through his ability to attract exciting changing exhibitions. I remember Cy's disappointment when he realized that his collection would not be permanently on display, but he also told me that he understood the need for continuous change.

The Katzen Art Center is a marvelous contribution to the city of Washington and was important to Cyrus as he aged. He came to love the center and was often seen sitting in the hallways watching students' faces filled with excitement as they moved from classes to workshops. He visited Jack Rassmussen on a weekly basis, contributing ideas and never letting him forget past promises. Cy told me that he planned to attend as many of the art openings that he could before he died. Several times a week he attended functions, especially enjoying his visits when foreign embassies displayed their country's treasures. Myrtle, who outlived her husband, continues to be seen in the Center for special openings.

Having a museum that bears my family name is a great honor that I share with my Washington cousins. The Katzen Art Center is a lasting legacy to American University and is a visual demonstration of how one philanthropic individual can effect change. Cy's story is one that shows the strength of good leadership as well as the pitfalls of working with a powerful man who wants to control his donation.

ACHIEVING BALANCE: LESSONS FOR PARENTS AND LEADERS

People are happiest when leading a well-balanced life. Participation in physical activities, going on vacation, quieting the brain, and just chilling out with friends are important ways to clear the mind. Daily exercise is not meant to be an exhibit in a science center, though many centers do devote quite a lot of floor space to them. I have always been conscientious about participating in a daily exercise regime. Passing bulging bodies on the street gives me great concern and motivates me to stay healthy. After reading how some businesses based in Asia integrate exercise in their workplaces, I decided to launch an experiment at Impression 5 where visitors were invited to join staff for fifteen minutes of stretching and movement. Our loud speaker announced the short break and suggested people to stop what they were doing, go into the aisles, and follow the leader's directions. Lively music enticed most visitors to give it a try. We chose to conduct the exercises at 2:30 in the afternoon, a time when fatigue sets in for most people. It was quite heartening to watch crowds of people bend and sway throughout the museum.

I loved participating in the physical activity and noticed that our staff had much more energy after the short interval.

Two-thirds of our visitors joined us enthusiastically while the other third were less willing, not wanting their attention diverted from what they had paid to be there for. I saw those breaks as a practical application of what the science center was teaching.

Nike is especially good at integrating exercise and work. Its corporate campus has several gymnasiums near office buildings, and staff are encouraged to leave work to exercise whenever they feel the need. This flexible attitude decreases work fatigue, promotes teamwork, and creates employees who are more alert and focused. It also serves to develop social contacts among distant staff members, increasing cross-departmental communication. Best of all, it makes Nike a place where work blends into play.

Getting away from daily stress with a break is imperative. Not only did I appreciate the change of scenery, but my staff enjoyed having me gone. I told myself that if everyone was well trained then my absence would be easily handled. Once a system is in motion, it is difficult to change course, and as long as everyone is moving in the same direction, it is fine to disappear for a while. I trusted that decisions made in my absence would be similar to my own. Cell phones and computers make it easy to stay connected today, but in the 1970s and '80s that was not the case. Unfortunately, these high-tech devices now make it more difficult to ever completely get away from work to fully relax.

Since I had children at home, most of my vacation time was spent with them ... but not all. My husband and I would hire a babysitter from time to time and take off to explore the world. It was our way of stimulating our minds and renewing our commitment to each other. When younger and could not afford the cost of help, a friend and I organized a sitting exchange. In my mind, there is no excuse for not taking needed breaks. In one instance all my husband and I did was get in a car and drive two exits on the highway, getting off to spend the night in a local hotel. After a great dinner, a soak in a hot tub, a movie, a mighty fine breakfast, and a walk through the nearby mall, we were ready again to face the world.

Vacations also are a good time for ideas. Refer back to the discussion on creativity where I spoke of taking a mental tour of a supermarket to find a repurposed use for the L'eggs plastic egg. Vacations are a bit like the supermarket tour. I often see, do and learn something new, and since my attention is relaxed, I find that I use this information in unexpected ways both at work and home. Inventiveness is simply a matter of paying attention to connections, and no matter where I go, I always have a low buzz of thought that will eventually affect my activities.

When on business trips, I usually stay an extra half or full day. Since I love art and culture, my wanderings during these precious free hours are often in art or history museums or along streets to view local architecture. These meanderings help me remain in tune with life outside of work while keeping me curious and playful.

All museum presidents are intellectually inquisitive and have outgoing personalities. These attributes are unwritten requirements for the job and are good qualities to develop. These same virtues are the ones I looked for in the men whom I chose as life partners. All three of the important men in my life shared my love for art, music, literature, dance, and science.

Canvas painting was a meaningful hobby that helped me reduce workplace stress. Exercise was not enough to alleviate tension, because whether jogging or in exercise classes my mind would never turn off. Painting became my freedom because it is impossible to decide what color to use and where to place it on a canvas while thinking of something else. Participation in the arts, crafts, music, or even bowling requires total focus on the task at hand. It is important for each person to find his or her personal diversion, some activity that is totally absorbing.

I believe that part of parenting is helping children identify after-school activities that might one day lead to a relaxing adult hobby.

You might wonder why I harp on this need for interests outside of the workplace. Doesn't everyone know that hobbies are important? The answer is no. There are a great many workaholics who do not know how to play, or feel guilty when they do. When they retire they have a difficult time because their identities are tied up in their workday personas. My doctor told me that he sees many patients who only live for a few years after retirement because they feel unneeded and become depressed. Entrepreneurs are especially vulnerable because they have so much time, money, and energy invested in succeeding that they forget there is more to life than work.

There are nose-to-the-grindstone families whose children are told that playing makes them lazy. I know of a young boy who was indoctrinated that it was sinful to attend high school sporting events and dances. He was not permitted to go to concerts, join the marching band, or interact with school friends who were not members of his church. When this youth reached adulthood he became bored and was unable to relax when not working. He escaped from idleness by taking long naps or watching television. It is quite troubling to see a twenty-two-year-old have difficulty finding engaging things to do.

My first education director, whom I will call Katie, was a perfectionist. She was an extremely talented and organized young woman who could develop detailed programs better than anyone I ever met. Her long hair bounced as she gave animated presentations to our visitors. Unfortunately she could not delegate responsibilities. She was absolutely certain that no one could do anything as well as she. Katie would observe various department heads make mistakes, become upset and want to take over their jobs. The result was that after a year working in the museum, she burned out and resigned. It was a sad day when Katie left, but I realized that she would never be satisfied because she could never be 100 percent in control. Balance in life, flexibility, and focus on long-term goals contribute to staying power. Perfectionism is a pitfall to be avoided. If you start an enterprise, you might need to be around for a long time, so burnout is not an option. People are not robots, and mistakes are bound to be made. The goal is to develop systems that help control those mistakes. Your desire may be to get to zero errors, but it will probably take forever to get there.

Inventors, founders, and managers tend to be quite talented and prone to perfectionism. The problem is no one has time to execute everything impeccably, and therefore we depend on others who are less than perfect. I—and I'm listing myself grammatically out of order here to emphasize my role in this—board members, volunteers, and paid staff made lots of mistakes. To develop lasting power, we had to have goals focused on details but also which allowed for human error without getting angry, stressed, or discouraged. By regularly evaluating progress, over time we became able to see growth. Too much attention given to daily minutia and inadequacies made everyone unhappy and insecure. Each year we conducted an evaluation and asked ourselves if the organization was better than it was the year before. When the answer was yes, then we celebrated with parties, trips, and friendly taps on the back. Throughout the year, I looked for ways to acknowledge the positive contributions of staff.

When I started the *Museum Tour Catalog*, good deeds were recognized weekly with PRIDE awards. Every person on staff, whether janitor or educator, was invited to share encounters that demonstrated exceptional work or helpful actions by colleagues. An employee might share a story of assistance he received from a colleague from another department when he found himself falling behind on a deadline. Another person would mention the strong arms that were provided to move a piece of furniture. Since I could not be everywhere, paying attention to these stories was illuminating and insightful. I learned quite a bit about how people interacted and helped each other and came to believe that most want to be helpful.

PRIDE awards (People Rising in Doing Excellence) were stuffed toy lions which live in prides. These toys were given to the recognized individuals to keep on their desks for one week. Passersby would ask why the accolade had been awarded. The act of recognition alone—no monetary achievement attached—made people feel acknowledged and, as a side benefit, contributed to the overall improvement of the business.

The PRIDE program was one of our company's best morale boosters because it drew attention to positive contributions rather than mistakes. We became a team of professionals who recognized that we were all in the educational entertainment business together. I think that if I still had a young family, I might copy the idea, giving out not just physical "trophies" but also public accolades. Wouldn't it be uplifting to sit around the dinner table and have family members mention a positive behavior that was appreciated by all?

All Things Safe and Secure: Care of Visitors and Staff

The whistle blew loudly through the neighborhood and my fear escalated, for it meant a tornado had been sighted. My fright-and-flight reaction told me to dash to the basement. Not so for the five women sitting calmly in my living room, laughing at my concern. They scoffed at me when I suggested seeking better shelter. Though twisters were not a regular occurrence in East Lansing, Michigan, they did occur from time to time. When sirens go off, most people step outside, hoping to see a twister. Once a tornado came within a half mile of Impression 5, bouncing off several nearby roofs, and still all anyone did was watch from the second-floor window.

Ignoring warnings is not a good idea at any time, so I was constantly on guard. Safety and security are always on the mind of a management group involved in entertaining the public. It was a high priority at both Impression 5 and OMSI, and employees took this responsibility seriously. Members of staff were trained in CPR, insisted that children walk instead of run in the exhibit halls, and were active in setting a tone for controlled exploration. Safety kits and fire extinguishers were kept up-to-date, and there were flashlights and emergency exit signs placed throughout the building in case of a power outage.

We quickly addressed corners of loose carpet and had aid on hand, including wheelchairs, for people in need. And, yes, we had fire drills! The fire department was always quite willing to visit and demonstrate how to use extinguishers properly. A safety committee of staff members helped keep the two museums as well as my catalog business claim-free.

Staff took the opportunity use local geological and weather deviations as teachable opportunities. Each state has its own disaster scenarios. Where I live in Oregon is ripe for a major earthquake and my home has fault lines crisscrossing nearby. From time to time I listen to geologists talk about the land formation under my feet and I resolve to move from the hills to flat land, though I never do. To better inform visitors about what to do in case of a quake, OMSI developed a very special sensory exhibit that is still on the museum's floor. Visitors enter a small room to Carol King singing, "I feel the earth move under my feet. I feel the sky tumbling down." Suddenly, the exhibit shakes, setting off emergency alarms. An announcer interrupts the radio program: "This is an emergency. You are experiencing an earthquake and must remain calm. Go to a doorway, stay away from windows or hide under furniture in order not to be hit by falling debris." For years this exhibit has been a popular example of learning by entertainment, and families are observed entering the shake room over and over again.

The Willamette River runs through my town, and I have always been concerned that the city's bridges will collapse with an earthquake, as happened in Oakland in 1989, and that people will be unable to get home. In my catalog company, I asked staff to bring a change of clothing to work, bought several days' worth of dried food for long-term storage, kept extra gallons of water on hand, assembled a box of blankets, ensured that first aid kits were well stocked, and put flashlights throughout the building in case of emergency. It seemed like it was better to be paranoid than sorry. Thank goodness we never had to use any of the supplies in a quake, but I did use them from time to time during snowstorms. There were several evenings when I could not get home, so I slept on a sofa at work, glad to be able to use these stored items.

Natural disasters are not our only concern in the museum world. Increasingly we worried about drugs, theft and violence, and child safety. Kidnapping does not concern most people, but as staff of a public institution working with children this issue was on our minds. We had to ensure that youngsters did not exit the building without their parents. Parents of children registered for classes are always signed in and out.

Once our operations manager went so far as to follow a father into the men's room because it looked like the man was going to physically abuse his unruly son. Thankfully, that was not the case, and there was no need for intervention, but eagle eyes are useful in preventing problems. Our early childhood teacher recognized an observing adult's unusual behavior, and we politely but firmly removed him from the premises. We learned later he was a convicted pedophile. Staying alert to uncomfortable situations is part of the job.

Staff was taken by surprise when a favorite display turned out to be a health hazard of our own making. A chicken incubator adjacent to newly hatched chicks had been installed at Impression 5. Children were permitted to take turns holding the baby chicks and did so carefully while staff supervised. Most city-born children have never visited a farm or watched a bird hatch from an egg. "Egg to Chick" was a delightful display that always drew a crowd, and we happily used it until the day we received a call from a parent informing us that his child had contracted salmonella. We were horrified at our lack of foresight and a thorough hand washing was added to the program. (Eventually we closed the display because it became difficult to get farms to adopt our newly hatched chicks.)

Another time I received an inquiry from the police asking if they could stage and film a mock burglary in our Lansing warehouse building for training purposes. We were shocked when told, "Your facility is perfectly set up for a burglary." Watching them act out what apparently could easily happen in my building spurred my resolve to beef up our security system.

I began by paying more attention to all of our doors. At closing time we routinely checked the exits, and noticed that the back door had been left slightly ajar for several days in a row. Once might have been an accident, but several times meant a call to action. We decided to investigate and asked a male guide if he would be willing to stay overnight. Our young guide now "guard" hid his car several blocks from the building, turned out the lights, left the slightly ajar door alone, and hid in readiness. At about 11:00 p.m. I received a call from our greatly agitated volunteer shouting, "I have him . . . I have him. What should I do?" Later he told me, "I was filled with adrenaline and felt super strong, so I grabbed the thief and hung on." Thankfully, the kid who was caught was young, alone, and unarmed, and police arrived quickly, but the guilt I felt afterward because of my own stupidity in placing staff in harm's way continues to haunt me. Just because I never really believed that someone was trying to break in (I assumed it was staff carelessness) was no excuse for not being cautious.

Those involved in nonprofit organizations work so hard and selflessly for small remuneration that it is difficult to imagine that some might not be honest. I was always sure that close colleagues were do-gooders above temptation. Unfortunately, I was not always right. Even when you have suspicions, it is never easy to catch a clever person in the act of stealing, and it is especially difficult if it is a senior manager.

A shocking wakeup call occurred when a trusted book-keeper was discovered to have stolen $40,000 of petty cash dollars over many years in order to buy antiques for his partner. He was our head bookkeeper, and our accounts always appeared in order. When our auditor first brought the missing money to our attention, the bookkeeper placed the blame on another employee, which resulted in firing an innocent and loyal woman. It took two more years before the real culprit was caught. This time the head bookkeeper was the one prosecuted and put in jail.

Over the course of my twenty-five-year museum career, I observed many instances of thievery, but one incident made me wonder how I could be so easily fooled and misjudge a person's character. After working for several years as my secretary, "Tricky," became increasingly agitated. The petite blond woman had access to one of my credit cards, and instead of using it exclusively for scheduling my travel arrangements, Tricky started making personal purchases and storing them in an empty closet. Her intention was to return the items for cash needed to support her prescription drug habit. Credit card companies have now closed that loophole by putting money back into the credit card holder's account when making a return. In those days, receiving cash was possible.

I was bewildered when several of our accountants walked into my office and asked me why I had purchased a bunch of teddy bears. They knew that I did not have small children at home and wondered at my sudden need for stuffed animals. Quite an accusatory discussion ensued. Suddenly, Tricky, who had been listening to the conversation from her adjacent office, jumped up, grabbed her purse, said, "I'll leave now!" and ran from the building. After Tricky had gone, the accountants and I inspected her desk, finding the most blatant clues as to what had happened. One of the most incriminating articles was a large sheet of butcher block paper covered with versions of my signature. In long neat lines, Tricky practiced how to forge my name. Another was a pile of prescription pads lifted from doctor's offices filling one desk drawer.

Tricky had chutzpah. No doubt about it. I discovered that this conniving lady had the nerve to go into the development office one afternoon, flash my credit card in the air, and make up this story that said, "Marilynne needs to rent a car but has forgotten her driver's license." She asked for a volunteer to rent a car in my name, saying that once I got to the rental office I would substitute mine for that of the volunteer. What actually happened is that Tricky went to the rental car office and used the volunteer's credit card. Her husband had previously taken her automobile away and she needed to have some way to get to the store in order to buy drugs. He did not consider his wife safe to drive and was especially concerned since she often took their daughter in the back seat. The evidence lying around the office was so poorly hidden that I often wondered if this addict was secretly hoping to be caught. It is unnerving to see a talented person with a three-year-old child become a victim of drug dependency. We learned later that Tricky had a long history of abuse and had been fired from her previous position.

You might wonder how this individual was ever hired by our organization in the first place. Part of the settlement around Tricky's previous firing was that if she agreed to go to a drug rehabilitation program, her boss would not say anything negative when asked for a reference. Tricky did attend a few rehab meetings but never completed the program. Our museum was the unfortunate beneficiary of her previous boss's largess.

Hiring good staff is not easy because of the many laws enacted to protect the job seeker. Often employers with limited resources find conducting a background check to be so cumbersome and expensive that they do nothing. What about references, you might ask? I found it rare to hear negative comments. No employee gives you the name of someone likely to give a poor reference. Many companies have a policy that only permits them to respond with a "yes, so-and-so worked here between x day and y day." The most helpful question that would produce some degree of honesty was, "Would you ever hire this person again?" If the reluctant reference answered hesitantly or with, "Maybe if I had a job that would fit his or her abilities," rather than "Absolutely! I would do anything to get that person back," I was cautious about hiring the individual.

During my presidency drug testing was not conducted at higher-level positions or in small institutions. Most often it was not part of the screening process at any level. Today the situation has changed due to federal grant requirements. Liability issues too have insured that drug and alcohol policies are put into effect and most centers now conduct drug testing. Yet there are ways to get the test to come out clean as I learned when visiting a head shop with a homeless youth. Job seekers have also become quite sophisticated when writing resumes, submitting professionally developed documents depicting that they are exactly what you are looking for even though in reality they are unable to write a clear sentence. Often when hiring, I ask for writing samples, sometimes requesting the individual compose a letter while still in my office. I am concerned if a person is a job hopper rather than one who stays typically at least three years.

A young man whom my husband and I have been mentoring recently took a job as a union painter. After his interview, he had to go through a great many drug, blood, and health tests before being hired. He went home with a thick document with all of the rules and policies of the company. After each section, he had to complete a test as proof that he had read the manual. I was impressed with the company's comprehensive system that insured that the staff manual was read.

Many of the applicants to jobs I posted had abysmal writing skills. Their public school education did not prepare them for the work world. Some schools and universities now require students to have internship experience, a trend I applaud. We did hire these young interns but quickly realized they needed quite a bit of supervision.

There were many occasions when I received more than two and a half feet of applications (stacked paperwork) for a job opening. Today those applications usually arrive in online mailboxes, but they take just as much time to review. Marketing positions are likely to produce the most applicants. It is surprising how many people consider themselves to be experienced marketers. It must be difficult and frustrating for talented individuals to get through the chatter to develop their careers. Poring through applications is tedious, and there definitely was a tendency on my part to pay more attention to early applicants. I recommend that anyone seeking a job stay on top of postings and try to be among the first to send in their resume. There were times when after three days of reviewing strong applications, I had less interest in reading the rest.

Networking is a must for job seekers, and getting everyone you know to help you is not a bad idea. Eventually some contact will be of benefit. I confess to being influenced by a woman who wanted her daughter to return to Portland from New Mexico, so pushed me to hire her son-in-law. I will never forget when she approached me at a donor party and said, "You should hire Jeff. He would be a perfect fit at OMSI." I politely asked her to send a resume, believing that would be the end of it. Yet when I read his credentials, I realized that he was just the type of person I wanted on staff. There were no job openings, but for nearly a year I kept his resume by my desk, looking at it from time to time. As soon as I had an opening, I asked Jeff to come for an interview, ultimately hiring him as director of education.

Interviewing is an art that is best shared by several people. I used a list of consistent questions to guide the process and, depending on the job, gave a test to the applicant. In positions that require public speaking or teaching, the applicant might be asked to give a lecture, teach a class, develop a design idea, plan a promotional campaign, or respond to a customer complaint. My son-in-law was once asked to participate in a role-playing exercise during an interview for a research position. "I did a pretty good job," he said, "until one surprise question was thrown at me. I did not think on my feet fast enough." Though he did not get the job, the experience was memorable. It is worth practicing and having friends and family throw questions at you before interviewing for a coveted position.

Our employees were always put on probation before starting benefits. After three months, we had a good idea of whether someone was a fit for our organization. Though a wonderful person, we needed to assess if he or she would blossom under our loose form of management. We looked for those who could manage their own time, act creatively, and participate as a team member. It is always difficult to let people go, but the three-month period allowed us to be rigorous in our assessment. I learned the hard way to cut the cord early if need be and not hang on.

I found group interviews of five to six people a successful strategy when hiring for temporary education and docent positions or, as in my last company, a seasonal call center. A silent observer usually sat off to the side evaluating body language, contributions to the conversation, and person-to-person interactions. The interviewer used ice-breaking exercises and relaxation games. The ensuing discussion enabled us to learn a great deal more about the applicants' experiences since they were comfortable and talking to their peers. Group interviews also give insight into problem-solving abilities because applicants are put in situations that require them to respond quickly. Inquiring about hobbies sometimes brought surprise responses that were used in unexpected ways. For instance, when we learned that someone was a musician, we explored the possibility of that person giving a public or at least a staff performance. Another man we hired with a strong interest in astronomy helped during many museum star parties.

Once I employed someone, it was important to orient him or her to the values and culture of the organization. Helping the newly hired feel a part of our group was always well appreciated. At times I brought a welcome balloon to the office and tied it to the new employee's chair. The presentation of a clean office, complete with supplies, a list of staff members with their extensions, and a tour of the facility were always given, along with introductions to all.

When I started Impression 5, I was so busy putting out fires that taking the time to conduct evaluations seemed like a luxury. I was mistaken in this assessment of needs, for evaluation meetings that are carefully designed actually make things easier in the long run. I learned quickly that every employee deserves to have the boss's complete attention in a private session to air concerns. A two-way conversation demonstrates caring and understanding. Evaluations became a time for setting goals that in the long run provide clarity, save time, and contribute to empowering committed, efficient people who understand their roles as part of a team. I now believe that evaluations are a right that should be demanded by every employee. To ensure that my senior managers knew how to interact with their staff, consultants were hired to run training workshops.

Whether an organization is small or large, an employment manual should be made available, complete with mission statement and values, spelling out the parameters of employment. In addition to discussing vacation time and benefits, the manual should outline a path to deal with conflicts. If you are employed by an organization, be sure to take the time to read literature that is given to you.

Having manuals in place does not mean that everything will always go smoothly. One young man we fired turned on his boss and proceeded to give him a bloody beating. The bruised manager came to my office quite shaken and bearing a bright shiner. From that moment on, I kept a medicinal bottle of wine in my office. In examining how that firing might have been better handled, I realized I had to do a better job training managers in how to hire, evaluate, communicate with, and fire their employees. The terminated employee should have been warned many months earlier that if his behavior did not improve, firing might be a consequence. Instead, the dismissal came as a surprise and developed into a situation that elicited anger.

Most of our employees and volunteers appreciated receiving management training, finding it stimulating and beneficial. When we were a small museum with a limited budget, we sought volunteers who were willing to donate their time to train staff. I was always pleasantly surprised at how many people offered to help.

— — — — — — — — — — — —

Marilynne's Lesson #16: Talk to others about how they handle difficult experiences.

— — — — — — — — — — — —

It is not OK to sit around complaining, but it is important to learn how to cope. I learned this by observing how a colleague handled a most horrific occurrence. For twenty-two years, Alan Friedman was the president of the New York Hall of Science. During his tenure, a high school rented the science center for senior prom. The evening started out quite lovely, with alluring gowns and lively dancing—and then a conduit pipe unexpectedly tumbled down, immediately killing a young woman. You might imagine how quickly the evening turned to one of horror.

Alan handled the situation in a compassionate, professional manner, immediately leaving what he was doing to respond and help a most distraught family and hundreds of grieving teens. As spokesperson for the Hall, he had to answer the many inquiries that came in from the press, school, politicians, and community, who wondered if the building was safe for occupancy. Alan was 100 percent available for the parents and school and did everything in his power to help them get through this painful time. The press could not succeed in baiting him into saying something combative and quotable.

Alan's response to the situation was a guide to me when I faced my own horrific experience. A child in one of our overnight camps went to the restroom at night without using his flashlight and walked into a tree limb, damaging his eye. I received a call near midnight and immediately went to the hospital to wait with the parents until their son arrived. This occurrence was a humbling and sad experience that demonstrated that even with all of our safety precautions, accidents will happen and that any chief executive working with the public needs to be mentally prepared to handle emergencies.

Alan shared a list of the lessons he learned from handling a severe sudden crisis. Anyone in a position of authority can benefit from his insights.

- Designate a sole spokesperson
- Have a pre-established decision command structure (who must be involved, how, etc.)
- Be careful about what is put in writing
- Remember the press and politicians have their own rules of fairness
- Anticipate likely crises

EVALUATING SUCCESS
FOCUS ON ALAN FRIEDMAN: NEW YORK HALL OF SCIENCE

Evaluating Success—Focus on Alan Friedman New York Hall of Science

Alan Friedman died unexpectedly in 2014, having just completed a consultancy in Saudi Arabia, and shortly after being interviewed for this book. He was consistently a creative and energetic influence on the museum field, emphasizing the need to institute evaluation methods. Alan's breadth of experience on several continents added to the wisdom he brought to the field.

There are lots of crises that face directors of public institutions, and it is impossible to be prepared for them all. One

Alan

of the most complex situations I reviewed for this book occurred in 1999. Alan Friedman, who was then director and CEO of the New York Hall of Science and also chair of the Cultural Institutions Group of the City of New York, a coalition of thirty-three publicly supported institutions located in all five boroughs, was called to rescue the Brooklyn Museum of Art from this defining emergency.

The museum's temporary exhibition, called *Sensations*, included work from Chris

Ofilia, an award-winning British artist. Ofili's submission, *The Holy Virgin Mary*, was an eight-foot religiously themed painting splattered with elephant dung and close-up images of female genitalia cut from pornographic magazines.

Rudy Giuliani, New York's mayor at the time and a man known for his quick temper, was outraged by the painting, shouting to the press that a black Madonna covered in dung was disrespectful. He threatened to close the 190-year-old institution within sixty days if the art was not removed immediately. The museum community was horrified, and fearful, remaining silent at first because of possible consequences to their own institutions if they chose to support Brooklyn. Most of the cultural organizations received city funds and were quite concerned about their own vulnerability.

As the newly elected coalition chair, Alan urged the group to stand together in support of the Brooklyn Museum of Art. The controversy initiated a confrontation over freedom of expression, religious tolerance, and public financing of the arts with Alan at the fulcrum. For months his world was in turmoil as he and several staff members did little else but respond. Phones rang day and night with queries coming from reporters, lawyers, the Civil Liberties Union, politicians, and members of the museum community. "These interactions were nasty." said Allen. "I was awakened in the small hours of the night by reporters hoping to catch me off guard. They would stretch the truth and in some cases even lied in the hope of getting me say something controversial."

Alan's board of directors at the New York Hall of Science trusted him implicitly and gave him the nod to lead the charge against the mayor even when unspoken threats implied that science center funding might be cut. The Hall had a lot to lose with $1.5 million of their $7 million operating budget coming from the city and $37 million pledged for capital projects being administered through agencies answerable to the city.

Adding fuel to the controversy, a computer hacker managed to acquire one of Alan's private emails to coalition-member museum directors. It was a draft of a letter to the mayor, being circulated for approval. A full-page article in the *New York Times* greeted Alan when he woke up one morning. "I was very upset and was convinced it would be more difficult to carry on future negotiations." He continued on, however, and with a great deal of persuasion got most of the thirty-three city institutions and ten private museums including the Whitney, Guggenheim, and Museum of Modern Art to sign a letter to Giuliani telling him of the "chilling effect" his actions would have. The letter spoke of "lasting damage, not only to the Brooklyn Museum of Art, but to all of our cultural institutions, and to our city." Giuliani was not swayed, but rather dug in his heels, trying to brandish his conservative credentials. Eventually, with help from the American Civil Liberties Union and the other museums, Brooklyn won a court injunction against the mayor that also prohibited retaliation against the other institutions.

Alan learned a great deal during this crisis, but he came to it with internal fortitude and an innate ability to think under duress. He handled the situation masterfully.

___ ___ ___ ___ ___ ___ ___ ___ ___ ___ ___

Alan's Lessons #1 and #2: The press is not your friend. Neither is your insurance company.

___ ___ ___ ___ ___ ___ ___ ___ ___ ___ ___

Alan warned his colleagues that journalists are not their friends. Their job is to tell a story, and the juicier, the better. He told me that "there is a fine line between following legal advice, which is generally to say nothing to the press, and to state your side of the case. To keep the press reasonable it is necessary for them to believe they are not being stonewalled."

He also grasped the need to inform trustees and supporters the moment such a critical issue arises. In the instance of the falling pipe that I spoke of earlier, Alan immediately phoned the borough president to insure that a surprise call from the press was not her first introduction to the tragedy. Previous to this incident, he had been a trusting individual, believing that his insurance company was there to help, but he soon discovered this was not the case. Insurers look for excuses not to cover costs of litigation and payments and would have been happy to imply negligence on the part of staff.

Following advice from a mentor who worked in the Parks Department he learned to deal with controversy by taking on the role of an offended party. When the accident occurred he came forth immediately by saying that he was personally horrified by the incident and pledged to get to the bottom of the situation.

What made Alan Friedman able to handle complex issues and become such a capable leader? Why was he in 1999 able to reengineer an obsolete World Fair facility located in the Bronx and turn it into one of the country's major science centers? Some of Alan's effectiveness had to do with his outgoing personality. He also had enough internal confidence that he willingly shared the limelight. The twinkle in his eye was infectious, and just looking at him, you knew that you were in the presence of a special person. I used to like watching his beard shift up and down as his mouth moved animatedly when speaking of his latest passion.

Alan spent his first five years in Brooklyn before moving with his parents and sister to Atlanta, Georgia. The family was all about learning. He had "education parents," willing to do most anything to ensure their child's academic success. To Alan's parents, education was the key to upward mobility. Though his dad never graduated from high school, he was a successful insurance salesman, returning home each evening to entertain his family with colorful stories of the day's events. His mom had an entrepreneurial bent and opened a small dress shop, which she operated for twenty years. Alan was a close companion to his younger sister, June, and the two siblings thrived with encouragement and support from their parents.

During Alan's youth, Atlanta had few museums to stimulate a budding scientist's mind, but the family made up for it by participating in many activities together. Attending musical events and readings was a regular occurrence for the Friedman clan. Alan's interest in science was stimulated by vivid images that flew off the pages of the science-fiction books he devoured. His public school education provided dedicated teachers to shape his young mind. These mentors made him realize that "a single good teacher is more important to a person than all the things that are wrong [in life]. Lack of inspiring teachers dooms everything else to failure."

Following high school, Alan enrolled as an undergraduate at Georgia Tech and studied electrical engineering, but over time he found the subject not satisfying. Most of the science-fiction characters he read about were physicists, and he was determined to turn fictional possibilities into reality when he began to study for a doctorate at Florida State. As is the case of most doctoral programs, his training was aimed at taking his place as a professor and research scientist.

This straight-and-narrow path was interrupted by an opportunity to spend six months at the Lawrence Hall of Science in Berkeley, California. He loved the excitement and energy of the interactive museum, and the short assignment stretched out to over ten years. He eventually became director of the department of astronomy and physics. Alan discovered that he could have fun and at the same time make a living by explaining science. He told me, "This realization was life changing, and from that moment on, the excitement afforded by science centers became my calling."

Opportunities are often random, and those not afraid to grab them can benefit immensely. While still at Berkeley, Alan was lent as a consultant to Cité des Sciences et de l'Industrie to help develop the ambitious new science museum in Paris. An American with science center experience was valuable to the French, who had no experience in this emerging field. He quickly became involved in new exhibitions and programs, was responsible for a children's area, and helped develop an astronomy section. His biggest contribution, however, was to convince the museum to conduct formative evaluation as part of the planning process. Formative evaluation is a method of gaining both qualitative and quantitative feedback in order to better understand educational outcomes. Basically, it is a way of getting an assessment that can be used to make improvements and offers accountability to funders.

Life in Paris was dynamic, exotic, and intellectually stimulating, but after six months, the consultancy was coming to an end. The experience, though, opened three new options to mull over. He was expected to return to his job at the Lawrence Hall of Science, but the Paris science center asked him to remain in France indefinitely. A third opportunity came in the form of a request that he apply for a job at the helm of the struggling New York Hall of Science. No, it wasn't just struggling—it was for all intents and purposes closed, and it was located in a Queens neighborhood that many Manhattan residents found beneath their dignity to visit. Even those residing locally did not respect the tired old museum. It had no endowment, the building was dilapidated, and nearly all of its operating costs were provided by the City of New York, which no longer wanted to do so.

Originally established in 1964 as part of the World's Fair in Flushing Meadows Corona Park, it was then one of only a few hands-on science centers in the United States. Unlike many other buildings vacated soon after the fair, the NYSCI remained open and served as a resource for students until 1979, when it closed for major renovations. A group of science museum consultants who had been hired to evaluate the space for redevelopment suggested permanent closure of the facility. Their recommendation was to build a new science museum in Manhattan. Alan told me, "This proposal was met with deaf ears by the Queens president who was adamant that the center remain in Queens." Manhattan had many cultural facilities, and Queens had few, so the push to keep the NYSCI local was on.

The City of New York agreed to continue to supply 50 percent of the funds for ongoing operations thus making more urgent the need for a knight in shining armor to take over the dilapidated castle. Enter Alan Friedman who would oversee the transformation to a modern science center.

What I have learned about museum developers is that they are risk takers who enjoy a challenge, and Alan was no exception. Even though many colleagues advised him not to accept the position as director, he was up for it. He saw it "as an opportunity to live with only my own mistakes. I can make the rules," he said. Alan quickly surrounded himself with competent assistants and was fortunate to hire Sheila Grinell to be his deputy director. As a past director of the Association of Science and Technology Centers (ASTC), Sheila had considered competing against Alan for the directorship in New York but decided that with a young child to raise, she should not take on that role.

Dr. Alan Friedman accepted the position and for twenty-two years, from 1984 to 2006, served as director of the NYSCI. After a great deal of fund-raising and planning, he and his staff reopened the hall in 1986, providing Queens with a "feather in their cap" museum. Major proposals were funded, such as a $400,000 expansion and installation of a display about the atom. An exciting science playground designed to accommodate children of all ages was added in 1996. It contained a giant lever, an Archimedes screw pumping water in a wet area, wind pipes, a climbing net, slides, sand boxes, and metal drums that meant hours of fun for the visiting school children. Traveling exhibitions such as *1001 Inventions* were rotated in to ensure that the center stayed fresh and relevant. From *Preschool Place* to *Sports Challenge, Microbes* to *Technology*, the displays offered visitors a window into mathematical and scientific thinking.

Continued growth and the center's ability to draw large crowds was a surprise to government officials. They were asked to allocate further funds for greater expansion. Fund-raising was a complicated activity because building and land were owned by the city but management was conducted by a non-profit organization. It was a devil with a two-pronged tongue, one side seeking funds for capital improvements and the other side reaching for operating dollars. "My strategy," Alan told me, "had to include making the local politicians shine. In fact, the entire organization is trained to celebrate those offering their assistance. Staff's job is to make me look good, and my responsibility is to make everyone else appear exceptional. Basically, the science center operates as a well-oiled machine. Everyone fulfills a different role, enabling the organization to thrive, and so credit is constantly being given out . . . to everyone."

— — — — — — — — — — — — — —

Alan's Lesson #3: Working with politicians takes tact and experience. It is not a job for the naïve.

— — — — — — — — — — — — — —

Alan claimed that it took him over ten years to comprehend New York politics. The system of boroughs, community boards, city council, and city hall was complicated. As he dealt with mayors and commissioners, Alan learned to dance—the budget dance, that is. "The way it works" Alan said, is that the mayor proposes an executive budget by the third week in January that for twenty-two years has always included cuts in cultural affairs." At first Alan took the lacerations personally, but eventually he learned that it all was part of a game. "In order to have negotiating leverage, the mayor cuts the items that the city council most cares about: libraries, museums, and parks. Money is then reinstated to these organizations if the council will agree to the mayor's current priorities which include police and fire department requests." Queens Borough President Clair Schulman, a woman Alan described as an angel, was a strong advocate for the center. She patiently guided him through the maze of complex political intrigue.

Raising operating funds was only one part of Alan's job. He found it more fun to try to seek grant money for grants for his education ideas, and he doggedly pursued leads. He acknowledged that "to succeed, you do need to believe in yourself . . . and you also need to gain the trust of others."

In 2006 the New York Hall of Science completed a mammoth, $92 million capital expansion. It was one of Alan's crowning achievements. Others included special recognition for encouraging new technologies, creating unique models for teacher training, and developing ways to serve an extraordinarily diverse audience. The New York Hall of Science had become a beacon for science education.

I asked Alan if he thought science centers really do what they claim to do: teach and inspire. He responded by describing a cherished program the museum initiated called the Science Career Ladder, which hired kids as explainers (display guides) for up to six years. This unique program provided training for science majors who could then continue their studies at nearby Queens College under a tuition waiver. The students pledged to continue in this work for an additional two years after college graduation by helping inner-city schools. Over five thousand teens have gone through this program, which has changed a great deal for the mainly minority and immigrant participants. Sixty-six percent of the students continue to pursue careers in science, technology, medicine, or science education . . . a staggering number.

A favorite story of Alan's was about a young Hispanic woman who had dropped out of high school because of pregnancy. Deciding she needed a job, she applied and was hired on as an explainer. This position inspired her to complete high school, and she eventually obtained a college degree. She landed her first job back at the museum as an assistant in charge of explainers. After moving up to became head of the entire explainer program, she left to take a position as a program officer in a charitable foundation for youth development.

Another woman, one of Indian descent, joined the explainer program in her sophomore year of high school after being told that it was a good way to meet boys. This young woman became inspired by study, eventually receiving a doctorate in science education. After returning to the hall as director of education she was hired away by the American Museum of Natural History. There are hundreds more stories that give testimony to the lasting effect science centers have on the public.

For his good work Alan became a recipient of the American Association for the Advancement of Science's Award for Public Understanding of Science, the Association of Science-Technology Centers' Fellow Award, and the American Institute of Physics Gemant Award. The American Association of Museums named him to its Centennial Honor Roll in 2006. In retirement, he traveled the world, visiting many countries as a consultant.

Today, NYSCI stands as New York City's only hands-on science and technology center. More than 450 exhibits explore biology, chemistry, and physics. NYCSI serves over five hundred thousand visitors each year, with an additional fifty thousand participating in off-site, school-based, and community-outreach programs. New York was fortunate to find a great man to create the thriving institution the New York Hall of Science is today.

Out into the Community

When I started Impression 5, the museum was very needy. Asking for and expecting help became second nature for me, and there certainly were good people willing to oblige. Once the museum was established, the community expected me to give back time and share newly gained expertise.

One of the more interesting activities I was involved in while in Lansing was helping a friend start a lighted boat parade. Our intention was to duplicate what San Antonio, Texas, had created with its wonderful canal procession and thereby stimulate our own riverfront renewal efforts. For many years, our museum staff contributed to the event by designing inventive floats. For weeks the shop housed volunteers and staff who used their creative talents in wild ways. What fun it was to glide through town to cheering spectators! I became hooked on parades and decided that every time I had a chance to be in one I would participate. Impression 5 later organized a bicycle parade complete with old-fashioned cycles with large front wheels and unicycles leading a rowdy group of adults and children of every age on their own bikes through the streets of Lansing. When the group arrived at the museum, we tested kids' bikes for safety, ran a bicycle maze, and challenged participants to see how slowly they could move on their one-or two-wheeled vehicles.

At OMSI, sponsors helped defray the costs of participating

in the Rose Festival celebration that takes place each June. My favorite float was built to honor the submarine USS *Blueback* that our museum had just acquired. Our board chairman, the submarine committee leader, and I popped out of the rose-covered funnel to greet the thousands of people who lined the streets. Practicing my queenly wave produced two very sore arms by the end of the event. I loved seeing happy, expectant faces and hands waving back and hearing the shouting as we floated by in our navy outfits.

By operating a nonprofit institution, I immediately became connected to many events and activities external to our operation. Though mainly focused on the trials and achievements of my own museum, I found it impossible to stay isolated from what was happening throughout the city, if for no other reason than others demanded my involvement. I was asked to join boards of other nonprofit groups as well as committees to improve the welfare of the city. In Portland, among my extracurricular duties, I served on the Board of the Visitor and Convention Association and on Rotary Club committees, and helped light the bridges as a founding member of the Lighted Bridge Brigade. For six years I was a trustee of the Northwest Regional Education Lab, participated on a committee at the School of Engineering at Portland State University, chaired a governor's task force for science and engineering education, served on the board of a nature center, and became a board member of the Giving Tree, an organization for low-income families entering assisted housing. The list goes on and on. Busy, busy, busy—that was my commitment, which became my mantra.

I was once asked by a newspaper reporter what the secret of Impression 5's success was. My response was printed in the *Lansing State Journal:* "Put on long underwear (we had a cold, poorly heated space), work like hell, and don't give up." I acknowledged that the museum was successful because of "the involvement of students, senior citizens designers, housewives, working people, industrialists and anyone with a spark of imagination, a desire to create or build." We took everyone who was interested in as volunteers and made the museum theirs. We also realized that we could not live in a cocoon, and that becoming involved in extracurricular projects throughout the area was our opportunity to influence education and the arts.

OUTREACH

Whether a museum is large or small, its walls form the limiting boundaries of activities. Large museums are usually constructed in major cities, and their spaces seemed enormous to me when I started in Impression 5's small building. (During my interview with Bob Russell, Impression 5's fourth director, he told me that I 5 seemed large to him. He came to Lansing from a 4,000 square foot museum. Everything is relative.) I was always envious but used the large institutions as models for improvisation—how could we do a version of what they were doing? Never one to let size get in the way of service, we developed a range of traveling programs to reach distant learners. This outreach continues to expand under direction of the many people who have taken over the museum's helm.

For its first fifty years of operation, OMSI also had limited space but it developed one of the most outstanding outreach programs in the nation, and it became that way in part because of the center's physical limitations. The museum owns a fleet of vans that take science activities into schools in Oregon, Washington, Idaho, and Montana. Airplanes carry educators to Alaska, where science activities are brought into small communities, sometimes with as few as fifteen children

One summer I observed OMSI classes held in a school in Fort Yukon, Alaska, located just north of the Arctic Circle. Teachers slept in apartments attached to the school because there were no other rental units in that small town of six

hundred residents. Since it was summer, these school apartments were available to our staff. At 12:30 a.m. on the first
evening of my trip, I heard children shrieking with laughter as
they played on jungle gyms outside of my bedroom window
in this land of perpetual summer light. I wondered how these
youngsters were ever going to get up in the morning to attend
our program but was pleasantly surprised when most did. In
my free time, I meandered down to the local health clinic to
pick up a Daily Food Guide, put out by the Alaska Native
Health Program, in which the benefits of eating such staples
as moose, bear, seal, walrus, porcupine, ptarmigan, and whale
were spelled out. I read that it was not a good idea to eat
polar bear liver; that porcupine, walrus, and caribou are good
for blood and muscles; and that seal oil and muktuk (whale
blubber) are excellent for eyes and energy.

The superintendent of schools for the district slept in
his office in Fort Yukon during the week, visiting by day the
dozens of tiny communities that the district served. He flew
his own small plane to these distant schools, returning home
to his family on weekends, flying two hundred miles to get
there. During the warm months, rivers and streams in this
area of flat land would melt, and kayaks and canoes would
be used to transport people from home to salmon fishing
grounds. Winter, however, was the best time for socializing
because when the waterways froze over, a bus service operated,
bringing family and friends for visits.

During this Alaskan sojourn, I flew in the school superintendent's four seater from Fort Yukon to a one-room school
house located by a river and built on permafrost. The newly
constructed school building had no indoor plumbing so students and teachers braced themselves against the cold to use
the unheated outhouse. Just looking at the privy made me
shiver. But inside the two-room building, there was no lack
of warmth or intellectual stimulation. The science activities

OMSI staff presented were engaging and the children lively and involved. Parents were invited to see the demonstrations, and they inspected unfamiliar creatures such as the lizards, snakes, and turtles that were brought with us on the airplane.

I was fortunate to attend a demonstration of the Inuit Olympics, featuring games rooted in hunting and survival techniques. Though originally a male-only event, women are now integrated into even the most arduous activities. I watched a one-foot-high kick contest for which competitors stood on one leg, preparing to jump to reach a piece of fur that was raised each round. The contestant had to kick the target with the foot he would land on, remaining balanced on his return to ground. There were several games of contestants either standing facing each other or back to back to see who could push the other person off balance. Another trial involved bending over, arms down sweat pants in order for the contestant to grab ahold of her ankles in preparation for a race. The ear pull tested the ability to bear pain, giving an inkling of what it would be like to have frostbite. Two players sat on the floor, a loop of leather cord over their ears. They both pulled until the cord either fell free from one opponent or the match was stopped because of too much bleeding. Ouch! The blanket toss was the most fun to watch. One person stood on a blanket ringed by people who lifted the blanket over and over, tossing the person as high as possible, the flyer's goal being to return to the blanket without losing balance. These games were another way to educate children to the rigors of living in an Arctic climate.

A political event I witnessed in Fort Yukon involved the local Native residents trying to oust the white mayor. The mayor was attempting to introduce new agricultural practices around planting and harvesting wild rice in the hope of the town developing greater economic independence. The denizens thought the man was crazy. They also claimed that he rummaged through the town dump (a regular activity for locals) in an attempt to obtain blackmail information. While I, of course, could not tell who was in the right and who in the wrong, what I did observe was that white people telling the Native Americans what to do and how to educate their children was not appreciated. Their distrust of white America was reinforced by watching the selection process for a new school principal. The town looked long and hard for a Native person, of any tribe, who was willing to relocate to the desolate area. They absolutely were not interested in a non-Native educator, no matter how well qualified the person was.

Back in Portland it was also important that we understand cultural differences before offering classes. When operating programs for Native Americans, OMSI tried to find partners. Quite a bit of attention was given to who should be in charge. One program was conducted on the Warm Springs Indian Reservation, where residents and scientists joined with OMSI to operate Salmon Camp. The goal was to have the Native children develop a sense of pride by learning how salmon migrate from inland waterways to the ocean. Campers started the program on the reservation, participating in special Native events that are secret to white Americans. The children then follow the rivers, counting fish and observing behaviors, until the salmon end their run in the ocean. When the campers returned to Portland their science program continued during the fall under the direction of the local chapter of the American Indian Science and Engineering Society.

Museum personnel have to be sensitive to every racial and socioeconomic subgroup in their community. When I was in Finland at an International Science Museum Conference, I gave a talk about outreach programs. During my lecture, I asked what museum educators in Europe were doing to attract the extensive Gypsy population. As soon as I touched on this subject, the room became silent with tension felt throughout the lecture hall. Apparently the subject of the Romani culture (Roma) was a taboo topic in European museum circles. I never was aware of any programs addressing this underserved population.

Teacher training, with its focus on inquiry-based learning, is a large part of the offerings of most science centers. The Exploratorium in San Francisco conducts the nation's most extensive and sophisticated training programs for high school teachers, scientists, and museum professionals. The influence exerted by Frank Oppenheimer, founder of the Exploratorium, was enormous. He showed the profession how to take scientific laboratory experiments and turn them into sturdy childproof exhibits. He invited the public to become part of scientific exploration. In 2013, The Exploratorium moved to its impressive location on the waterfront of San Francisco Bay, managing to retain the chaotic magic of their original home. When you step into the facility, you feel like you are in a combination of workshop-garage-factory. The atmosphere is dynamic, with space filled with hundreds of devices that invite visitors to conduct science experiments. The Exploratorium, as do many other museums, holds workshops for teachers and museum professionals that are conducted both in their home base as well as in various locations throughout the country. Quite a few of these training programs are held in conjunction with universities giving credit toward a master's degree.

Schools regularly conducted field trips to our museum and were given special tours of the exhibit floor. Private demonstrations and activities could always be arranged for a small fee. Sometimes schools sprung for those programs, but also birthday parties became an important boost to the budget. A science center party is a major source of delight for the lucky child who, along with friends, participates in science activities before eating cake and ice cream. Parents find these parties easy to manage and a hit with the kids, and rooms are reserved for most weekends.

Overnight camps are another activity offered by many museums, and OMSI developed many. More intense camping opportunities available at places like Camp Hancock, located in Oregon's high desert, offer unique weeklong expeditions that explore flora, fauna, and fossils in the area. My son still talks about a Hancock camp that specialized in teaching aboriginal skills. My son found himself to be strong and accurate with the atlatl, a device used for throwing spears or darts. The atlatl consists of a rod or board with a projection at the rear end to hold a weapon in place until it has been launched. Flint knapping in order to make spear points was another specialty of the camp. I have watched knappers work with all types of stone and greatly admire their dexterity and accuracy in fashioning a stone knife or arrow point. Stone tools were considered "new technology" for those ancients living so many years ago. Parents who enroll their children in their museum's summer program provide them with unforgettable experiences.

Many years before my time as president, Camp Hancock gave away some of its land to the State. Now it needed more space to house its programs. I was always on the lookout for a way to facilitate its growth.

During the early 80s, a communal experiment was started on a 64,229 acre parcel of land not far from OMSI's Camp Hancock. Many of our counselors were hired, unbeknownst to me, to work at the ranch known as Rajneesh. Our young teachers developed private contracts, enabling them to work during the less active winter months. The Rajneesh was a cult, operating a Utopian experiment with many highly educated people trying to develop sustainable agricultural practices, educational offerings, and loving communal activities. Yet because of greed the cult eventually failed due to criminal activities by their leaders.

I was on the grounds for their garage sale and purchased A-frame huts for Camp Hancock. Rose colored chairs for my board room and several other pieces of furniture also made their way into OMSI's new building. Several years later I returned with Secretary of State, Norma Paulus, to consider forming a collaborative to purchase the ranch. My plan was to move and expand Camp Hancock on this developed compound that had extensive housing and classroom space. Our collaborative was unable to negotiate a reasonable price, however, so Camp Hancock stayed in its original location. Instead of expanding Hancock, programs spread to other communities—the mountains, central Oregon, the San Juan Islands and on the coast.

In 2016 OMSI completed construction on a new camp on donated land located in Newport for the purpose of teaching coastal and oceanic science. The city is now a center for oceanic study because of the presence of the National Oceanographic and Atmospheric Administration (NOAA), the Hatfield Marine Science Center, the Oregon Coast Aquarium, and Oregon State University. The area is a bustle of well-educated people involved in environmental impact studies and it is anticipated that campers will have a chance to be exposed to "real scientific research."

For those not interested in overnight camping experiences almost all museums offer extensive day programs with a rich variety of classes. Summer is a busy time because so many parents are looking for ways to enrich their children's vacation while getting them out from underfoot. Children can learn everything from videography to robotics or how bridges are engineered. They study natural science, chemistry, and holography. In order not to turn away children with limited income, there usually are opportunities to apply for full or partial scholarships. Thousands of children, and adults too, are educated in individual, family, and Elderhostel programs throughout the United States by museum-sponsored offerings.

If you think that you have heard enough and are exhausted just thinking about so many opportunities that have to be coordinated and overseen by those who manage museums, please rest a moment before continuing. My mother-in-law once said that she thought I was always flitting from one activity to the next. Her insight was a good one that probably led to my career choice. To the public, I appeared focused: one museum, one job. The reality was that the museum is an umbrella for many businesses: gift shop, restaurant, classes, exhibits, travel programs, fancy fund-raising events, etc. I liked them all and was lucky to be able to participate broadly.

Travel excursions are an active part of the educational offerings of most museums. Trips are sponsored that cover every aspect of science, art, history, and nature imaginable. Subject-specific experts, curators, and educators lead excursions to such sites as the Galapagos Islands, the Grand Canyon, the San Juan Islands, Easter Island, the Louvre, the fields of Gettysburg, etc. Numerous national and international research sites and nature preserves are often willing to host special programs for young and old. The list goes on and on. These travel programs are fee based and at times are designed to support serious research as well as earn money for the institution. They have the added benefit of keeping moderately paid staff motivated. Those involved in development often lead tours to help them become better acquainted with potential large donors. A great deal of endowment money is acquired because of the personal friendships developed on travel excursions.

I mention these wonderful programs in part to show you that no matter how large or small, life is the "whole wide world museum." Everything we do and want is at our disposal as long as we are alert and recognize possibility. When starting Impression 5, I was envious of major institutions that had been in existence for over one hundred years. I was impatient and wanted everything they had to offer to be in our possession. Thank goodness I learned to slow down and take baby steps toward our vision of comprehensive educational offerings.

Though small, even before it had a building, Impression 5 offered day programs and science classes. Today, summers are filled with a very active education program offered in themed day camps called L.A.B.S (Learning About Basic Science), with Lego Science, Frozen Science, and Duct Tape Science among the offerings. There is also a science-based playgroup for the very young, scouting activities, and a continuation of home-school program offerings. Over time, the lower level of the Museum Drive building was renovated to add classroom space. Many years after its inception, Impression 5 became involved in outreach offerings such as Science on Wheels, which goes to schools, libraries, churches, and anywhere inquiry-based learning is desired.

In sharing the many educational opportunities offered by museums, I cannot forget overnight adventures or Camp Ins. *A Night in the Museum* was a fun movie, but lots of institutions offer this type of program (without the scary drama) on a weekly basis. Most science centers and some children's museums entertain large groups of children who arrive with pillows and sleeping bags ready to learn, play, and sleep in the museum. Programs offered vary and are developed to meet the needs of the group reserving the experience. In the morning after such a camp, I would arrive at work to see cars lined up with parents picking up their sleepy children. OMSI has the largest Camp In program of any museum in the nation.

The museum also has the added benefit of owning the USS *Blueback* submarine, enabling those who are interested to actually sleep and work in the crowded conditions on board. Local submarine vets have developed a complete program of activities for the lucky children or families who are given tasks in the engine, communication room, or galley. They learn about how the submariners put cases of food on hallway floors and sometimes throughout the sub, crawling from room to room until those onboard had eaten their way down to a lower level. They discover that the crew could take only occasional three-minute showers and that they slept in bunks called "hot beds" because when one person left for a shift, another one took his place in bed. The best place to sleep, I was told, was where the missiles were stored, because it was well air-conditioned and quiet.

There are also opportunities for young and old to participate in research expeditions. For example, dinosaur digs that permit volunteers to work beside scientists are offered by such institutions as the Museum of Western Colorado, the Wyoming Dinosaur Center, the Museum of the Rockies, the Museum of Geology in South Dakota, and Dinosaur Provincial Park. Since dinosaurs never lived in Oregon or Michigan, we would recommend those interested to attend programs in other states. However, Oregon does have quite a few fossil beds that are incorporated into various camp programs.

In my early twenties, my first job offer was to work at the Boston Children's museum to assemble anthropological kits that school teachers could rent for use in the classroom. This active program continues to expand and is a fantastic support to Boston area schools. The Brooklyn Children's Museum has a busy rental program as well that astonished me when I reviewed the depth and breadth of their offerings. As if that is not enough exertion, many museums share staff knowledge through consulting services. Exhibit designers may be asked to assemble displays for other museums and businesses while educators design interactive curriculum options for public schools. Sharing among museums is extensive as these cultural entities lend and circulate their vast collections. In general, you will find museum personnel to be collaborative, going out of their way to respond to requests for specialized programs.

All museums work to attract funds and share best practices in reaching underserved audiences. Surprisingly, one such audience is the young adult crowd, and appealing to them is not always easy. While still president of OMSI, I started a monthly evening event that brought in a live band, opened up a dance floor, and made drinks available. After 8:00 p.m., the museum closed to anyone under twenty-one years. The bands varied, which helped attract different cultural groups. Salsa night was filled with students and teachers who demonstrated the most graceful, sexy Latin dance renditions, from tango to mambo. Jamaican music brought a bit of trouble because the band spent their breaks in the parking lot smoking marijuana. It bothered a number of people on staff, and we had to change bands. I thought people were a bit strait-laced. I love reggae music, but I had to go with the flow. In general, the idea of an evening for young adults was a good one, and after I left the organization, it evolved to be better executed by a later administration.

Now OMSI offers several programs for thinking young adults who want to meet and greet each other. OMSI After Dark caters to this age group so successfully that there can be as many as eighteen hundred people visiting the museum in an evening. I attended one clever After Dark event that themed around the science of beer. Many local breweries conducted beer-making science demonstrations, which spiced up the evening. In addition to admiring the main activity, I was impressed by some of the ancillary displays. Vidal Sassoon, for example, demonstrated their products for free on people's hair, though it had nothing to do with beer but rather with going out on the town in general. Singles found it easy to mingle in the safety of the exhibit halls, and it was effortless to start a conversation between two people perusing the same display. Around the country many museums invite young city workers to share the cocktail hour with them. Treats and good music make popular venues for the single crowd. By catering to the needs of these young people—catching up with friends, meeting new people in a safe and fun space, and experiencing something new—museums are carefully enticing the next generation of visitors and donors.

Lectures in pubs are another unique way of involving adults. Through OMSI, these science presentations have enjoyed such an overwhelming success that the initial program in a local brew pub was expanded to include multiple locations. Local and national scientists are brought in for a lecture discussing the latest research being conducted in their field. A pre-lecture slideshow of science trivia is given while attendees are purchasing food and settling in to their seats. A fun trivia quiz tests attendees' knowledge, giving them a chance to win tickets for gift shop items and OMSI activities. The question-and-answer period is always quite animated.

Usually in mentioning the underserved, it is not the young adult being discussed but rather those who live in poverty. Museum personnel are especially interested in reaching low-income families in need and work hard to develop ways around the issues that keep them from attending programs. There often are problems concerning transportation, lack of adult supervision, and limited funds for admission or class fees. An active scholarship and admission program is a must in order to serve more than the wealthiest members of the community.

When OMSI made the move from its first building in Washington Park to the riverfront, instead of putting our exhibitions in storage we decided to open a temporary exhibit in a mall in a part of town that skewed toward lower income. The mall display attracted a new audience because it was placed on the opposite side of town from the old museum. It served as a good advertisement for our new location. The move also made a statement that OMSI was for everyone in the community and not just the wealthy.

Once the move was completed, we didn't forget that neighborhood. We developed a variety of low cost after-school and weekend activities that we ran out of a local church basement. Bus trips occasionally brought the children to OMSI. Parents were also invited to join some of the computer classes and participate in excursions. The institution raised funds from generous donors to help underwrite the costs of supporting the program.

Trouble started with our selection of a program manager who decided, unbeknownst to me, OMSI was a "fat cat" he could manipulate. For instance, I agreed to let him hire a photographer friend to take pictures of the children. The man worked for a few days and then to my astonishment sent in an $87,000 bill, way out of proportion for the work done. I was forced to go to court to fight this abuse and luckily the judge agreed that the bill was outrageous. This was a time when a volunteer lawyer was of great assistance.

Poor people live in a state of continuous crisis where there never is enough money to take care of personal needs. The man managing the after-school program was strongly tied to the community, understanding the issues. He was able to scare away a drug house that was across the street by threatening the dealers with constant surveillance if they did not move. We were thankful for his savvy knowledge of what was happening in the surrounding area.

Unfortunately, the more imbedded in the community he became, the more he acted like a local precinct boss instead of a representative of OMSI. He kept the fifteen-dollar annual registration fees he collected in a strong box under his desk instead of handing the money over to accounting. When a neighbor asked for a handout for food or shelter, he would lend them or give them the money from OMSI's coffers. As he continued to dispense money, he became a more powerful local figure and eventually decided that he wanted to split from OMSI and create his own neighborhood museum.

I had to confront a very difficult situation without making waves in the press. We could not let this program director, no matter how well intentioned he was, continue to use the collected fees at his own discretion. Our donors were the ones underwriting the program, and the purpose of the tuition was to ensure commitment to attend. Nor could I recommend that the neighborhood consider dividing OMSI to start their own museum. I watched this type of division occur in other communities and fail dismally. Knowing the tremendous expense of operating a museum, we did not think it would survive to serve the best interest of neighborhood children.

After quite a bit of soul searching I decided to let him go. The man was uncontrollable and doing damage to OMSI's reputation. The community had other thoughts than I and was outraged. A meeting was called with a full contingent of press invited to attend. Not knowing any better, I went to the meeting to explain the reason for my decision to fire the manager. As soon as I opened my mouth, before I could say one word, the audience started screaming and drowning out my comments. Submitting to an hour of abuse, I left in great confusion, wondering what I had gotten myself into. Later I was told that the mistake I made was attending the meeting in the first place. The way I was treated was a game to the meeting organizers.

I felt concerned for the manager, who was acting in accordance with his values and knowledge of his community. Many of his actions were charitable, though done with other people's money. It was not long before someone local stepped forward and offered him a job that would be less contentious, and media attention quickly died down.

A Two-Class Society: What Museums Can Do To Help

The short time I spent working in mental health and the many years I worked with low-income families through museum programs and nonprofit boards have contributed to my strong concern that America is in trouble—great trouble. Though with small efforts I have tried to make a difference, the only way society will really change is if there is an uprising of sentiment to do so. And what we need to do is to follow one of the great teachings of all of the religious leaders. We need to care for one another.

There is a controversial Harvard University author by the name of Charles Murray who with Richard J. Herrnstein wrote *The Bell Curve* and more recently *Coming Apart: The State of White America, 1960-2010.* His thesis is that there are two Americas, an upper and a lower class which no longer share values involving marriage, hard work, honesty, and religion. He uses lots of statistics to show the difference between the upper class community he calls Belmont with a working class one labeled Fishtown. (83% of people in Belmont are married as opposed to 48% in Fishtown.) In Fishtown the highest academic attainment is a high school degree. It is also a place where high dropout rates are not thought of as failure. Those residing in Fishtown work in low wage, low skill service and blue collar fields. Belmont residents on the other side of the tracks have advanced degrees with their residents serving as doctors, lawyers, professors, engineers, scientists, etc.

Murray claims that the upper class today is more isolated than ever and does not know or understand the lower classes. (John Edwards said the same thing when he said "We have two Americas".) He also says that class division is not focused on money alone but on intelligence and education. I believe there is truth to his arguments and that as a society, we have a lot of work to do if we want a country with shared values and work ethics. The 2016 presidential race between Clinton and Trump provides a good example of the disconnect that exists in our society.

Museums traditionally have appealed to the upper classes. My catalog company also appealed to the wealthy who could afford to purchase our products. We attracted the educated and planned to continue to do so. We had values that include a love of learning, honesty, curiosity, family, hard work, and compassion. Though not all museum visitors have advanced degrees they all distinguish themselves as valuing education. Most museum staffs cherish the obligation to inspire visitors in the value of learning and try to demonstrate in a way that is entertaining, creative and comfortable.

In a previous era one of the giants of the industrial revolution had an aggressive approach to educating the diverse immigrants who came to the United States. Henry Ford required those who worked in his factory to participate in a training program promoting American values. There were pros and cons to his approach. The pro was that his program inspired a common outlook and system of values; the con was the loss of individuality and ethnicity. The early school system was also a great leveler, with people from many nations learning English as the accepted language, practicing common values, and becoming part of our democratic history as a melting pot of ideas. In school children would learn to think of the Pilgrims as though they too had arrived in the 1600s. Military service as well had a huge influence in leveling values and combating bigotry by providing a place for social mixing and cross cultural camaraderie. The draft brought all sorts of people together who had to learn to live in harmony.

"The times they are a changing," sings Bob Dylan. Currently we have an enlisted army that does not draw from such a wide range of people, causing the difference between officers, contract workers, enlisted men and the uninvolved citizen bystander to be more pronounced. The wealthy and most educated among us rarely serve. School dropouts are not welcome as military personnel become increasingly more technological.

In the United States the wealthy either send their children to private schools or live in "good" zip code areas. They support education and do not rub elbows with those who do not. There are exceptions, but even so, contact is sanitized. It is difficult to comprehend what it is like to grow up in poverty, though some do try. In my neighborhood two nearby teens participated in a church run program aimed at improving understanding and compassion for the poor. The participating high schoolers spent several days living on the streets in order to learn about homelessness. Each of these pretending-to-be-poor teens was given $1 a day for sustenance and told to find additional ways to get food. At night they were guaranteed a place so ate and slept in the church's homeless shelter. They were clever and stayed somewhat clean by washing as best they could in the church bathrooms. These intelligent youth strategized to obtain good begging advantages and pooled their dollars with others in order to buy food. Together they purchased a loaf of bread and some peanut butter realizing that $1 alone does not go far. Their experience was more simulated than real, and the actual street kids resented them. To those living in abject conditions my neighbors were viewed as upper class children on a slumming party who created competition in begging. Though the class divide became acutely obvious, the experience did open their eyes to the underprivileged. It made me wonder what a museum's obligation is to help the poor. The issue is complex.

So what can we as caring people do? We can continue to be strong advocates for our own families and values. Teach, learn, share, and take constructive action throughout life. I remember reading about concepts of *noblesse oblige*. It is a European idea that obliges the wealthy classes to help the poor. This notion needs to evolve to a definition of classes that includes education, not just wealth. The educated have an obligation to assist the uneducated and teach them about justice, work, living creatively and lifelong learning. The Roosevelts were taught these values and turned them into Social Security, the United Nations, WPA projects, and a host of other programs to benefit all of society.

The Bible frequently instructs followers to help the poor. In **Deuteronomy 15:11** we read, "For there will never cease to be poor in the land. Therefore I command you, 'You shall open wide your hand to your brother, to the needy and to the poor, in your land.'" Today we need to heed these messages by increasing funding for organizations like the Boys and Girls Clubs, Job Corps, parks departments, museums, and a long list of community-based organizations that attempt to inspire youth.

The poorly educated often have limited entertainment possibilities, so they spend free time watching TV or YouTube, looking at programs that are increasingly filled with anger, fear, foul language, and killing. Violence is presented as an everyday occurrence. Filmmakers routinely display images of women being treated women poorly, and sexual exploitation abounds. It is not surprising that so many children grow up believing that the world is a violent and uncaring drug-filled place.

If we pay attention to pollsters, the upper classes want their taxes lowered and government handouts decreased. The wealthy feel safe living in gated communities or having front door security for their apartments. Wondering whether uneducated people wandering the streets have the skills to hold down jobs is a depressing subject to contemplate. Apathy contributes to a growing sentiment that uneducated people and immigrants should not participate in our democracy because they neither know the issues of the day nor share our common values. I queried a twenty-one-year-old street kid to find out what he knew about the Fourth of July. He responded that it was about fireworks and picnics, and in further exploration it was obvious that he did not know that our country ever had a revolution. This child was a high school graduate. The shared remembrance that the United States was founded with a vision for people of all classes has been forgotten, yet these thoughts need to be revitalized if we are going to have a country that works well for all.

If we are not careful, the wealthy will increasingly be living in gated communities, much as they do in parts of China, where they have been erecting Villas for a half-million or more people to live surrounded by high walls by high walls and armed guards. These communities contain their own shopping centers, restaurants, hospitals, and schools. Women, especially, never leave the confines of the wall except to travel for a vacation with their families. In our own country we need to be concerned as well. The question of who lives in a constrained environment will become mute if we do not combat this situation; it will be the wealthy whose freedom of movement is limited.

It is time to think of class as more than just rich and poor. The class equation must include intelligence, learning, truth, creative problem-solving abilities, and ignorance. A dialogue is needed to discuss common values and how to reach out and educate the 25 percent of children who are school dropouts. We may not always agree on the best way to provide health care or a common religion, but I do believe we can agree on the importance of education, trust, caring, honesty, family, and community. Because of the nature of museums as entertainment centers, keepers of community memories, and promoters of creative expression, they too play a large role in assisting the undereducated become better integrated in society. Second and Third World countries such as India, China, and Saudi Arabia have been constructing multiple science centers throughout their vast lands in order to improve access to information. These centers with their committed staff are making a difference in introducing many populations to a technological world. By inviting youth to participate as volunteers they also open new avenues to learning. Museums have numerous examples of teen explainers, or guides influenced by their experiences pursuing scientific, social scientific, or artistic careers. The following tales are of two such youth.

BEATING THE ODDS: STREETWISE

Several years ago, my husband Ray and I became involved in the life of a nineteen year-old street kid I'll call Streetwise. He and his eight siblings lived in poverty in a small town about one hour north of Portland. The elder four children did not graduate high school. Two served time in federal prisons, and several have wasted away with black tar heroin, and other drugs. Three do have minimum wage jobs.

When Streetwise was a child, I occasionally brought him to my house in Portland, hoping to show him another way of life. One summer, after I no longer worked at OMSI, I was able to get him a scholarship to a summer camp. He was enthusiastic about doing engineering activities, enjoying the opportunity to learn with his hands rather than by reading. We discussed art, politics, and history, and I read nighttime stories to wet his appetite for adventure. When Streetwise entered high school, our contact lessened, and eventually we lost complete track of him. Later we learned that he often cut school, was always hungrily scrounging for food, and escaped home whenever his mother's back was turned.

From the age of sixteen, Streetwise lived on his own, bouncing from shelter to shelter, sleeping under bridges and in doorways. It was impressive that he managed to graduate from high school. Streetwise described sleeping in layers of clothing under a bush and going into school at 5:00 a.m. in order get a warm shower and eat the free school breakfast. Though he graduated with math scores at grade level, a note on his diploma mentioned that his English did not meet state standards.

When Ray and I again saw Streetwise he was clearly very ill. He had moved to Portland and happened to be walking across the street while we were stopped at a red light. We feared that he had pneumonia, and so we brought him home to nurse him back to health. He regained his strength during the cold and wet month of November, and it became obvious that we could not put him out to continue his wanderings during the winter. Ray and I did not know what to do, and our friends were quite worried about us getting involved. Neighbors who saw Streetwise in the driveway called to warn us about a vagrant person on our property, advising us to call the police. Streetwise stood hunched over, wore torn clothing, had plugs in his ears and long straggly unkept hair. When he spoke, he mumbled and would not make eye contact. A university friend of ours who spoke to him told us, "There's not much there."

The first thing we did when we decided to keep him for the winter was to pay for a haircut (Streetwise was not happy about losing his long locks). We then took him to Goodwill to buy clothes, a warm coat, gloves, and hat. We set rules and insisted that he shower daily, keep his room clean, and make his bed. Ray made him get up early and exercise for at least one half hour daily. Sleeping until noon was not acceptable. I took him to museums again, challenging him to pay attention and talk about what was going on. To get him to say more than yes or no, we worked on verbal expression over dinner. Each evening he was asked to share a story about his day, as did we all.

Then what? I was in the middle of the busy catalog season, and needed people to work in the warehouse. It was easy to provide Streetwise a temporary job, though to keep it, Streetwise had to prove that he would do the work. He amazed us all! Always early to work, late to leave, it turned out that he was very competitive and worked hard to do the best job with the fewest mistakes. What a surprise to learn that there was something to this kid.

After the catalog's busy period, however, Streetwise was once more unemployed. Though he had a good recommendation from his manager and he registered at many temporary agencies, he could not find work. The job market for an unskilled person is brutal.

Ray, a wood artist working out of our house, was going crazy trying to keep Streetwise busy doing odd jobs. We decided that he had to do volunteer work while looking for paid employment. Volunteering was not part of his upbringing and Streetwise, as he did with most of our suggestions, rejected the idea. But, since he could not come up with an alternative, we decided to sign him up for one of our favorite organizations, the Audubon Society. You might imagine his reaction. Birds? However, when he went for orientation, he was surrounded by young, beautiful female volunteers who immediately came over to sit at his table. He returned from this meeting with the broadest of smiles and told us that he had had one of the best days of his life. Over the next months, he helped clear hiking trails and went on bird-walking trips with Ray. We gave him his first binoculars, a bird book, and a camera. An amazing transformation began that continues to this day. Streetwise pays attention to our feathered friends, has learned some of their names, and even photographs them occasionally.

I encouraged Streetwise to read, something he rarely did, claiming it was unnecessary for succeeding in life. When we visited OMSI and he was asked to read exhibit signs out-loud he became agitated. I had to help him through the words until he understood the information presented. We perused the daily newspaper during breakfast and talked about issues of the day. He had limited vocabulary and found it difficult to pronounce words. I discovered a great graphic novel by an MIT historian, Larry Gonick, who wrote the *Cartoon History of the US,* and gave it to him. Because he knew so little about the history of our country, reading the book became one of the conditions for remaining in our house. The bribe worked, and the book was enjoyed. By that summer, the kid who before thought the Fourth of July was all about picnics and fireworks, now understood the holiday. Since Streetwise was enthusiastic about one activity, skateboarding, I bought seventh grade-level books on the subject. He devoured them. It was a start.

The task of finding work continued until finally we heard about Job Corps, a government training program run military style, for youth just like Streetwise. Even Job Corps takes perseverance and knowledge of systems to get accepted, and he had to select an area to focus on. Ray and I lobbied for weeks to get him into the program. It was very difficult for him to choose a trade; his response was "I don't know. I get bored after a week or two." He finally selected commercial and industrial painting, thinking it was better than going to jail, another option as a way to be fed. When accepted, Streetwise's initial attitude was, "At least I will have a roof over my head and food in my belly for two years." Once there, however, his outlook on life changed, and he blossomed. It was an amazing transformation.

The painters union sponsored his training, and he learned how to apply paint safely, put up scaffolding, deal with hazardous material, drive a car, become a flagger, and many more skills. He took classes in leadership, even discussing kindness and personal finance. Each skill required him to read training manuals and take a test. He thanked me for having made him read because it kept him from having to take remedial classes. He became a stronger reader and was able to get through the many technical pamphlets required of a professional painter. Job Corps gave monetary rewards, certificates, and privileges for each positive step on the way. It was such a smart way to reward positive behavior. Most of these kids did not care at all about grades, but they were interested in food and clothing and were willing to work for points to that end. Streetwise was so very happy when he was recognized for his accomplishments. For his final exam, he received 100 percent (a platinum) on his math test and almost as good (a gold) on his reading.

Streetwise graduated from his program with honors and certificates. He stands straight as a result of the many pushups and jogs that he was required to do. He has lost his ear plugs, dresses well, smiles, and is helpful, looking and acting like a middle-class young man. He has a lot to say because he has been exposed to interesting experiences, and he has become a more curious and observant person. Streetwise is presently a journeyman union industrial painter, working on bridges, ships, and containers. He reads with ease and is constantly asking questions and looking up answers on his computer. With his energy and internal fire, he should do very well in life. In one year, he went from no future to future. In four years he completed his training. To me, he is a hero, as are the people who supplied school breakfast and lunch to him, the teachers at Job Corps, and the museum that provided a scholarship when he was young. At OMSI he learned basic mechanics and realized that he enjoyed hands on learning. Importantly he saw how other middle class kids dressed and interacted with each other by talking rather than cursing and fighting. Streetwise was helped to recognize a world of opportunity outside of the confined space of his dysfunctional childhood home and with the support of so many people he was able to succeed. Now when we go to a cultural attraction, Streetwise pays attention and is willing to contribute his thoughts about the experience. He has become a good companion.

YOUNG SCHOLAR

Jeff Gottfried, one-time director of education at OMSI, initiated and received NSF funding to conduct a unique Young Scholars program. High school students were selected from a national applicant pool of those interested in working alongside research scientists during summer vacation. There was no difficulty in finding applicants with a 4.0 grade average who wanted to take advantage of this opportunity. Most of the teens came from caring middle- and upper-class families who encouraged their children to exceed. But Jeff was interested in looking beyond the obvious to see if there were children who had talent but, for reasons of poverty or family dysfunction, might not have been able to achieve their potential. He asked teachers to make suggestions of students who might fit into this category of unrecognized youth.

Sure enough, one of the local high school teachers mentioned a boy, whom I will call Young Scholar, who had been moved each of the past five years by his family who lived near the poverty line. Young Scholar's father was a Vietnam vet who, if entering treatment today, would have been diagnosed with post-traumatic stress disorder (PTSD). In the '70s, the military was slow to acknowledge that diagnosis as valid. His mother suffered a variety of illnesses and was also incapacitated. They moved from house to house as they faced evictions, and there were many times when Young Scholar spent months sleeping in the family car.

His teachers, recognizing the boy's intelligence, encouraged Young Scholar to apply for the summer research position at OMSI. Though Young Scholar's appearance and manner of speaking appeared to be mismatched to his knowledge, his teachers were able to see through the superficial to a spark of genius. His grades were low B's, and his command of English was marginal. The boy's dress was shabby, like that of a street kid, yet his application essay was compelling as he spoke of his life and challenges, so the OMSI program decided to take a risk on this young man. Jeff's intuition was good, and throughout the summer Young Scholar became energized and hopeful.

The research he participated in was an environmental study of water quality of rivers in eastern Oregon. Jeff visited the site one week and noticed that the youth was not around during dinner hour. In inquiring about his whereabouts, he was told that Young Scholar was so wrapped up in the research that he did not want to stop what he was doing until it became darker. Later that evening, Jeff overheard Young Scholar asking another youth if there would be a possibility of living with the boy's family the following school year, since his parents were planning to move once again. Jeff immediately discussed the young man's situation with his wife, Emily, and they decided to take the boy in during the following academic year. Jeff went to Young Scholar's apartment, loaded his few belongings into the car, and brought him home to a new atmosphere with caring people who lived creatively and applauded learning. The following year, Young Scholar never missed a day of school, receiving a 4.0 grade point average by year end and winning a Bausch and Lomb Science Award upon graduation. This prestigious award was accompanied by a four-year full scholarship to Rochester University. It was quite an accomplishment for this awakened student.

Young Scholar accepted the scholarship and went off to study science while he worked cleaning dorms to augment his stipend. As Young Scholar continued to return to Jeff's house for vacations, the family grew to accept and love him as a son. Upon graduation, he accepted a job as a teacher in private school in New Orleans and eventually returned to Oregon to obtain a master's degree in environmental science, in sedimentology. With diploma in hand, he was back to New Orleans, for a doctorate program at Tulane University. Young Scholar lived through Katrina, almost losing his entire PhD dissertation in the disaster. This man, who understood the difficulties of overcoming adversity, managed to find help in rescuing his thesis from flood water when the campus was closed. Presenting and defending his thesis was not easy either, because his thesis committee was now spread throughout the United States. He had to undertake the arduous task of reassembling his dissertation committee before he could graduate. Today Young Scholar is married with two children and is a professor in a Louisiana college. Because of recognition by his teachers, inspiration gained from participating in a museum program, and a dedicated museum professional willing to go the extra mile, this young man is a contributing member of society.

A great many museum programs help children escape the constraints of their environments. During my tenure at OMSI, we opened several after-school programs in low-income areas of the city. We collaborated with groups like the Urban League to ensure that both children and adults became computer literate. The wide variety of offerings included field trips for entire families to and from OMSI. Though OMSI grew to have many square feet of exhibit halls and classroom space, it always recognized the importance of specifically designed local programs. In some instances, classroom hours are extended to accommodate working parents, and attention is given to the racial diversity of staff.

LEADERS COME FROM ALL BACKGROUNDS
FOCUS ON FREDA NICHOLSON: DISCOVERY PLACE

Growing up in an orphanage in the mountains of North Carolina and overcoming the stigma of poverty, Freda Nicholson created a life of service to her community. How she rose from her difficult childhood to become part of the upper classes of Charlotte is the story of an individual with a can-do attitude, one who created opportunities for herself. As an example of a rags-to-riches woman she never, never let class snobbishness stand in her way, nor did she forgot the lessons of her past. Freda played an pivotal role in not only her institution, The Discovery Place in Charlotte, N.C., but she impacted several museum associations at the national level.

Have you ever thought of reserving an entire four-hundred-plus-person ocean liner to take you and your acquaintances to the Amazon? How about chartering a 747 plane? Sound a bit risky? Would you do it if it put your job on the line and also risked your personal finances? That is what one very gutsy woman, Freda Nicholson, did.

Museum presidents always have their attention centered on fund-raising, and in 1986, when Halley's

Freda

243

Comet was due to make an appearance in Brazil, Freda was there with interested amateur science aficionados in order to observe its passing. Wanting to become a major player in developing OMNIMAX/IMAX large-format films, Freda realized that she needed to have more money than the museum presently reserved for new ventures, so she set out to find the funds in a way that allowed her to control the outcome. Freda was not inexperienced when it came to the tourism industry. For a great many years, she organized excursions for wealthy donors, using the camaraderie and intimacy that develops among fellow travelers as a way to get into the hearts and wallets of potential philanthropists. In 1986, the year Halley's Comet was going to be visible in the Americas, she had her chance to do something extraordinary. At first she contacted a Greek shipping line that was headed for the Amazon and reserved only fourteen cabins. The space filled immediately, with a waiting list of one hundred people. Freda was amazed that the rooms filled so quickly and realized that the interest in the comet was something special.

There was only one thing she could imagine to do next. "Let's rent the entire ship," she said, and so she did. Letters were immediately sent out to numerous science center presidents, asking them if they wanted to participate in this once-in-a-lifetime opportunity. With overwhelming response, they quickly filled the ship. What then? Getting so many people from North Carolina, the planned rendezvous point, to Brazil was not going to be an easy task. So Freda then rented an entire 747, the first to ever land in the Charlotte airport. Staff were called into service driving people from their hotels to the airport.

Planetarium personnel from the Franklin Institute were on board along with science specialists from Discovery Place and other participating museums. Halley's was strong motivation for teaching astronomy and nature while on the Amazon, but it was a risky venture, one that could have cost Freda her home if it had not succeeded for she felt compelled to personally insure the venture. She admitted that the museum's board of directors hardly knew what was happening so she accepted ownership of the undertaking. Fortunately the Amazon cruise was a grand success. When all of the accounts were finalized, Freda did net enough money to participate in the large format film industry's new productions.

Freda's Lesson #1: Running a museum is a job for a risk taker.

You might wonder how Freda came to have a strong enough sense of self to be able to tackle such a venture. Her story is quite remarkable and an inspiration to those who start from the bottom. It is a rags-to-riches tale that I find intriguing because it demonstrates that the United States' claim as a place where a person can climb out of poverty to reach success has roots in reality.

Freda Nicholson was an Appalachian girl growing up high in the mountains of North Carolina. To a northerner she has a mesmerizing southern accent to prove her birth right. One of five children in her father's second family (there were three older step-siblings) she was firstborn to her mother. As the oldest in this poor family, she was thrust into a position of responsibility at a very early age. Her mother spent many years in and out of mental hospitals due to severe depression, and her war veteran father contracted tuberculosis, taking him away from home as well. By the time she was eleven, her older half-siblings had left home, so Freda was the only one left to care for the youngsters, feeding and nurturing them as best she could. Though it seemed like it took an eternity, social services finally became aware of the family's plight and made arrangements for the three older children to be placed in foster care at the Crossnore School in Crossnore, North Carolina. The younger children were placed in Oxford Orphanage, leaving the siblings wondering if they would ever see each other again.

Most of the time I hear terrible stories about life in an orphanage, but the Crossnore School turned out to be an exception. Freda claims that it changed her life and more particularly the founders, Dr. Mary Martin Sloop and Dr. Eustace Sloop, became mentors and a source of inspiration. They taught her an important life lesson.

Freda's Lesson #2: You can do anything if you try hard enough.

The Sloops were exceptional people who started their boarding school in the middle of nowhere, bringing hope to impoverished children. They began the school in 1913 in their own home, at first providing unheated attic shelter in the cold of winter to their young boarders. Their belief was that "education is the best way for a child to rise above his circumstances." Experiential learning and focused individualized care developed into the school's mantra with fund-raising becoming a way of life for the Sloops, who wanted to support a boarding school, hospital, and dental clinic. As pioneers, they brought electricity and the first telephone and paved road to Avery County. Today, Crossnore Academy has grown significantly and is operated as part of the state's charter school system.

The Sloops never understood the words "it can't be done" and always found a workaround to make things happen. For instance, Dr. Mary Martin approached the Daughters of the American Revolution (DAR), asking for discarded clothing for their young orphans. The donations she received were quite inappropriate, so she sold the clothes and then used the proceeds to clothe her school's children. This initial effort has turned into a massive retail outlet much like that of Goodwill, and several hundred thousands of dollars are earned each year to support the school. The couple was always on the move, searching for money and opportunities for their children. They went to Raleigh, North Carolina, looking for government funds and gave speeches to community-minded groups to raise awareness. When there were no resources for a hospital, Dr. Sloop organized local work parties to collect riverbed rocks and haul them to the site to be used in construction. The Sloops built their hospital. When they needed a power plant, it also was built with Sloop muscle and brains. Freda told me that Eustace Sloop had a real mountain person's "can do" mentality; "let nothing stand in my way," she used to say. They were masters of the work-around philosophy of getting things done.

Young Freda arrived at Crossnore feeling depressed and ashamed. Living with others in a large dormitory room, she was afraid that she too might develop a mental illness like her mother or wind up in the hospital with tuberculosis like her father. The Sloops consistently reassured her that she was not her parents and that her future lay elsewhere. She was taught to have good manners and keep clean. The Sloops contributed greatly to giving the young woman courage and self-esteem, observing that Freda was a hardworking student who liked math and science. Upon her high school graduation, they managed to arrange for a full-tuition scholarship to be given by an anonymous benefactor. Later in life, she tried hard to discover the name of the donor, but it was never revealed.

Freda graduated from St. Joseph Hospital School of Nursing in Savannah, Georgia, and met Nick, a surgeon, while working at her first job in New Orleans. Love, marriage, and eventually six children and fourteen grandchildren followed after the couple moved back to Charlotte. As of this writing, the two have been married over sixty years, a record in my book.

Life was easy in the early days of marriage . . . and a bit boring. The neighborhood wives were friendly and took the young mountain girl under their wings and introduced her to the ways of Charlotte society. At first she followed the custom for young women of comfortable means, playing cards, visiting friends, and passing the day in gentile chit chat. But Freda didn't like the lifestyle of the idle rich, so she announced to her surprised husband that she was taking a job as a nurse at the hospital where he was employed. I got the impression that he was not very happy about that decision. Freda eventually went back to school to receive her BS in nursing, followed eighteen years later in 1976 by an MEd in education from the University of North Carolina in Charlotte, where she majored in supervision and administration.

Ever looking for new challenges, even with a full plate, Freda taught for a while upon getting her degree. When an opportunity to assist in developing a health exhibit about the body at the Charlotte Nature Center came up, she decided to leave teaching and accept the part time work since it fit into her schedule, permitting her to take care of home obligations. The small nature center, located in a wealthy white suburb unfurled new and exciting opportunities for Freda. The body exhibit was fun to work on and opened to great acclaim, stressing the little museum to its limits.

Just before her arrival at the center, the board had decided it was time to move to a larger facility so it could serve more of Charlotte's residents. The new site was in a dismal part of downtown where sidewalks were filled with prostitutes and drug dealers. The city wanted to clean up the area. In the midst of planning and though fairly new on the job, the director of the Nature Center was relieved of his position due to personal problems. Being left with a vacuum, the center asked Freda to take over the helm. With her background in health science, a degree in administration, a husband with some standing in the community, and experience at the Nature Center, she seemed like the ideal candidate. And so Freda said yes and immediately discovered that the new project needed $1 million more before it could open on its scheduled date eight months later.

When a doubting Tom newspaper reporter told her that it couldn't be done, her answer was, "Oh yes it will be complete. We will be open in October as planned." Within two weeks, with the assistance of Bank of America executives pressuring the city, she obtained the $1 million needed. This never-say-no woman was proving her worth.

A massive call went out for retired people to volunteer their carpentry skills. While the men pitched in with their brawn and engineering know-how, a woman's group formed to fund-raise. This was like a museum barn raising, the likes of which could probably never happen today because of building codes and construction laws. What a time of hustle it was as volunteers worked alongside paid coordinators to get the exhibits made. Multiple workshops were set up throughout the museum, and the sounds of sawing and pounding could be heard throughout.

Consultant Joe Sonderman helped with the original design and is credited with coining the new name, Discovery Place, out of consideration of the uniqueness of the Charlotte community. After traveling the country on a grand tour to see other facilities, the founders did what perceptive people do, which is look locally to identify strengths and needs. Charlotte was too small to have an aquarium, a natural history museum, and a science center. So Discovery Place was born without a strong bias, committed to accommodating multiple educational desires. Included was an aquarium, the first museum-built rain forest, and an area with open stacks permitting visitors to explore the museum's vast natural history collections. Discovery Place became a trendsetter by permitting the public to view items that many institutions hide in back rooms.

Did everything happen smoothly and without problems? Of course not. There was behind-closed-door criticism for hiring a woman instead of a well-respected local man. There were questions raised about installing a rain forest in a science center. Some of the small natural history museums throughout North Caroline felt their territory was being invaded by the plan to include natural science exhibits in the science center. The local newspapers enjoyed printing editorials and stirring up controversy.

***

Freda's Lesson #3: It takes backbone to manage board and community differences.

***

As already emphasized, museum presidency is not a job for the weak. The board, general public, press, educators, government officials, and staff all believe they know what is best. It would be easy for the job to be turned into a nightmare under a weak director. Freda and I have both observed museum presidents who were fearful of their boards. We listened to worries from colleagues about losing their jobs and how they felt the need to please pushy board members and donors, with the result being that they were handicapped, finding it hard to make difficult decisions. When I first arrived at OMSI, board members told me who to hire for certain positions and, like Freda who faced similar situations, I had to set the standard for board behavior. Freda was even stronger than I. Her word was law.

Museum staff are professionals who have dedicated their careers to serving the public through exhibitions and education programs. Board members are not trained to manage education-entertainment facilities but the need to become supportive and ensure that the institution is financially stable, ethically appropriate, and managed for growth. Upon hiring the right person to lead the organization, they do not need to be involved in daily operations. A new president must develop credibility with the board of directors by appearing confident, setting clear goals, and communicating progress.

The director of any non-profit must insure that the staff is professional by seeing that they are continuously educated, not only in their subject areas of expertise and general museum operations but also in sensitivity to the needs of their local community. Freda instituted a policy that encouraged ongoing training, sending staff to trade shows, paying for classes, and involving them in national and international travel. As a result, she takes great pride that many on her staff were able to leave their positions to advance their careers, with some becoming the heads of their own organizations.

Twelve-year-old John Mackey became enamored with science by attending programs and volunteering at the Nature Center, which is still under the proprietorship of Discovery Place. He was eventually hired full time and worked his way up to positions of greater responsibility until he was selected to be president following Freda's retirement at the age of sixty-seven. Now John too has announced his retirement and can look back proudly to a life of service to his community, all because of a science center.

Freda's Lesson #4: Let stress go at the end of each day.

The job was challenging, and Freda's stress level was high. As the museum gained credibility, she became more involved in community and professional boards. She served as president of the Association of Science and Technology Centers as well as the American Association of Museums. She recalled one International Museum conference held in Barcelona that was attended primarily by male colleagues. The hotel had listed her as Fred Nicholson and was quite surprised when a skirt-wearing Freda arrived to register. Her hotel suite was complete with a complimentary list of women she could call for companionship and was well stocked with cigars. The conference introduced her to the man who headed the Russian Science Museum. This was at a time when the Cold War was at its height and her initial reaction was hesitant. Over the years, the two became close friends and maintain their friendship to this day. His contribution to handling stress was a smile along with vodka.

Though Freda too enjoyed her drink, at the end of each day, her real love was the mountains. Her family retreated there whenever they could, and in retirement most of her time is spent with her husband in their mountain home. Located near Crossnore School, where she spent her youth, Freda remains involved on the board of directors Crossnore School and continues to help them raise funds.

During her career, she was honored with a great many awards, including an honorary doctorate from Queens College in Charlotte and the Woman of the Year recognition from the City of Charlotte. What does Freda believe gives meaning to life? "Be the best you can as a parent and set an example to rest of the world in everything you do."

A Source of Energy

Impression 5

Oregon Museum of Science and Industry

SECTION IV
THE PRACTICAL SIDE

BUDGING AT THE SEAMS:
LESSONS FOR MOVING

S uccess brings a new level of complexity. It was not long before
people found their way to our Impression 5 warehouse
museum even though it was tucked away in an obscure industrial park. There were days when the noise level was extreme,
and we worried about the overuse of our facility and marginally
well-made displays. The landlord who rented the space with no
money down was continually amazed that we were able to hang
on for so many years. He beamed with pleasure at our success.
After three years of operations in the warehouse, the search was
on for a new more permanent building.

During that time I was divorced and started dating a man
who eventually became my husband. Marty had his art studio
on Mill Street adjacent to a vacated building that once operated a small mill. The site was centrally located along the river
in downtown Lansing. He kept telling me that Impression 5
should purchase the land with its three buildings, one of which
was his small workshop, and become his landlord. The largest
structure was an 86,000 square foot two-story brick warehouse
that at one time was used for milling lumber. It was in poor
condition but intriguing. The large second floor rooms exuded
a warm feeling that came from old heavy wooden beams, a huge

dinosaur of a freight elevator and wooden floors throughout. The third structure had rental potential for a variety of uses. (It was later sold to a nonprofit community theater.)

The location was perfect with a reasonable price tag of $526,000 though thousands more dollars were needed for renovations. Areas in the building had been previously used as offices and could accommodate our staff needs. With a bit of ingenuity from a local architect, a newly designed entrance allowed for a second-floor museum. The plan was to use the lower part of the building for offices and storage and later turn it into classrooms. A slightly larger area on the lower level, near the freight elevator, was a perfect location for an exhibit production shop. Heating the uninsulated warehouse was going to be expensive and difficult, electrical coverage was adequate and air conditioning nonexistent. After much debate about future growth and renovation plans, with assistance of local and state government officials and lots of contributions from local citizens and generous foundations, the property on Mill Street was purchased.

The building's shortcomings were brought home one winter day when I was out of town at a workshop at the Exploratorium in San Francisco. I received a panicked call informing me that there had been a heavy snowfall and the roof had caved in. "What are we to do?" the voice on the phone asked. Not much could be executed from my location across the country, so I depended on the staff on hand to prop up the roof, cover the hole, and call the insurance company. They rose to the occasion magnificently by shoring the structure up and covering the roof with plastic until it could be repaired.

A nonexistent cooling system was another major handicap everywhere except for office areas. Summers when children were off from school should have been a perfect time to visit Impression 5. Instead the building was a sweat box that kept people away. It wasn't until years later, after I had left, that there was enough money to renovate and add a cooling system. When I imagined the previous occupants working away in the Mill Street factory, I felt very sorry for them.

In time the city improved the street and renamed it Museum Drive. What a good decision the officials made! Our museum became the impetus to clean up the dilapidated area, increase tourism to the capital, and promote business growth in the center city. A few years after our opening, the R.E. Olds Museum moved in next door, featuring displays of antique automobiles that honored Oldsmobile's history in Lansing. Strip clubs and bars that fronted our property eventually moved out, and the Lansing Convention Center was built down the street, giving the area quite a boost.

Moving OMSI

OMSI presented quite another story. When first hired, I inherited an 86,000 square foot facility located in a beautiful park laced with hiking trails that also housed the arboretum, zoo, and World Forestry Center. The museum's exhibit hall did not share the richness of the outside environment. It was tired and painted black. I felt like I was entering a cave every morning when arriving at work. My goal was to brighten the space and find a way to bring the institution into the twenty-first century. The following story tells how that was accomplished.

Everything has a tipping point, that moment when an understanding of circumstances allows for a new reality. The instant it happened for me was the moment an Explainer interrupted a conversation in my first-floor office.

Chatting animatedly around a large polished table were eleven semi-inebriated men and one woman, relaxing after a five-course celebratory dinner and swirling drinks while talking with our guest, John de Lancie. Better known as Q on *Star Trek: The Next Generation*, John was in the building to sign autographs during the opening of the *Star Trek: Federation Science* exhibition, which was already very popular, largely because of John. The crush of bodies compelled us to escape the display as quickly as possible for my office.

"Some kid just knocked down an old lady," the Explainer shouted as he entered. "There are too many people. Should we stop letting them in?"

The floor was a mad house of children running from display to display, long lines of people waiting to get into the transporter room, and parents peering over heads to keep track of their families. The din of babbling voices and noise created by the exhibit itself was overwhelming. Autograph seekers shoved invitations at John when he periodically took his seat at the signing table inside the glass doors. *Star Trek: Federation Science* was predicted to be successful but no one imagined that there would be a herd of humanity trying to get into our members-only reception.

The idea for a *Star Trek* exhibit had come three years earlier from our "Trekkie" gift shop manager, Terry Hiller. He was enamored by *Star Trek* and knew every character and nuance of each episode, even corresponding with Gene Roddenberry from time to time to discuss the possibility of an exhibit. As soon as he presented the idea, I became intrigued and saw a chance to make a statement, not only locally but nationally, presenting a testimony of where I wanted to go with the museum's exhibitions. Using popular entertainment as a base for teaching science would create marketing advantages that could lure science-fiction buffs of all ages into our museum. Visitors would be shown current scientific advancements and compare them with fictional predictions that were so vividly portrayed in books and movies. Our goal was to merge entertainment and education in blockbuster exhibitions that would leave a lasting impression on the participant. In the early '70s this blending of fields was a new concept, as was the idea that education could be enjoyable.

We had evidence that "edu-fun" works. OMSI had successfully tried this approach a few years earlier when developing a superheroes exhibit in conjunction with DC Comics. To get started on that display, I had to get permission at the DC Comics' headquarters in New York. Seated in the chair opposite me in the waiting room was a man hunched over and engrossed in reading a newspaper. Because he looked familiar, I became curious, embarrassingly glancing in his direction several times before realizing that I was staring at a life-size sculpture of Clark Kent. When finally summoned to my meeting, I continued to be surprised while walking through the narrow hallways. Punched through one wall, practically hitting my nose as I walked by, was the tight-fisted arm of Superman, ever-ready to come to the rescue. I was definitely intrigued and saw how little was needed to make a strong statement of their brand. My timing with DC was perfect because it was Superman's fiftieth anniversary, and the company was pleased to comply with my request to develop a traveling science exhibit. The Smithsonian had also been given license for an exhibition, but they planned to take a more historical approach, displaying artifacts and costumes used in feature films throughout the years, while our design would be more interactive. Superman would have good exposure through our two museums.

OMSI's goal was to demonstrate how ordinary people are superheroes today because of modern technology. Superman may have x-ray vision, but so do we, because of various imaging devices that let us explore the inner depths of our bodies. We wanted to show archeologists and detectives as superheroes because they dig up items to be subjected to technological tests that help determine origin and history.

Our staff quickly became engaged in designing real-world connections to DC's science-fiction heroes. When complete, the

Superheroes exhibit became a favorite reason for visiting OMSI, and it continued to bring the museum recognition for the many years it traveled throughout the United States and Europe.

After that blockbuster success, we looked for a follow-up idea that would be even more spectacular. When the suggestion for a Star Trek exhibit was unveiled it did not take much encouragement to contact Paramount for an appointment with series, and then franchise, creator Mr. Roddenberry. Gene was most obliging and invited me to visit. Feeling like a Hollywood insider, I excitedly flew to Los Angeles. Once there, negotiating the highway system in my rented car, with other vehicles whizzing by, was a challenge for one used to the more manageable roads of Portland, but I was able to make it to the front gate without an accident.

Since I was expected, I sailed through security and was directed to Gene Roddenberry's unpretentious office on the Paramount lot. My eyes traveled everywhere to watch costumed actors walking nonchalantly toward various windowless buildings, entering through Alice-size doorways. It seemed as though within those walls was a kind of Wonderland where actors would go through a metamorphosis. Open-topped vehicles whizzed back and forth, taking riders and cargo to huge metal studios lining gridded streets. My feeling of awe continued through the afternoon when I was given a personal tour of Paramount back lots and sound stages where so many familiar films had been shot.

Our proposal to Gene was to develop a traveling science display that demonstrated special effects and scientific achievements that inspired the Star Trek series. Because of OMSI's participation in an eight-member national exhibit collaborative, I convincingly explained the importance *Star Trek: Federation Science* could have on education. Through our network, the display would visit each member site, giving it an audience well beyond the population base of Portland. Once the initial travel schedule was completed, *Star Trek: Federation Science* would be made available worldwide to institutions willing to pay a rental fee for a three-month showing.

Gene Roddenberry turned out to be a down-to-earth, approachable man who loved science, and he immediately embraced our vision. We chatted quite a while before having lunch in the star-studded cafeteria where he explained he would have to get Paramount's permission, but quickly added, "I think I may have some pull there." Sure enough, after many conversations and a yearlong wait, we received positive approval from Paramount. OMSI was on its way to developing its most comprehensive and challenging exhibit to date.

Staff stayed in touch with Gene, who had to approve exhibit plans as they were developed. Fortunately everything was in place before he died in 1991. His death left a great sadness for all of those involved who had admired his genius. We certainly missed having him attend our opening. The *Star Trek* franchise has produced story material for almost five decades, resulting in six television series consisting of 726 episodes, and twelve feature films. We were pleased to be counted among the many spin-offs of their successful run.

OMSI's exhibit was valued at $1.3 million dollars and filled the entire first floor of our building. The success of *Star Trek: Federation Science,* along with praise from Q, who spoke eloquently about the uniqueness of the exhibit and the specialness of OMSI, was the tipping point that convinced the board of directors that it was time for the museum to grow. And though I had been talking nonstop about the need for more exhibition space, public response to our last several changing exhibitions did more to promote the cause for a new building than all of the speeches I ever gave. Media attention and attendance numbers were giving the museum the credibility that was needed before undertaking a costly capital campaign. There was no doubt about it—an overcrowded building demonstrated that we had reached the tipping point. OMSI was on a roll and ready to provide Oregon with a desperately needed contemporary science center.

The up-scale community around OMSI loved the Museum where generations of children visited the small building located in Washington Park near the zoo. Thousands of kids attended camps and classes, walked through the aorta of a 10 foot heart, and visited the Kendall planetarium for star shows. Families stood in lines for hours when the first moon rock was put on display after the nation heard the inspiring words, "One small step for man, one giant leap for mankind" spoken by Neil Armstrong. The only downside to expansion was whether loyal members would ever sanction a move from the museum's pristine location in the wealthy West Hills.

Choosing a site in a downtrodden neighborhood may be appreciated by city planners, but it is not always welcomed by the general public. The move across town was quite a stressful time with corporations lobbying for OMSI to move into their blighted neighborhood in order to jump-start redevelopment efforts. Some museum members sent hate mail when they learned of our planned move, threatening never to visit the new east-side location we selected. They told me that they would not feel safe getting out of their parked cars, and it would be dangerous walking from parking lot to our front door. Our architects assured us that this was a problem easily resolved with proper lighting and landscape design.

The site eventually selected offered numerous riverfront amenities even though it was considered the wrong side of town by west-side residents. It was more centrally located, had easier access to public transportation, and was visible to the west-side promenade, a popular walking trail. An added incentive was that Portland General Electric was willing to give us the land and huge turbine buildings for free, agreeing to clean up, at their expense, any toxic waste left behind. Portland's

Development Commission saw it as an anchor for future east side growth.

The emotion I experienced when the board finally embraced the idea of a new building was that of déjà vu. Moving to a new facility was an undertaking that would once again occupy every second of my waking hours. It was an adventure that I suspected would be fraught with a great many demons and unexpected horrors as the project progressed, and I asked myself if I was ready for this next challenge. Most of the turbine halls had to be removed with the original building gutted and kept as a historical reminder to be integrated into the general layout. We planned to add a new planetarium, OMNIMAX Theater, and fortuitously, a submarine. Building new space was intriguing because the move gave me a chance to test organizational skills developed while president of Impression 5, thirteen years earlier. It also provided a platform for the many architectural ideas I had about location and size of exhibit halls, offices, public spaces, etc. I wanted staff offices to have windows overlooking displays and parents not to fear that their children would get lost in huge multi-exited spaces or a maze of hallways.

The opportunity to build from scratch pushed forward my first challenge, that of redefining the museum's philosophy. The 1944 OMSI building in Washington Park that was first envisioned by John Stevens as a natural history facility was going to be moved and enlarged to bring it into the twenty-first century, but what would that mean? By 1990, we were serving over six hundred thousand people in a facility designed to hold one hundred thousand, and as president it was my job to spearhead its evolution.

Though I had been involved in two previous expansions as director and president of Impression 5 Science Museum, this was going to be the most ambitious undertaking of my career. Not quite as naïve as I was back in the Michigan days,

I still was inexperienced in managing a large construction project and a sizable staff. The venture was going to be quite a learning trial, and my energy had to come from the citizens of Portland who loved OMSI and were ready to help it grow. For each piece of hate mail I received, I heard from dozens of people who supported the move.

The 1985 call to move the museum to the riverfront provided insight into city planning as I witnessed amazing transformation and development spurred by our museum's move. At times I felt like I was living through a sped-up movie clip, with bleak areas quickly so artfully converted.

Hundreds of scientists, educators, leaders and parents were brought together to reimagine a museum for the 21st century. My goal was to ensure community buy-in while incorporating the unique advantages of Portland. In their enthusiasm, many founding organizers wanted to duplicate everything they saw rather than stop to understand their own community's strengths and weaknesses. Yet there are those who direct museums embarking on major expansion who tend to be ambitious and dream of leaving a unique and lasting contribution to society. Personal goals are motivating as long as ambition does not supersede what is right for their particular community. Just because another museum's philosophical plan is impressive does not mean that it should be duplicated. We strove to understand Portland's needs.

When we were ready to build OMSI, a committee of board members, architects, and staff whizzed around the country, visiting museums in a private jet provided by one of our trustees. By the time we returned from our travels, we had a pretty solid consensus of what we did and did not like. It was easy to put in words and on architectural drawings a plan that we could all embrace. Our $31.1 million fundraising project was ready to begin though there were many skeptics that said it could not be done. Ours was the largest community project of its kind to ever be attempted in the Portland area. In four years we did manage to raise $32 million.

Over the following year senior staff officers became responsible for planning operations, exhibitions, education programs, facility management, marketing, publicity, signage and opening events. Each person played a critical role in the success of the undertaking. We became an inspired family, motivated to put our best ideas into action. Detailed attention was given to ensuring that both male and female bathrooms had infant changing tables, electrical outlets were usefully placed, there would be smooth flow through the exhibit halls and theaters, and that the size, shape and location of exhibit halls and classrooms worked effectively.

Developing or expanding a museum is exciting and exhilarating as well as frustrating and exhausting. No matter how carefully you plan, the unknown always occurs. Personal jealousies and ambitions abound side by side with genuine desires to help. Bureaucratic idiosyncrasies get in the way of speed and efficiency. Labor unions face off with contractors, slowing down the work; banks play games with loans while impatient volunteers wait in the wings ready to pitch in with donations of time and money.

I felt like I had a noose around my neck when the country went into recession during construction phase. It starred with the stock market crash in 1987 and evolved into the Savings and Loan Crises in the early 90's. At first our fundraising efforts were strong and community response was rewarding. We had enough money to start construction and several board members were concerned that if we waited for all of the funds to be deposited the delay would cause cost of materials and construction to rise significantly. So, we started work on the building knowing that we had Mitsubishi bank to back us up with a loan until all of the pledges were received.

But once the economy started to sink, bank regulations

stiffened, and Mitsubishi shockingly pulled out, leaving us with dire consequences. We did not have enough money to continue construction so the project halted. The union workers and contractors, however, charged fees even though they were off the job. I remember attending one negotiating session where my lawyer turned to me and said, "Don't look at the union representatives or smile." That was difficult, because I was a consensus builder who believed everyone in the community was trying to help OMSI succeed. I did not like the idea of being confrontational with those whose families would benefit from our new center. The contractors eventually sued us $11.3 million for the delay that occurred during the middle of 1991. A settlement of $2.2 million was eventually reached. Costs continued to mount.

We finally did get backing from the Oregon Department of Energy and a consortium of five banks but the interest rate was higher and the cost over-run so great that it took many years to crawl out of debt. I became a persona-non-grata for my leading role. With the savvy political knowledge of Pat LaCross, a subsequent president, and help from the State of Oregon, the museum finally brought the budget back into balance. Once more it is blossoming and able to grow under Nancy Stueber's able leadership. OMSI received a donation of additional land adjacent to the current property that will be turned into some sort of science oriented development.

— — — — — — — — — — — — —

Marilynne's Lesson #17: Success is measured by the buildup of relationships that support a project and help it to survive many deviations along the road.

— — — — — — — — — — — — —

Whether the undertaking is small or large a driving force for success is a clear vision sprinkled with an appropriate amount of fear. Once ideas are put into writing, speeches given to community groups, and funds or volunteers solicited, the project is launched and there is no turning back. People quickly put their trust in leaders who in turn are not expected to fail.

When completed, the $34.2 million museum built on Portland General Electric land with adjacent shops and storage facilities became a beacon of progress for the city. The building was brightly lit with an environmentally friendly parking lot, becoming a beacon of design and a major city attraction. The east-side promenade initiated on our site was eventually extended for miles, offering bicycle riders and walkers the opportunity to carouse the river along what was once a dark and scary bank. Connections throughout the east-side were made in ways that I had not previously imagined possible. A community college annex went in next door adding the the educational emphasis of the development. More recently a pedestrian/light rail bridge and transportation hub were built near the museum, making OMSI easily accessible from every part of the city.

Today, no one remembers that the property was once blighted, that there were financial difficulties or that the board and I were asked to make difficult choices that garnered a great deal of criticism. Memories are short-lived. The museum that was once perceived as being on the periphery of the city has suddenly become center stage. Newly acquired land adjacent to the museum is now in a planning stage that will lead to new ways of honoring developments in science and industry. As it presently is, there are additional attractions, such as a submarine, that is a story of its own.

Acquiring historical property from the federal government is a complicated undertaking. Whether it is a space shuttle, rocket, airplane, or submarine, the acquisition comes with pitfalls and responsibilities. Since OMSI is situated on the Willamette River, I wanted a submarine. In earlier years, I visited the Chicago Science and Industry Museum and toured its WWI submarine. Once on board, I moved throughout trying

The USS *Blueback*

to imagine how men lived in such tight quarters while knowing that they were enemy targets. Submarine movies such as *Das Boot,* about the first German submariners, intrigued me. OMSI's board of directors were completely tied up with raising funds for the new facility, so I was on my own when it came to a submarine. The idea stayed dormant in the background of my mind until opportunity came knocking once more, and realizing that when it does, I had to act.

Everything changed one spring day when three men walked into my office and asked if it would be possible to put a torpedo on OMSI's property as a memorial to submarine vets. I replied that a torpedo was inappropriate for our science center but that if they could get a submarine, we would turn it into a memorial. The men left laughing. As they later told me, their laughter was in delight, as they felt they'd come with a small request and left with the "whole enchilada." I, on the other hand, assumed they thought a submarine was a dream, like I did, and I never really expected to hear from them again.

The veterans went to work immediately and contacted the navy, discovering that the USS *Blueback*, a barbel-class World War II submarine was about to be decommissioned, but we had to apply immediately. It was an especially attractive boat, a movie star sub that had been used in *The Hunt for Red October*. The museum was given an unbelievably short three-month deadline to develop a plan for installation and operation. The navy informed us that we would have to sign a document agreeing that there would be no financial help from the federal government. The trustees informed me that though they liked the idea of a submarine, it could not be a fundraising priority. They were still raising money for the building.

Passion for a project at times demands finding a way around obstacles. It involves organizing many people to work against great odds for what is perceived as a community good. One person who had a real belief in Oregon and was known for helping ideas become reality was Senator Mark Hatfield, then chairman of the Senate Finance Committee. A second person who made the project happen was Rear Admiral John (Jack) Barrett, who had recently retired to White Salmon, in the State of Washington. He brought with him experience gained by helping Hawaii acquire the submarine USS *Bluefin* for a memorial park in Honolulu, Hawaii.

I called Senator Hatfield to ask for his assistance, which he willingly gave. With a great deal of help from the senator and many submariners, we were able to obtain $1.6 million, of which over $1 million was taxpayer money. Unfortunately, by the time we were granted the funds, we lost our submarine, because it was three months past the application deadline. The lobbying effort intensified, and to our great joy, we got the sub. It was then that President Bush, the elder, decided to rescind all pork barrel funding. Guess what funding was considered pork barrel? Once again we had no money to install the submarine.

Our volunteer submarine-veteran lobbyists, along with Senator Hatfield, went back to work, making phone calls and writing letters. A massive organizational machine sprang into action to get the funding back. We received the answer we wanted in the spring of 1991, though we were not home free yet.

The navy did another about-face and decided it wanted to use the *Blueback* for target practice. It turned out that years before, the USSR had stolen plans for the submarine and proceeded to build an entire fleet based on its hull design. Once the Soviet Union dissolved, their fleet of WWII subs was sold off, primarily to Iran. Navy officials wanted to target practice on our sub in case we ever had to fight ships with our own design.

Re-enter the admiral and veterans, who convinced the Secretary of the Navy that education served a much greater purpose than destruction. Finally, after many months of frustration, a compromise was reached that the military would keep the sub for one more year to conduct nondestructive target practice using sonar. We were assured that we would receive the *Blueback* at the end of that year.

It should not surprise you by now to find out that by the time we got the sub back, our funding had once again disappeared. It helped that Senator Hatfield was a powerful man in Washington who chaired the Senate Finance Committee. This time we acted quickly and were reallocated the money. There were further delays, but finally we received permission, and with an Act of Congress, the sub was released. By the time the Blueback actually sailed into the Willamette, we had only five months to prepare and polish the waterfront exhibit. Elated submarine vets developed a tour for visitors and spit-polished the brass for our May opening.

The story ended with celebration and excitement. A row

of handsome young sailors, clad in US Navy whites stood at attention on top of the boat under colorful flags while a bag piper rose from the stack to play an emotional "Amazing Grace." The memorial opened with a dedication presided over by Senator Hatfield along with the Secretary of the Navy, John Dalton, who had served on this particular sub. It was fun watching him take his wife on a tour of the *Blueback,* showing her every nook and cranny of the quarters and asking her to crawl through tight spaces. She followed him politely. The occasion was emotional, and there were many teary eyes, mine among them.

This project benefits the community today by providing a historical connection to WWII veterans; it also opened a new path to OMSI's future success. Over the next several years, volunteers continued to upgrade the sub's interior and improve its interactive features. Recordings of stories given by actual men of service amaze and thrill all, including those who cannot physically navigate the tight spaces. We developed a detailed video tour for disabled people to enjoy.

FUNDRAISING IDEAS AND INTERACTING WITH DONORS

"There is no such thing as a free lunch," my father used to say. I think a lot of fathers used to say that and probably still do. Money is always on the mind of anyone running a nonprofit organization, especially a museum. Door receipts are never enough. Museums raise funds in many ways, from individual donors to public and private grants, from admissions to gift shop purchases, and from fee-based education programs to fundraising events. Exhibits, marketing, class offerings, building upkeep, and staff cost a great deal, and earned income is considered outstanding if it can cover 70 percent of operating expenses. There rarely are leftover funds to pay for exhibitions, so a great deal of staff and board energy is expended in getting donations and grants.

Corporations, foundations, governments, and wealthy individuals are solicited for large donations to underwrite special program and building needs, to provide access for those who cannot afford to pay, and to underwrite specific exhibitions. Most museums initiate several annual events in order to attract different types of donors. At the high end, there are dinners, auctions, and even golf tournaments. Appealing to the middle, there are concerts, charity races, and haunted houses.

Philanthropic events, however, may not the largest source of donated income because they require a great deal of staff time. Their greatest benefit is that they tend to generate publicity.

Fund-raising events are often used as friend-raisers. They keep the organization in the minds of the area residents and raise awareness of exciting program changes. These appeals also are an avenue for reaching the multitude of smaller donors who would like to feel a connection to the institution. It is important to recognize that some donors seek recognition for their contributions and others prefer to remain in the shadow. Both types need to be acknowledged in their own way. Community buy-in that is demonstrated with a great many small donations is extremely important for an institution's long-term viability. Your five dollars counts. Obama proved in his presidential internet campaigns the effectiveness of getting a small amount of money from a large group of donors. A crowd of people behind a cause demonstrates to foundations that there is a broad base of support that will not let the institution fail. They validate to city and state officials that the organization has a following, and it makes it more likely to receive a public grant.

Impression 5's staff considered several ideas before embarking on our first fund-raiser. After hearing about a successful Halloween extravaganza that raised $50,000 annually for the Boston Children's Museum, we decided that was a perfect activity for our creative crew. Planning began for what would be a fun, child-centered, safe, artistic experience that would be enhanced by a cadre of local goblins and ghouls. Once assembled by our ambitious exhibit team, we expected the house to become a special annual attraction for the area.

Our first effort was in an abandoned house scheduled for demolition in a seedy part of town. The structure had already been stripped of running water, heat, and electricity. We designed it for visitors to enter the building by climbing through a basement window before touring the upper two stories. They exited it by sliding down an airplane chute attached to a second-floor window. I went to Michigan State University's planetarium staff for help, soliciting suggestions and equipment from their master special effects personnel. We borrowed projectors, ghoulish images, and color gels that contributed greatly to a mysterious ambiance. Quite a few friends and supporters volunteered their time by decorating various rooms. My favorite effect was in an upstairs bedroom with black walls. White balls hung on strings from the ceiling in one foot intervals in every direction. A strobe light focused on two slow-moving sheet-clad ghosts who vibrated the balls. Early visitors had a mind-altering, very beautiful experience in this haunted art extravaganza.

In order to secure the house once our precious props were in place, various acquaintances volunteered to camp in it overnight. On the first night a couple arrived with sleeping bags and camp stoves ready to inhabit the cold, creepy building. Skeletons, floating heads and an uncertain neighborhood made the experience quite unsettling. It wasn't long before they heard the sounds of pranksters trying to break in on a search for a bit of fun. The police had to get involved to frighten them away. The second evening, our "guards" were four MSU fraternity brothers. Unbeknownst to us, these rowdies invited dozens of their friends to a loud, drunken Halloween party. Since the house had no running water, the backyard served as their potty. The next day beer bottles and garbage littered the house and yard. The neighbors complained, but no equipment was broken or stolen.

Local children were trained and employed as volunteer spooks. Several of the kids were hellions who added chaos to the house. One twelve-year-old slightly disturbed male spook brought a crow bar to his station and used it to smack visitors as they passed his haunt. It took a few hours before we discovered what he was doing. Another young man stole a strobe light, and when confronted, denied taking the prop even though several people saw him leaving with a bulge under his costume.

The visitors themselves were unpredictable. While waiting in lines outside of the house, groups of friends would tell each other ghost stories, building their anticipation of fear until it reached a fever pitch. The teenage girls were especially wild and would shiver, scream, and fall into each other's arms. Then when it was their turn to enter the house, they would use their heightened fright as an excuse to grab and destroy everything in sight. The delicate room of balls and strings became one large massive tangled knot.

After the strobe light theft, I told the neighborhood kids they could not return to spook until the strobe was returned. An accommodating Boy Scout troop agreed to don costumes and help out on a moment's notice. How did our neighborhood hoodlums react? They hid in the back yard near the end of the exit slide and threw rocks at descending visitors. The following day, after many negotiations and a treat at McDonalds, the local crew apologized and were invited to return. I never did get the strobe back but instead was given an additional surprise. On the last evening, not one child showed up to spook. Without ghosts and goblins the house no longer felt haunted.

We only made about $7,000, but acknowledged that it was the first year and the event was bound to have shaky results. Never succumbing to defeat, we pledged to continue the Halloween venture the following season, though we decided to obtain a facility in a better neighborhood. A local shopping mall had a vacant anchor store and was willing to let us use the space for the weeklong occasion. The building had eight wonderful, large display windows that were perfect canvases, ideal for children's imaginative Halloween paintings. Local classrooms submitted designs, and we purchased the paint. The afternoons were warm and pleasant so it was fun to be outside in October with these energized children. The completed windows formed haunting murals, and we were sure that they would help increase attendance.

Inside the building, a maze of walls funneled people through a shadowy experience. At each turn in the tunnel, a special effect surprised visitors with vampires, ghosts, or skeletons.

The day of the opening approached, and I excitedly went to inspect our handiwork. As I drove into the parking lot, I noticed that something appeared to be horribly wrong. Seven of the eight display windows had cracked. The cool October evening reacted with the day's warm black paint to create a science experiment gone bad. Calling the mall's manager to inform him of our fiasco was extremely embarrassing, not an enjoyable experience at all. The windows had to be covered with plywood, and all of our hard work was, so to speak, out the window. We had turned the mall into a blighted zone that really did look haunted. The generous and understanding owner lived with those covered up plywood windows for another year before attracting a new tenant.

Opening night saw long lines of children and parents waiting to get in as early as 6 PM. To our dismay, the first person who came lumbering to the door was the fire chief. He took one tour of the haunted maze and declared it a fire disaster waiting to happen and closed the house down before it opened. I lost my composure, and a waterfall of tears began to stream nonstop from swollen eyes for the next four hours. It was the first and only time since starting the museum that I completely lost my cool and was incapable of continuing to operate in any rational direction. I sobbed the night away with a friend in his automobile outside of the mall. I was not alone, however, and wonderful volunteers saved the day. They called in union electricians, who worked throughout the night to correct wiring mistakes and then sprayed a flame retardant on all of the cardboard and fabric throughout the haunted maze. To great fanfare, the house was approved by the fire chief, and the event got underway the following evening. After these various disasters, Impression 5 dropped the haunted holiday event, deciding it was much too risky a venture. We never collected more than $20,000 which barely compensated for the costs and amount of work required.

OMSI held a different kind of annual event, which brought its own successes and difficulties. Upon my arrival in Portland, I inherited a most elaborate and sophisticated community auction. OMSI was the first museum in the nation to conduct a charity auction, and it was truly spectacular. Three full-time employees and hundreds of volunteers operating in competitive teams solicited donated items year round. There was even a day when local pilot-owners of small airplanes flew auction volunteers to cities throughout the state to collect donations, often being treated to lunch by the donors. OMSI serves the entire state and most communities wanted to contribute to its success.

The event was held over two evenings. It was designed to appeal to a general audience on Friday evening and to high rollers at a black tie Saturday extravaganza, both at the Hilton Hotel. The first night, hundreds of chairs were arranged in rows to seat those who attended for a nominal fee. Food and drinks were made available by the hotel from cash bars located around the ballroom. Those in the main auction room enjoyed a lively show put on by a team of professional auctioneers. Adjacent to the live event were several side rooms arranged with silent bidding tables.

Friday's reasonable entrance fee and cash bar did not mean the items were shabby. One year a distressed, wide-eyed woman burst through the auction hall doors into the hallway, exclaiming, "I just bought a horse. What am I going to do with it? I live in an apartment. I don't even ride." She was quite upset, but since all sales were final, I asked her if she wanted to donate the horse to Hancock, our high desert camp. The woman was relieved and agreed immediately, receiving a tax write-off for her contribution. The next day we loaded the horse on a trailer and the surprised, yet pleased, camp director took him away. The horse was most appreciated at Hancock because there now was a speedy way of going off-road into the hills. Years later when a senior couple got lost during an Elderhostel program our camp manager was able to gallop to the rescue. He also helped local ranchers during cattle roundups thus endearing him and the camp to neighbors who often returned favors.

Saturday's elaborate gala, the social event of the season, required a handsome entrance fee in exchange for the privilege to bid on items even larger than a horse: jewelry, Humvee rentals, fine art, use of a cheetah for a private party, and antique cars, among other luxuries. At the end of the evening, a well-known band kicked off one of the best dance parties in the state. An elaborate breakfast was served in the wee hours of the morning.

I will never forget when my husband Marty and five other men hovered around a bid in hope of being the last person to sign a silent bid sheet that offered a property lot in an undeveloped Arizona border development. I remember the look on Marty's face when he came into the main auction hall to tell me what he had just purchased. The photo of the property that was eventually mailed to us portrayed two car tracks in the desert with a cactus growing on the side of the road. Since that acquisition there have been numerous assessments and taxes to pay as the development slowly improved. It still remains to be seen if the land was an investment or not.

The Portland community loved and looked forward to OMSI's auction, but it did have downsides. Indeed, I stopped the annual event after conducting a detailed financial analysis. From a $10,000 auction purchase, perhaps $2,000 made it to the museum coffers, after event expenses. We ended up still needing money but were unable to request additional donations from benefactors who believed that the total amount was a usable contribution. Staff costs, storage facilities, food for volunteers, and ballroom rental made the event quite expensive to put on.

There was also a significant risk from the fly-around effort to collect gifts statewide. For years we were fortunate that the flights went smoothly, but I feared our luck would eventually run out. Pilots are not permitted to drink before flying, but there were many times when we noticed the smell of alcohol on the breath of our volunteers. The men donating their planes tended to be wealthy donors, and it was not easy to ground them without direct proof. The fly-around chairman often let infractions slide. The pilots also didn't always heed warnings of bad weather. One blistery year I spent an anxious four hours waiting in the airplane hangar until all of the planes returned safely. That gathering was the last time OMSI held a fly-around. I did not want to be the museum's president when a plane went down.

Today's auction is much more in keeping with the educational mission of the institution and does succeed in producing solid program underwriting. Costs for the event are more reasonable since the gala is held at OMSI in a tent rather than at a hotel. Rather than watch a promotional video before the auctioneer hits his gavel, donors are given a chance to explore the exhibitions, marvel at large-format films, and gain a first-hand understanding as to the purpose of their contributions.

Instead of auctioning objects for personal acquisition, museum programs are auctioned off. For instance, the auctioneer might ask people to pay $20,000 to support the chemistry lab; $1,000 to underwrite class visits for a group of underprivileged children; or $200 to send a child to camp. There is opportunity created for both large and small donors to contribute, and by the end of the evening everyone participates. To increase the likelihood of wealthy donors attending, celebrity guests sparkle. Free admission is given to senators, the governor, mayors, movie stars, astronauts or anyone who could make the event more special.

Whenever staff proposed a new fund-raiser, we had to decide if it would improve our credibility and standing in the community. The goal was always to give a "we couldn't possibly miss" event aimed at all of our donor groups. It is hard not to be discouraged the first time a fund-raiser is held because they all tend to lose money. It is not unusual to take two to three years before the event is considered successful. What this meant for OMSI is that when undertaking anything new, we tried to find an underwriter to defray costs. As in everything else in museum work, patience became a virtue. In fact, I think I will make that a lesson.

— — — — — — — — — — — — —

Marilynne's Lesson #18: Patience is a virtue.

— — — — — — — — — — — — —

There are ways to raise money that are win-win rather than based on pure benevolence. Sponsorships are a mainstay of museum fundraising but, as in all monetary transactions, it is necessary to be aware of pitfalls. On the positive side, corporations and individuals donate quite a bit of money to support exhibitions and build museums, exhibit halls, and programs that bear their names. Most of the time donations are benevolent, but that is not always the case. Corporations are usually quite sensitive to the media attention their donations will bring their businesses and want to ensure that their brands are well represented. In seeking sponsorships, it took us a while to learn to set guidelines outlining what we would or would not do. Issues arose as to the size of the company's logo on signage, how much radio or TV coverage the sponsor would receive, and whether to allow corporate products to be placed on display in the lobby. Consideration also was given to the appropriateness of a sponsoring corporation for a particular exhibit.

During our early fundraising days OMSI received a generous donation from a local donor. Not wanting to have a museum full of company names and logos, we put what we believed were appropriately sized signs on exhibit halls in recognition of donations. Unfortunately, this particular major gift giver was most unhappy, expecting his name to be displayed with a great deal more fanfare. Eventually the sign was changed, but not before an important donor felt slighted. It would have been wise to discuss signage in advance.

Sometimes, even if you follow what a donor wants, the result is not favorable. I even slighted myself. My husband and I gave $10,000 to the new museum and decided to have metal tabs put on 10 chairs in the planetarium in recognition of our family. Every time I go into the domed theater, it is dark so I cannot see their names. I have yet to find them, even though I have looked many times. I would have felt better putting our family name on a sidewalk plaque.

There are companies that act diametrically opposite to the educational message of an institution but offer such large donations that it is very difficult to turn down. Examples we had to be wary of was having a fast food restaurant sponsor a nutrition exhibit or a tobacco company's support of a healthy heart and lung display. Staff always has to be on the alert as to the ulterior motive of the donor.

I threw caution to the wind once and accepted a donation against all set policies when an anonymous donor, via an attorney, offered to pay for the installation of a display on fetal growth. Included would be fetuses, suspended in formaldehyde, showing weekly, early stage, and monthly, later stage specimens, illustrating growth through the nine months of pregnancy. Three plasticized late stage fetuses would also be mounted as part of the exhibition. The specimens were acquired from third world countries, adding to our unease.

The question of the donor's motivation was high on our minds. Was the anonymous person altruistically wanting to educate, or was there an antiabortion statement in the background? A few of our staff members were adamant about not accepting the donation. Some found the idea gross and unsettling while others did not want us to deal with possible political implications. Most, however, were quite excited by the sense of wonder that this exhibit would create.

Having seen a similar exhibit as a child in Chicago's Science and Industry Museum, I did not find showing the miracle of birth at all disturbing. In my mind, sharing fetal development with expectant parents could only serve to motivate them to eat and live in a healthy manner. With board approval, we accepted the donation and put together a committee of school sex educators, health professionals, and scientists to consider the best way to exhibit the fetuses and develop accompanying written material. Our educators held a staff training session to deal with expected visitor questions. The fetuses were tactfully installed inside a horseshoe ring of cabinets with one entrance so that any parent who did not want his or her child to enter could easily bypass the display.

On opening night staff were braced for controversy and were surprised, almost disappointed, when there was none. Instead of negative reaction, the exhibit brought overwhelming praise. Over the years, I observed pregnant women visiting monthly to see what was happening within their own bodies. Parents would also bring children in to prepare them for the birth of their siblings and as a way of explaining some of the facts of human development.

In another situation where I sided with a political issue that resulted in a large donation, my uneasy conscience still concerns me. When seeking funds for the new OMSI building, our organizing committee decided that we should approach the state legislature for a $1 million grant. Our lobbyist and I arranged for an appointment with the chair of the appropriations committee. We were greeted warmly but were quickly told that if I would get OMSI's directors to lobby the legislature to pass a video poker bill, and assuming it succeeded, then we would be given the money through the state lottery commission.

I was quite conflicted, but when the proposal was discussed at the next board meeting, most in attendance agreed to speak in favor at a public legislative hearing. There were a few naysayers among the trustees who were not happy that OMSI was being called upon to be promoters of video poker. One man in particular outlined vividly how machine gambling not only promotes addictive behaviors but involves Mafioso types who have a monopoly on selling the machines. My main attention was on dollar signs and getting money needed for our building project, so I disregarded negative concerns and spoke positively at the congressional hearing about how gambling would benefit and support the arts. Our lobbying efforts worked, and we did receive our money, but once video poker passed into law and I watched the behavior at a few sleazy halls, I was horrified. I have since asked myself if what I did was right. I gave up one ethical position by justifying another and have felt ashamed ever since. Friends say that video poker would have passed anyway, with or without OMSI's input, but as a person who generally believes that you should stand up for your convictions, I consider this action a low point in my job as museum president.

A surprising number of donors use their museum contributions for personal benefit. Art museums have to be especially careful of pressure from board members and wealthy donors who offer large monetary contributions in exchange for mounting an exhibition of an artist whose work they have been privately collecting. By holding such an exhibit, the museum gives tacit approval to the specific artist, increasing the value of the donor or board member's collection overnight. In an earlier chapter I discuss the sizable donation of Dr. Cyrus Katzen to American University to build an art center and gallery. His main goal was to have a home for his personal collection which was included as part of a donation. A portion of his art was museum quality while many pieces were not, causing conflict with the university who had to negotiate a way to appease his ego while keeping a $20,000,000 donation.

There are horrendous examples of museum staff who have acquired artifacts illegally. Even with full disclosure of the provenance of an artifact, there are times when it is wise to be leery and take extra time to have trustworthy experts reevaluate. There is a juicy read called *The Medici Conspiracy* by Cecilia Todeschini and Peter Watson that discusses clever rogues and museums involved in suspect acquisitions. The book details how reputable museums wind up purchasing illegal artifacts from what most would consider reputable businesses. Museum and collector purchases can unintentionally help further rogue archeological digs in unapproved locations. The removal of antiquities, theft of paintings, and art forgeries unfortunately are real concerns for those managing museums. There are enough black market con artists to make a collection museum wary of the source of an artifact. Certain large museums have lost a great deal of money because of these deceits. For example, art that is documented as having been stolen by WWII Nazis from a Jewish home may have to be returned to the owner.

There was a time when Native American mummies were featured in museum exhibits. In recent years our society has acknowledged the need to respect the dead, and most mummies have been repatriated to their tribes for reburial under the Native American Grave Protection and Repatriation Act. When I arrived at OMSI in 1985, the museum had a small natural history collection, among which were several Native American mummies. They were eventually removed from public display by the curatorial staff who made arrangements for their return to a local tribe. The repatriation act does not impact Egyptian or South American mummies, which are widely included in displays throughout the world.

Though most tribal mummies are repatriated, there is still controversy about doing so. The return of several finds, including that of Kennewick Man in Oregon and a ten-thou-sand-year-old Spirit Cave Man discovered in Nevada, were held up in court for years. Scientists debated the age and affil-iation of some of these ancient finds, claiming that there is no biological, cultural, or physical evidence to prove that these fossils belonged to local tribes. Sensitivity to this information and how it is presented involves money as well as emotions. Congress designates certain tribes as being First People eligible for financial assistance. DNA analysis affirms that there are other Americans who arrived earlier, but they have not been readily acknowledged, thus making designation controversial.

Sensitivity to the animal kingdom is a strong part of the ethics of museum curators and educators living in the twen-ty-first century. There was a time when it was common to have stuffed animal trophies on display in dioramas. Wealthy people in the nineteenth and early twentieth centuries would go on safari and bring back their kills, which were often pre-served with the aid of arsenic. Today, very few museums add to these exhibits that were installed in an earlier era and do not want to encourage hunting of endangered species by showing mounted specimens. I was once offered a very large exhibit by an avid big game hunter. I turned the display down, preferring to use wildlife photography and films to teach about animals.

Poachers have decimated elephant herds in Africa and India in their lust for ivory. In 1989, an international ban was placed on elephant ivory in an attempt to keep this magnificent species from going extinct. Only ivory acquired before the ban, or ivory taken from mammoth tusks excavated near the Arctic Circle, are allowed to be displayed in museums since that type of ivory does not involve killing live animals. Unfortunately there are too many poachers and prospective buyers who ignore the law and we are seeing mass slaughter continue.

For my own edification I went to Kenya in 2008 on an Earthwatch excursion and as a volunteer accompanied a research scientist on a study of elephants in Tsavo National Park. During our ten day stay our team observed 164 elephants walking, eating and playing with their young. It was a site to behold as these giants freely lumbered along the African savannah in female groups shepherding babies playing friskily by their side while being minded by older sisters. We watched as they showed signs of tenderness (mostly toward the young ones), play, rage (at our bus for surprising one at a bend in the road) and happiness. We were thankful to miss seeing grief, which elephants strongly exhibit when an animal dies.

When the animals took their short 45 minute rests, they would form a circle, facing outwards with the babies in the center. The oldest female, the herd's matriarch, was always on guard for her close knit family. It was her job to notify the rest when it was time to continue their wandering. We learned from our research leader that elephants can communicate over long distances by producing a sub-sonic rumble that travels over the ground faster than through air waves. Their messages are received through their trunks and the sensitive skin on their feet. Teenage males that had been evicted from the pack would often join other young males, following the herd at a safe distance, while older males were seen foraging by themselves. In one alarming incident our vehicle surprised a feeding elephant who turned on us, starting to attack. Our driver backed down the mud path at record speed to get away. Enraged elephants are certainly something to avoid. I came to love these magnificent intelligent animals and now feel very sorry to see them in confined conditions at zoos where they suffer from foot diseases, mistreatment and boredom.

Asking a company to sponsor a display that has illegal contraband not only puts the museum at odds with the law but impacts the sponsor in a negative way. We always had to be aware of ethical practices, stay on top of the law, and act with caution and care. It is easy to make well-meaning mistakes.

EXPANDING SCIENCE CENTERS
FOCUS ON SHEILA GRINELL:
ARIZONA SCIENCE CENTER

Expanding Science Centers—Focus on Sheila Grinell Arizona Science Center

Sheila Grinell is a dynamic attractive woman with a huge winning smile, a wonderful wit, and to top that off, is very intelligent. You can't help but be drawn into her circle of cohorts and get involved with her many projects. When young she understood what it meant to make your own future, and whether it was assisting at the Exploratorium, working in Japan, directing the science center association or developing her own museum she made a difference. She was a clever fundraiser who knew the ropes and insured that her programs met with success.

"How do I get ahold of Sheila Grinell?" I emailed Alan Friedman. "Funny you should ask," he replied. "We are both

Sheila

in Saudi Arabia conducting a workshop and she is 30 feet away." Sheila, in one room instructing the women, and Alan, at some distance with the men, were communicating back and forth through microphone and phones.

Over the previous four years, Sheila and Alan had been helping the Saudi government prepare to open four science centers, one in each quadrant of the country. The goal was to inspire and help the country's citizens appreciate math, science, and new technologies. Always at the center of the fire, from the start of her career to retirement, Sheila was an instrumental part of the movement to expand science centers.

Born in 1945 in a Manhattan taxi cab on the world's last non-nuclear day, her dramatic entrance was the first of many commotions. (Robert Oppenheimer, with Frank at his side, conducted the first nuclear test the following day, July 16.) Never one to be marginalized, she fought for survival throughout her life, using her razor-sharp brain and moxie to better educate society. Brought up in the Bronx by a podiatrist father and a housewife mother, Sheila claimed that she matured despite her parents. Her active mind was not challenged in a household that was sans books, movies, and cultural activities. This young woman was bored. By fourth grade, she was walking quite a distance to the library, and by sixth, the subway system became her umbilical cord to the riches of Manhattan. Sheila made quite a statement when, at the age of eleven, she decided to run away from home. Her newfound desire for independence gave her the courage to travel to Macy's, though she shortly realized that she had no place to go from there but back home. Sheila took life into her own hands, took the bull by the horns, and just went for it (Nike would be proud). She signed her own report cards (all A's) and influenced and helped raise her younger sister, a successful artist. At a very young age, Sheila had learned quite a lesson:

— — — — — — — — — — — — —

Sheila's Lesson #1: Depend on yourself: Don't be
afraid to make a move to get what you need.

— — — — — — — — — — — — —

Passing the test to attend Bronx High School, nicknamed
Science High, was easy for this academically talented student
and, after skipping eighth grade, Sheila had the opportunity
to participate in honors math classes. Dr. Irving Allen Dodes,
her math teacher, made all the difference in her young life
by becoming that one significant individual willing to mentor
an intellectually starved student. He was her magic and her
patron, inspiring not only Sheila but the thirty-two boys and
one other girl who graduated from his class. These were Sput-
nik-influenced years, with science education having become a
national priority. Most teachers in Science High had PhDs and
worked with a math-and-science-rich curriculum, providing
fertile ground for quick minds to flourish.

During Sheila's senior year, Dr. Dodes surprised Sheila
by calling her mother to his office. His message was that her
daughter was bright and he would like to see her attend Radcliffe College. Sheila's response? "What? I don't want to attend
an all-girl's school." When she finally realized that Radcliffe
was the female part of Harvard, and then won a scholarship,
with the support of her mother, Sheila was ready for her college adventure.

An entire universe opened for this young co-ed who
had been ravenous for scholarly challenges, and she quickly
became immersed in the stimulating Cambridge environment.
Since she loved math, her first thought was to become a math-
ematician. But after taking physics classes, her interest waned.
Eventually her love of languages triumphed; she majored in
English and thrived, being elected to Phi Beta Kappa in her
senior year.

Sheila's Lesson #2: It's not about the subject. It's about learning how to learn.

During the four years spent studying at Radcliffe, her sense of self-worth became stronger, and she felt more at ease in her own body. Having an analytical mind, she considered her strengths, weaknesses, and interests in order to come to grips with just who she was.

Being interested in learning led her to accept a Fulbright fellowship in the south of France. What an eye-opening experience this European year was for a girl who grew up in the Bronx. The value of travel to gain new perspectives became imbedded in her spirit.

When the year abroad came to an end, a more advanced degree seemed like the logical choice so Sheila headed for Berkeley during the turbulent confusion of the late '60s and early '70s. There she enrolled in sociology, which, considering the political upheaval and ongoing changes, was a timely subject.

It is easy to imagine the craziness of her campus life. One incident I observed when visiting Berkeley during those years was of a man standing outside the student union shouting that he was going to give away all of his money. He then proceeded to open a shopping bag and started throwing dollar bills high in the air, in turn producing a mad scramble of students grabbing for the floating papers. When his bag was empty, he announced that he would be back the next day to do the same. I watched in awe, afraid of entering the fracas and being knocked down. The political and social atmosphere was very strange, yet electric and full of promise.

Upon earning a master's degree in 1968, Sheila started to search for her first real job. An acquaintance told her about a science museum that was being created and was looking to hire an assistant. That possibility sounded worthy of pursuit, so she applied for an interview with Frank Oppenheimer at the Exploratorium. The two had an immediate connection. He appreciated her diverse background in science, humanities, art, and sociology. On the spot, he invited her back to his house where during their chat she mentioned in conversation that "the thing I liked best about what you showed me today was that you could walk between the screens." Evidently Oppenheimer appreciated her sensibilities; he hired her immediately. She was twenty-four. From the beginning, she was put in charge of developing the explainer (guide) program and quickly became involved with every part of the developing center. She planned exhibitions, started educational programs with local schools, and eventually wrote the first catalog. Sheila was so important to the young science center that as second in command she helped Frank define just what the Exploratorium was. The five years she spent there were tremendously exciting—even though she froze each time she left the trailer that served as an office inside the cavernous Palace of Fine Arts building. The building was so cold that at one point she threatened to quit if Frank didn't get a heating system; taking her seriously, Frank got radiant heaters installed before the next chilly season.

Because of her work for the Exploratorium, she was invited by Richard Gregory to travel to England to work with *The Story of Art* author Ernst Gombrich on a traveling exhibit called *Illusion in Nature and Art*. Upon returning from the UK, Sheila discovered that Frank had hired a man to be his heir apparent. Realizing with a shock that she had been passed over without discussion, it became obvious to her that it was time to move on, though Frank claimed not to understand her decision to do so. Sheila was not the type of person to wait around and feel sorry for herself.

As a curious linguist, and for her own enjoyment, Sheila had been studying Japanese, in part because it was a language based on characters rather than phonetic letters. So when she left the Exploratorium, the energetic young lady traveled to Japan. You might think that this was a gutsy move. In fact it was, but true to form, it was not long before she was offered a job. For three years, she worked for a Japanese publishing house in its English-language subsidiary. On each project, the company paired a native English speaker with a Japanese colleague, giving Sheila the benefit of rapidly improving her language skills as she gained a broad cultural understanding.

Sheila's Lesson #3: You learn about yourself as an America by living abroad.

Though Sheila's time abroad was enjoyable, the United States beckoned, and she returned home. She did a stint with New York News for Kids, but before long she had heard of a position in Washington, DC, at the newly established Association of Science and Technology Centers (ASTC). The impetus for this organization came from the directors of the nation's twelve large science museums under the leadership of Joel Bloom of the Franklin Institute. It was conceived as an organization to serve their needs, which were not being met by the American Association of Museums (AAM). There was a philosophical battle going on in Washington DC, with AAM not accepting interactive science and children's museums as "real museums," primarily because they were not based on having collections, but on having interactive exhibits.

ASTC started in 1972 (the same year I started Impression 5) with Lee Kimche hired as the first acting director. A few years later, Michael Templeton, the man who ran OMSI before my tenure, took over the reins, and in short order he needed someone to coordinate special exhibits. Michael quickly hired the feisty, personable woman who would eventually succeed him in 1987 as director. Once at the helm, Sheila was a no-nonsense change maker. I met her the first time in Iowa at an ASTC conference that catered to only sixty-four attendees. Realizing that ASTC's start-up funding was going to dry up, she started instituting ways for ASTC to become self-sustaining. Sheila decided to change the meeting format, substituting one large annual conference for the two smaller ones that had previously occupied the calendar. A development director was hired, a publications division strengthened, and changes made to the internal operations to insure long-term stability and survival.

It was not long before love enveloped Sheila. For many years, she had a commuter romance with a New Jersey businessman by the name of Tom Johnson. They married in 1980 but never lived together during the time she remained in Washington. Perhaps their separation was one of the reasons for their long life together. "Part of the marriage deal," said Sheila with humor, "was having a baby." Just before son Michael was born, Sheila moved to New Jersey, but never one to rest, she remained active from home, continuing as a consultant, often to ASTC. By the time the New York Hall of Science was looking for a director, Frank Oppenheimer recommended her and called to urge her to apply for the position. The selection was quickly narrowed down to two people, Sheila and Alan Friedman. On the day of the interview, after having consulted with a child psychologist about the pros and cons of accepting a high-pressure job while caring for her infant son, Sheila withdrew her name from the selection process. Alan and Sheila were close friends, so when he became president, Sheila accepted a three-quarters-time position as associate director.

— — — — — — — — — — — —

Sheila's Lesson #4: Your baby is only young once. There will always be another job.

— — — — — — — — — — — —

The two colleagues worked well together developing the New York Hall of Science. At the end of three years, much to Alan's regret, Sheila resigned, believing that the center no longer needed two high-powered people. In addition, working from home as a consultant better fit her sense of family obligation and her interest in new challenges.

Opportunity continuously knocks when talented people become available, and for the next 5 years she was hired by ASTC to run a training program called the Institute for New Science Centers. As a NSF backed grant project, the Institute was at the heart of the science center boom. Once more Sheila found herself in a core position to influence the growth of science literacy. She was a promoter of hands-on learning and encouraged the building of science centers around the globe. But in the back of the mind she wondered. She had consulted and helped others, but could she successfully be the CEO of a museum?

The time had come for a change. Michael was in sixth grade, and Tom had just taken early retirement from IBM. Sheila believed that she had "one more in her," so she decided to put her name into the national searches. It was not long before she received a call from Phoenix about the need for someone to be the founding director of the Arizona Science Center. "Great," Sheila thought, "I will be warm, my husband Tom can play golf, and we will find a good school for Mike." When she was called for an interview, the entire family went to see Phoenix. As a group, they made a good impression. Sheila remembers one interview question: "How do you make all of the parts fit together: entertainment, education, mission, and market?" Her answer was, "Well, that's my job." The board reaction must have been one of relief to know they had found the answer in Sheila. Within a matter of days, she was offered and accepted the job, and the family moved into the sun.

What she inherited had been started many years earlier. The Junior League had initiated the idea for a science center and had set up a demonstration center in a small storefront. The board then spearheaded passage of a City of Phoenix $20 million bond issue for construction of a building, planning to spend an additional $6 million on the interior. Almost immediately, Sheila informed the board that the capital budget was inadequate by at least $10 million. They already had an inkling that they were underfunded, but reality had not set in. When asked what she thought of the staff, Sheila was upfront and responded that a new one was needed. This frank feedback was also accepted by the board.

Sheila decided to help the trustees learn about what would really be required by taking them on a weekend trip to see science centers in Toronto and Pittsburgh. Nine trustees and a friend signed up, on their own nickels, for what would turn out to be an exciting and bonding excursion. When a second trip to California was scheduled to explore giant screen theater technology, it was even easier to get takers. A third trip to Salt Lake City to check out planetarium technology pulled even more people together. At board meetings following these trips, stimulating discussions culminated in solid forward-moving momentum.

Of course money occupied Sheila's mind. Through the State of Arizona, she was able to apply for money for energy education from the Exxon Valdez reparations fund. She did not shrink from contacting her buddies at the Exploratorium and elsewhere, calling in chits and asking for assistance with various planning issues. In the very short time of three-and-one-half years, the building went from concept to completion. You might wonder how that was possible.

Sheila began the capital campaign by seeking high-tech support. She and trustees approached Intel, Motorola, and Honeywell to get the task started. By lucky coincidence, she had interacted with the director of the local Flinn Foundation when he worked at Robert Wood Johnson, and it was the local foundation's fiftieth anniversary. The new center, which Sheila and the trustees named Arizona Science Center, became the recipient of a $1.5 million gift in exchange for naming the IMAX Theater for Irene P. Flinn. In an amazingly short time, $20 million was pledged to match the original $20 million bond issue so construction of the museum, theater, and planetarium could proceed. The Arizona Science Center was completed on time and on budget, and the first nine months were fantastic, with attendance greatly exceeding expectations.

As with most new science centers, attendance decreased in year two. A great many people came once to see the new building but did not return. The center addressed the challenge of boosting attendance by booking blockbusters, a strategy which proved so successful that it led to the need for even more space. An additional $5 million bond was obtained in order to add a traveling exhibition wing, bringing the size of the total facility to approximately 160,000 square feet.

Some people are builders, and others love to manage operations. Sheila gets charged by creating something new. When she tried to increase earned revenue by initiating a for-profit investment business focused on creating traveling exhibitions with a local design/build company, the board got cold feet. Greatly disappointed, Sheila took stock. She understood that in ten years the building would need a facelift and an endowment would have to be developed for long-term stability. She decided that she was not the one to carry on. A more traditional-oriented person was needed than an individualist who developed her own story line. So what next?

— — — — — — — — — — — —

Sheila's Lesson #5: Prepare your organization for change.

— — — — — — — — — — — —

One of the most creative succession stories follows. Over the next two years, with the aid of an executive coach, Sheila mentored Chevy Humphrey, who was serving as development director, to take the top position. Chevy's responsibilities and sphere of influence were continuously increased while Sheila prepared to leave. By the time Sheila was ready to say goodbye—and had talked individually with all forty-five board members—Chevy was unanimously supported and appointed to be the next president. Sheila is pleased that after leaving her job at the helm she remained friends with Chevy. She watched proudly as her successor built an endowment and became president of ASTC, taking part in the international museum arena.

Consulting once more provided a way for Sheila to take her accumulated knowledge and apply it as a spark plug where needed. She wound up helping out as interim CEO for three organizations: the Tech in San Jose, Mobius Science Center in Spokane, and the Center for Teacher Success in Phoenix. (The latter is now absorbed by the Arizona Science Center.) The challenge of an interim CEO is to prepare the way for institutional change. The job is especially important if the organization must transition from a beloved founder or long-time director to someone with new energy and new ideas. Many churches have institutionalized temporary ministerial positions for the purpose of opening up congregants' thinking and willingness to embrace change, and the museum profession has started recognizing the same need. In this spirit, Sheila managed to prepare her three organizations to get ready for the next CEO.

Today, when Sheila attends social events in Phoenix, it is not unusual for her to be stopped by people who say, "I am indebted to you for the first five years of my child's life," or, "Thank you for what you have built; Phoenix is a richer place." She takes pleasure in the many explainers and staff who have been influenced to pursue science center careers.

At the conclusion of our discussion, I asked Sheila if she

thought that people were intrinsically curious. She responded, "Yes, but if you take away burgeoning interests by telling youth to think or act in specific ways, then you bleed the curiosity away." She sees science centers as places to experiment with alternative forms of communication while marshaling curiosity. Sheila remains an inquisitive individual with a vivid imagination who in retirement is reimagining herself as a novelist. The world needs to get ready—her first novel, *Appetite*, is a great read.

Passion, Sexuality, and Community

Much like a song that you cannot get out of your head, there are three life concepts persistently call: passion, sexuality, and community. Together the three form a melody which manages to become part of most of my decisions.

Passion

Passion has many definitions. It can include love and rage, sometimes at once. It can mean fear and hate as found in the writings of Mao Tse-Tung or joy, a feeling that is natural to all people. When I watched the movie *Gandhi*, I observed a man feeling a rage so intense that it moved him to action. Gandhi was willing to die for his cause. His love for his homeland and his compatriots was so powerful, so overwhelming that he was able to justify sacrificing himself. In the process of freeing India, he provided an important model of peaceful resistance. Martin Luther King based his civil rights marches on Gandhi's lead, as did Nelson Mandela. The passion of these men helped win their fights for freedom.

Many evenings were spent with my children discussing the pros and cons of passion. My most fervent hope was that they would be willing to take the risk to live honestly and with commitment. I did not want them to be afraid to experience the rewards and the pain that comes from following opportunity. When they were young, I tried to help them discover things to do that they would find absorbing. It did not make any difference what their interest was as long as it was legal. I wanted them to experience what it felt like to be totally invested in an activity and to be consumed so that it occupied their minds for hours each day. My hope was that when they became adults they would crave the feelings experienced as a child, and transfer their desire for passion to selected careers.

My views were influenced to an extent by my parents. Mother was a Republican and staunch capitalist. She believed nothing was beyond my grasp if I became focused and passionate about my undertaking. Mom convinced me that at the very least it was my responsibility to try wholeheartedly to reach my goals. As a side value I learned how important it was to have family support for my activities. My mother believed it was part of a family's responsibility to their children to provide a consistent and positive foundation. She encouraged me to participate in various ventures and, if I failed, to view it as a learning experience—no problem. I am sure that is why I see failure as a precursor to success. It is also why I am not afraid to try.

Dad was a social democrat who dedicated his life as a physician to serving the poor. He believed it was his responsibility to care for others less fortunate than he. His actions led him to seen as a saint to his patients and an eccentric to his family. We all paid a price for his passion as he worked around the clock to take care of those in need. I remember him getting up at two or three o'clock in the morning, rushing to see a patient in hospital or home. Observing Dad's total dedication to his profession was inspiring to a young mind.

Martin Luther King Jr., the Kennedys, and Nelson Mandela knew the risks of advocating social and economic changes.

As the nation honored these men of conviction, surely their families anguished over whether the risks taken were worthwhile. Janis Joplin, Judy Garland, and Jimi Hendrix were passionate about their music and yet were never satisfied with their accomplishments. With every performance they were compelled to do better, to be more perfect. They were afraid of slipping, of being ordinary. They had passion for their art, but they lived without compassion for themselves. All three committed suicide. There is a delicate balance between dedicating yourself to a cause and maintaining a sense of identity. This is a great challenge in a meaningful life.

My passion is education of others through informal means, and I believe that creative problem-solving skills are important to teach. I enjoy helping people learn how to learn, how to research their own problems, and how to analyze their findings. The tools I prefer to use are drawn from science, math, engineering, and psychology. When studying to be a mental health counselor I became acutely aware of what happens when a person loses a job to outsourcing and becomes unable to deal with the situation. I observed a great many individuals unable to adapt to changing technology and shifting social norms. I watched once-friendly neighborhood streets become drug exchange sites, teens visiting pregnancy clinics in increasing numbers, and dirty, bent figures pushing shopping carts on busy downtown streets. How different life might have been for these people if they were better able to think problems through to find constructive solutions. A good counselor is really a teacher or coach, an instructor in decision making skills. The scientific method (a system of collecting background information, forming a hypothesis, testing that hypothesis, and coming to a conclusion) is used even if it is not the final outcome. Our personal lives are a continuous evolution that comes from repeating the process over and over again.

Work in mental health convinced me that the time to

learn decision-making skills is not after the fact when one's life has fallen apart, but rather before the crisis. Enter the contemporary museum: a new breed of institution dedicated to hands-on methodology as a way of training in how to live in an ever-changing society. But museums are not enough, which is why I started the *Museum Tour Catalog*, to sell educational supplies, toys, and games that encourage families to practice decision-making skills at home. Those who surround a child on a daily basis have the greater influence.

And so the major passion in my life, developing informal approaches to education, evolved to embrace several outlets. Whether in a museum, girls or boys club, at home, through a print toy catalog, or in a church, I promoted experiential access to learning, creative thinking, and holistic living. Passion . . . I certainly embraced it, though it did cause difficulties.

In hindsight I see that I lost a husband with each museum job. At Impression 5, my twenty-year marriage to Ron, my childhood love ended in part because of the turbulent times I was living in and to a great extent because the dedication I gave to the museum was so encompassing that I had little time to consider that my husband may have had a career that absorbed his time and emotions as well. One day we both realized we were in separate orbits. When I accepted the position as president of OMSI, I foolishly fell into the same trap of working around the clock, being completely focused on a difficult and stressful job and finding it hard to give my second husband, Martin, the emotional support he needed in establishing his own career. After eighteen years, we parted ways, though a friendship persists. I believe I finally got the message, for I have been in my present relationship for over twenty years, and Ray and I both pay attention to the other.

It took years to realize that family and friends need ongoing attention. Many of the people I worked with seemed like friends, but when I left a job, they rarely remained in my close circle. When your work life is over, it is your family and friends who are your lasting companions. This means making the time to lend a listening ear. I advise colleagues to take a moment (many moments) to speak of their love and to thank significant others for support. In retirement, I am spending much more time visiting and supporting friends.

SEXUALITY

What does sexuality have to do with life? Femininity is everything. It matters greatly that I am a woman, and as such, have made choices influenced by our male dominated culture of the 1950s. I was raised in a family who believed that boys were important and needed to be well educated in order to support their families. Girls were considered cute and adorable. They were encouraged to learn music and dancing, to participate in cheerleading. It was not necessary to study serious subjects like math and science. My parents wanted me to be a nice, friendly person who would someday become a mother and take care of marvelous children. I did fulfill their wishes with my five children and eight grandkids (who of course are all above average)—but I also did so much else.

When registering for high school classes, I asked my parents about studying physics. The response from Mom was clear: "You don't need to know that—besides, it will be too difficult." Dad responded hesitantly. He said, "Physics isn't necessary," but there was something about the way he answered that made me believe he was hiding the truth. There was a mystique about the subject that I had to discover for myself. I was quite shy then, and being the lone girl in the class was awkward, but I was determined to get good grades. It was a fascinating class that involved lots of experimentation, and I found it easy. Physics gave me a feeling of power because it gave me some understanding of how things worked. I could look at ordinary machines like automobiles, Ferris wheels, and merry-go-rounds and know what made them move. Best of all, the subject introduced me to the notion that there were techniques to be employed in solving problems.

Though I was not encouraged to study science, I was expected to become cultured by taking a variety of lessons in the arts and was encouraged to join school clubs to aid in socialization. After-school lessons were serious business because I was also expected to practice regularly. Every day there was a rotation: from dancing, to piano, to homework, to religious studies, and finally to whatever extracurricular school activity was engaging my time. I even took singing lessons to learn how to "put a song over" since I was a pretty bad vocalist. To this day I remember the words of the song I was made to practice:

> *"My mother made me practice every day. I went fa, la,*
> *la, la, la, la la.*
> *And thought it made the neighbors move away I went fa,*
> *la, la, la, la, la, la."*

It was pretty bad.

These activities were seen as providing the foundation that a future mother and housewife would need. As a by-product of being so busy, I also learned how to focus and manage my time. Without organization, it would have been impossible to accomplish all that was required. And I discovered that the only way to really have fun was to concentrate on what I was doing and enjoy small successes. I remember trying to practice the piano when my younger siblings were crashing and running around the house. When I complained, Mom told me to tune them out and focus on what I was doing.

My main devotion through high school was dance. I planned to be the world's greatest prima donna and beamed proudly when selected to be on the *Ted Mack Amateur Hour.*

That opportunity was an exciting affirmation in my young career. I told everyone I knew to tune in, and my high school announced the time and station to the entire student body. Rehearsal day for the show arrived, and I was next up to perform my dance. The music started, and the first steps came easily, and then I froze, completely forgetting the second half of the dance that I had performed hundreds of times. Humiliated, I was immediately informed that I could not be on the show and risk having a repeat performance on national television. Going to school the following Monday was embarrassing.

Mom, however, brushed the incident off and would not let me stop dancing or performing in recitals. "Hard work," she reiterated, "is what it takes to be good at anything." The TV debacle, she implied, was just a blip on the path to reaching my heart's desire and a small thing that should not get in my way. Through all of this, learning to be okay with failure and distractions, I also gained that deep-down feeling of being okay.

I have not talked much about surviving as a working woman in what was primarily a male environment because I never gave it much thought. At Impression 5, it was a given that I would be the director, and I didn't think about being the only woman in the country managing a science center. There were a few occasions when the chairman of the board believed that he should be in control of the organization even though he knew nothing about running a science center. I gently but firmly educated him that a professional is needed to manage a museum.

Remember the research project previously mentioned about women who learned to relax, change the way they dressed, and put their work in perspective? They were the executives who rose to the top because they developed an understanding of the complexity of responsibilities each person experiences in his or her life. Managing compassionately is sometimes thought of as a feminine trait, but in most contemporary businesses, this attribute is increasingly an expectation for those in leadership positions. It is possible to simultaneously embrace a feminine side yet be a determined and focused businessperson. Passion, feminine qualities, masculine qualities, and the ability to work with others are all needed to operate a successful business, or manage your family.

COMMUNITY

World events can never be ignored. A milestone occurred when I was young turned the entire country looking skyward. Sputnik was launched. This was the first time a spaceship was successfully placed in orbit. I remember my mother saying to me that she always prided herself in keeping up with change, but somehow she could not understand what it meant to be putting objects in space. She felt lost and confused about the future.

Many adults today feel like my mother did in the Sputnik era. Technology continuously introduces changes at such a rapid rate that it is not surprising that coping is difficult. We watch many former jobs disappear, and at the same time sophisticated technological positions stay unfilled because of a lack of technical education. Streetwise once told me that he wished he were born one hundred years ago. He did not like the competition and fast pace of city life, rebelled against using computers, and was fearful of driving on freeways. Thankfully, over the past years he has learned to cope with all of these realities.

This young man's reaction was similar to that of many of his peers who lacked an understanding of basic subjects, current events, and scientific advancements. Yet these are the men and women who will be voting and making decisions that affect society in the future. The high school dropout rate in the United States is 25 percent, which is a concern since democracy depends on an educated populace.

As a museum director, I remained cognizant of our

continually changing society with ever-evolving community issues, and soon realized that the job was filled with push-pull opportunities. I had ideas of what I thought the community needed, but it was not until citizens pushed me to accomplish what I preached that I could succeed. If I had not spearheaded the museum's growth, it would not have happened, but it was the community that did not let me fail. People grabbed on to ideas and would not let them die. In some respects, I was set up to succeed as long as I was just willing to put in the hours, accept the pain and pitfalls, and not think about anything but the end result. Absolutely no one wanted me to fail.

Informal education, teaching about science and new technology and working within my community was the passion I embraced in order to succeed. To do so I had to understand my own motivations, skills and weaknesses. Education may not be everyone's driving force, but if your passion does involve a public institution, it is imperative that others are willing to join in your vision. It is a hard road to travel alone. Community, society and collaboration is the mantra that must be embraced.

RELATIONSHIPS AND PARTNERING
FOCUS ON AL DESENA: CARNEGIE SCIENCE CENTER

A l DeSena and I have a lot in common. We both were grounded in educational psychology and shared ambitions to develop world-class science centers based on the learning philosophies. We constructed our institutions about the same time and shared notes on our development. When Al acquired a WWII submarine for the Carnegie Science Center I was inspired to do the same. Al still inspires me with his musical acumen and work at NSF. He understands the concept of community and knows how to work with various partnering organizations.

If you listen to Dr. Al DeSena, you might come away thinking that life is just a matter of luck, of being in the right place at the right time and of being open to unexpected opportunities. That may be true to some extent, but how you get to that place takes a person who has paid attention to details all of his life. Al is an interesting man, one who has a lot going on in a mind that quietly combines all he has learned with action aimed at influencing society. Not content to just jump into

Al

311

the fray without context, Al is steeped in history and understands that the past creates the building blocks for the future,
just as his past has influenced the person he is today.

Born in 1947 in Queens, New York, he was an only child
surrounded by a large Italian American family bursting with
aunts, uncles, and cousins. His grandparents had made the
move from Naples to Brooklyn in the early twentieth century.
Looking for a better life, much of the extended family made
a move to Queens, which at that time was mostly vacant lots.
Though only achieving a high school education, both of Al's
parents were businesspeople. Dad was in the sugar brokerage
business with an office on Wall Street while Mom worked as
a supervisor in the garment industry until her son was born.
As with all of the people I interviewed, Al's mother cared for
him at home, only returning to work when her child was older.

Though his parents never went to college and could not
help much with his homework, they were attentive to and supportive of all of his interests. Al fanatically watched programs
on television like *Mr. Wizard* and Disney's science series. He
was given telescopes and microscopes, chemistry sets and
science kits that would occupy him for hours. Never setting
off an explosion, he still got in trouble for the occasional bad
odors and smoke coming from the basement. As children of
the Sputnik era, he and his friends would wander outside
with their instruments to watch the Soviet and USA satel-
lites fly by. The entire nation became interested in science;
after all, we could not possibly let the Soviet Union surpass
us with their achievements. Unfortunately, St. Claire's School
did not have science lessons until the eighth grade which was
when Al actually had his first opportunity to be inspired by
a subject he grew to love. High school at Archbishop Molloy
made up for this lack of early focus, and he was thrust into a
strong program complete with labs and summer science programs. Because he'd grown up with a great deal of freedom—a

commonality among children of his generation, who were allowed to devise their own activities with friends and were not constantly booked with extracurricular sports, additional classes, or play dates—by high school Al was taking himself into Manhattan to visit the city's many art museums and to explore science-oriented facilities such as the American Museum of Natural History and Hayden Planetarium.

By the end of high school, Al's career choices included biology, chemistry, physics, engineering, architecture, music, chemical engineering, and patent law. As Al said, "My interest quotient was always high." When he stumbled on a slim booklet explaining what it meant to be a biochemist, the answer revealed itself to him. Never pushed, and always a good student, it was not difficult to be accepted to Fordham University, schooling supported in part by a NY State Regents Scholarship. At Fordham he had the opportunity to work four years as an assistant in the biochemistry research lab where he felt he was doing real science, not just preparing for it. The warmth of Florida State University and an NIH Traineeship beckoned, so he started a PhD in biochemistry, with the goal of being a research scientist.

During the Vietnam era, when the military was calling for more young men to enter the fracas, and Al had to decide what type of service he wanted to give to his country. The confined space of academia felt specialized and limiting to this young man who wanted to discover what life out there was all about. After two years at Florida State he left graduate school to fight on the Homefront by becoming a VISTA volunteer. He was informed that he would be placed in Appalachia. It turned out that Appalachia translated as Pittsburgh in the minds of the coordinators, and Al surprisingly found himself on an airplane to western Pennsylvania. His VISTA placement in a welfare office certainly helped fulfill his goal to better under-stand society. There he had insight into a completely different segment of the population than the one that surrounded him as a youngster. Working with mostly African American colleagues helped Al raise his awareness of the city's cultural and economic issues. His wife, Mary, also assisted underserved populations and would bring youngsters to their house for writing activities, which often included the children telling their life stories. Many of the tales were not easy to read.

Though young, Al was given an opportunity to have the impact he wanted by involvement in community organizing and in the complexities of public housing. As he demonstrated his competency, Al was asked to go to the state's capital in Harrisburg to focus on policy and law related to heath care problems of people who lived in poverty. These were the early days of HMOs, so it was stimulating to observe the beginnings of a new system of organizing health care. Back in Pittsburgh, Al also worked with adults who were trying to get their GEDs. Without literacy in many subjects, so many people were doomed to a life with no future.

In many ways, Al's early experience in assisting underserved people was similar to that of Bob Russell's, who started tutoring programs, or mine, when I worked in community mental health. What we learned about low-income and poorly educated populations affected us throughout our careers, making us more inclusive of staff, board, and museum patrons. We spent much of our lives trying to combat ignorance and educational apathy.

As Al's stint at VISTA came to an end, the young scientist knew that he wanted to stay on the action side of life rather than pursue a completely academic career. Science education combined many of his interests. Though not looking for a job, when he walked in to the University of Pittsburgh's Learning Research and Development Center (LRDC) for an informational interview and told the interviewer that he had developed chromatography kits, Al was hired on the spot to contribute to the development of a K-8 science curriculum. Al sort of just fell into a career path, and it was a good thing, for his young wife found out that they were soon to be parents of twins.

The work was fascinating and led him to enter a doctoral program to do research in education and sociology. The Individualized Science Program was multi-disciplinary and built in part on Piagetian and other theoretical foundations in cognitive psychology. During the 1970s LRDC was a hotbed of activity in this field. The program of study that Al pursued was eclectic and went beyond the ordinary. The University of Pittsburgh had a strong program in the history and philosophy of science and Al loved to hang out with these philosophical types along with those in his own department. Over time he started believing that he now had the breadth of background that he wanted. He eventually obtained his doctorate in Education with minors in higher education and sociology. Al now had a clear path to follow, yes?

No . . . academia was the beginning and not to be the end. When the Buhl Planetarium and Institute of Popular Science needed someone to do an evaluation and help with a planning study for developing a new science center, Al (who just happened to know David Henderson, the executive director of the Buhl Foundation and Board member of the Planetarium) spoke to him and was immediately given the job as a consultant. The work he had been embroiled in the university included developing inquiry-based curriculum very similar to the goals of the new science center. Interactive school materials were easily converted into hands-on exhibits. Al felt comfortable and at home with the challenges he was facing in his work.

Since Al worked well with the board, during this time of transition for the Buhl Planetarium he was asked to stick around and become director of programs. Remaining a full time consultant to help with the change, he was asked to accompany board members and planetarium staff on a grand tour of museums, and found it to be stimulating! Al described himself as being naïve as he accepted new responsibilities but was fortunate to have a board of directors who were savvy. The head of the Buhl, Joshua Whetzel, proposed a name change to the Buhl Science Center, and the city decided that a new science center would be just what was needed to spur an upgraded waterfront.

In 1987, the Buhl merged with the Carnegie Institute of Pittsburgh, to form a most unique grouping of nonprofits. The Institute at the time was also a headquarters for fundraising, which has both advantages and disadvantages since their board presents adds another layer of bureaucracy to go through for approvals. In this case, everyone was behind a move and magnificent sites were offered along the river. All the organization had to do was pick one and morph it into the Carnegie Science Center. The Buhl Planetarium, a prominent part of the new center, kept its former name. When Dr. Whetzel decided to step down from the Buhl, Al was the logical choice to be its director. Why did he say yes? "I guess I was ready." Al replied. "It was not a totally rational decision, but it felt right. I would have an opportunity to pull things [ideas] together."

The Institute made it easier for a person with few fundraising skills to manage a building project. Since Al had little experience acquiring donations, he was fortunate to be able to learn on the job by association with and being supported by the efforts of experts, including fund-raising consulting firms. When I heard him talk about this aspect of his job I must admit that I became a bit jealous. He could help the process out without being required to lead the effort. Leading fund-raising can bog a director down, especially if that director's main interest lies elsewhere, as mine always did.

In 1987 there was a lot of money in the Pittsburgh area. Private and corporate foundations, wealthy individuals, industrialists and generations of people who owed their livelihood to the prosperous city were pleased to step forward. Though the central district was losing population a renaissance begun in the 1950s was underway in Pittsburgh that was changing the area from steel and manufacturing to one that was highly technical. The city was evolving and a very energetic place to be.

— — — — — — — — — — — —

Al's Lesson #1: It is helpful to have a broad perspective and be interested in all things.

— — — — — — — — — — — —

Experiences Al had as a youth combined and eventually influenced the new museum. Even the course Al took in theater at Fordham was applicable to the museum, where storytelling became part of the visitor experience. Science centers often use theatrical techniques and interdisciplinary approaches in their displays and classes. Contemporary hands-on museums like to entice visitors to enter emotional environments that include exploratory opportunities.

— — — — — — — — — — — —

Al's Lesson #2: Everything is connected, but you can't do everything.

— — — — — — — — — — — —

It is easy to get overwhelmed with possibilities once a decision has been made to proceed with a new museum. Decisions have to be made about such routine things as the size of the exhibit halls, the placement of electrical outlets, and lighting. More unique choices such as whether to have stages for demonstrations, to have live performances, what type of signage or video presentations will be used, and just how interactive is an interactive exhibit, require debate and discussion. In the planning stage, good ideas seem to multiply, and visits to other institutions only add to the confusion. It doesn't take much to get caught up into an, "I want to do everything mentality," so a great deal of time has to be spent culling ideas to form a cohesive whole before promoting a unified concept to the public. This becomes a pick and choose phase where the overall philosophy and plan become an essential roadmap.

— — — — — — — — — — — —

Al's Lesson #3: Life itself is a teacher.

— — — — — — — — — — — —

Pay attention to the cues! Younger Al was surprised to discover that he had leadership inclinations, but he did. He organized a jazz combo and street baseball teams. While in college, he became president of the student affiliate of the American Chemical Society Chapter at Fordham. Each of these activities involved organizational skills and putting people together around a common mission. He realized early in life that he enjoyed coordinating activities and was "inclined to do it." As a graduate student, the university classes he took in organizational psychology laid the ground work for his future job running museums.

Al enjoyed opening festivities of the new science center in 1991 and stayed at the helm until the end of 1993. As director, Al lived a seven-day-a-week job, always having to work during the busy summer season and on holidays. His activities affected the entire family. They took vacations to science museums. His children had free run of the Buhl Planetarium facility and were enrolled in Saturday science classes. The entire staff interacted with his children, and the regular exposure with the museum made them comfortable with science. Today, one son is an electrical engineer at Johns Hopkins Applied Physics Labs. Another son has both a PhD in percussion and a master's degree in clinical social work while his daughter is employed as a paralegal. A most successful family!

Al had a grand and no doubt stressful time expanding the science center to include a state-of-the-art OMNIMAX Theater, a digital dome planetarium and acquiring the USS *Requin,* a World War II submarine. He had to deal with frequent frustrations around architectural and staffing issues as well as balancing the emerging philosophy of a science center with the interests of potential donors. Hidden agendas that served as corporate marketing ploys created mine fields to be averted.

He complained about how difficult it was to make attendance projections. Since there were not many hands-on science museums in the country, no one really knew how many people would be willing to pay admission. Without much data it became difficult to develop a sustainable business plan.

There were other problems to face, such as where do you find staff to work in a hands-on museum? At the time there were no schools of higher learning training educators to work in this manner though conference workshops and a few summer programs were offered from time to time. In Pittsburgh there were skeptics who did not see the value in interactive learning, wanting a more traditional approach. Traditional teacher education courses taught their students to run classrooms that were not set up as open ended, multi-generational playgrounds.

Among his other concerns Al was committed to integrating the old Buhl Planetarium staff with the new, and convincing them that a subject such as chemistry had as equal a role to play as astronomy. Coming to his aid was Peter Anderson, a very helpful consultant who had originally worked at the Ontario Science Centre. Al was relieved because, "Peter knew the ropes of participatory learning." Peter's company had a wealth of experience, and assisted in developing the early science center displays. His personal resume brought needed credibility to the project. Best of all, Peter had a great way of working with the staff.

An ASTC conference was held in Pittsburgh in 1996 (two years after Al had moved to Wichita) during Carnegie Science Center's early days, and I saw what a fine facility had been developed for a city in transition. I expected to see steel plants and smog throughout and instead had to search to take a tour of the last remaining factory. The city's air was clean, the sky blue and great restaurants were placed atop a hill that one reached by tram. The museum staff were great hosts and hostesses. The conference was energetic and a lot of fun for those of us who love to play with ideas and materials. We talked non-stop with colleagues, ate great food, danced the evening away and watched a great many of the large format films presented.

— — — — — — — — — — — — —

Al's Lesson #4: No one is perfectly suited to all the needs of a growing and evolving organization.

— — — — — — — — — — — — —

Dynamics change over time. Nothing stays the same. Eventually the board changed, which brought about some conflicts and differences in values, perspectives, and expectations. It became time for a personal change that would let Al use knowledge gained to help another institution grow.

After fourteen years with the Carnegie Science Center, Wichita, Kansas presented an interesting new challenge. Having already raised $20 million of a $40 million construction project, the Wichita board decided to expand their vision. They wanted a world class architect to spearhead their new museum. Moshe Safdie, an Israeli native who had immigrated to Montreal before joining the faculty at Harvard was hired, and with his design, the costs escalated to $62 million due to enhanced architectural design.

Each community presents a different set of challenges. In Kansas the leaders decided to merge a not-for-profit children's museum and a city-operated planetarium with the new science center. The new board wanted to keep the interactive concept of a children's museum but have it evolve as a multi-disciplinary adventure for all ages. The name they coined for the new facility was Exploration Place. As a combination of science center/children's museum, they did not want to identify the facility in a traditional way, but rather have it be known as a "creative learning center." They hoped Exploration Place would bring images to mind that included science, art and the humanities. Unfortunately the name turned out to be somewhat of handicap, making it difficult to brand the center. The media would ask, "What are you?" They kept calling them a children's science center. "Well no," responded Al. "That is not it at all."

Wichita is a city of 350,000 people with a market region of nearly 2 million. It is an industrial hub town that considers itself to be "the air capital of the world," a title given to them by the American airplane manufacturers national trade association in 1929. Wichita residents call their home "Travel Air City." Cessna, Beechcraft, Stearman, and Lear Jet all had their start there in the early 20th century. This strong interest in aviation became a focus for the new museum. A second theme that helped to redefine the new organization in people's minds was the environment. The facility itself overlooked the Arkansas River, and visitors were invited to travel through the river's geological and agricultural history through interactive exhibits were combined with theatrical presentations.

After ten years of managing the development and operation of Exploration Place, Al and his wife were ready to return to the east coast. Al sat near David Ucko on a flight to an ASTC conference one year, and David asked him if he would ever consider working at NSF. Though his response was at first, "I never considered the idea," over the course of the next few days he pondered the move and his curiosity grew. On the return flight, Al was ready to respond positively.

Ten years later Al was in an enviable position to continue making the difference he always wanted to make. He is a grant giver and a program supporter with a great deal of influence in the way science education develops. The people he works with are educated and committed to improving education throughout the United States. NSF continues to work with science centers but has broadened its support beyond museums. Most recently the National Endowment for the Arts, the Humanities and NSF joined together to discuss collaborating on a variety of projects. More recently Al has had opportunities to explore possible collaborations with the national Endowment for the Arts and the Humanities. Once more it is an interesting time for Al who enjoys drawing ideas from many sources. These he stirs in his creative mind in order to produce amazing outcomes. As an accomplished pianist and composer he practices what he preaches by integrating arts with the sciences in his daily activities.

Join me!

Exhibit floor at OMSI

SECTION V

CONTINUING THE EXPERIENCE

AFTER THE VISIT: GIFTS AND EDUCATIONAL TOYS

The museum gift shop is a place that provides continuity and remembrance. Everything from postcards, trinkets, and books to serious educational toys are available for sale. If the museum has done its job, it has made visitors curious. Material that can be used at home is a perfect way to extend the experience. I have always considered the gift shop to be an inspiration store.

The design and philosophy of a sales area is given a great deal of attention when being established, and many museum directors do get involved. The store manager is often the lowest person on the hierarchy but is required to bring in a large amount of money. Unfortunately during annual budget negotiations the manager's requests are often passed over. When I had my catalog company and made gifts to member museums, I often gave money directly to the gift shop manager to be used without the development office able to siphon off the funds for general operations.

Recently more and more institutions are making arrangements with private companies to manage their gift shops with a percentage of sales returned to the museum. The upside is that museum directors have one less thing to worry about in a job that carries a multitude of responsibilities. The contracted company has wholesale buying advantages that come from economies of scale. The downside is that we are witnessing the homogenization of museum stores. They start to look similar everywhere you visit. It is the shopping mall mentality.

My concern is that museum gift shops are losing their individuality and connection to mission. If a museum is unique, and they all are, then the gift shop needs to be a reflection of that uniqueness. I also view nonprofit organizations as training grounds for jobs. By removing top management positions, you eliminate the opportunity to learn how to be a buyer, to set budgets, and to respond to the creative needs of the organization.

In 1995, I left my position at OMSI to develop Informal Education Products (IEP) publisher of the *Museum Tour Catalog*, which sold the types of items found in museum gift shops. I was ready for a new challenge and wondered if I could succeed in a competitive national climate by operating a for-profit company.

The idea for a catalog gained momentum while I was still running OMSI. Over a span of five years, twenty-two museums met to consider forming a cooperative to operate a catalog company. We did so because in our way of thinking, the gift shop was an extension of the exhibit floor, a museum "to go," so to speak, that played an important role in continuing the day's experience. My colleagues and I were interested in providing children with the best quality toys and educational materials needed to carry on investigations at home. We wanted parents to have access to the tools that would enable them to assist their own children learn. And lastly, in a self-serving manner, we wanted to increase our earned revenue.

In 1994, the annual ASTC conference was held in Portland, and I took the opportunity to invite those directors interested in forming a catalog cooperative to a meeting in my office. Several of the museums, including my own, had just completed a study on the feasibility of undertaking such a venture and had come to the conclusion that it was too expensive and risky a venture. Getting started was projected to be a $1.5 million investment, which was beyond the scope of any of our organizations. I listened to all of the reasons why everyone loved the concept, believing that the catalog could turn a profit in three to five years, but no one was willing to sign up. I decided that if it was going to happen I would have to resign my position as president of OMSI and start the new business on my own. Twenty-two museums (Woods Hole is a research center) were willing to give me a small amount of start-up money and to lend their names for credibility. I promised to make a donation to these founding museums each year, which as of this writing has amounted to over half a million dollars. Several of my board members agreed to invest in the catalog company and with additional assistance from vendors, I was able to get started.

80% of educational toys are made in China with varying attention paid to quality. Craftsman products made in European countries are very expensive, carrying a price tag many parents are not willing to pay. Early on, I received a great many letters complaining of child labor practices in China. I decided that I had to see if their concerns applied to my primary factories, so in 1996 I went on a tour of major Chinese toy manufacturers. Showrooms were across the harbor in Kowloon but factories were primarily located on the mainland. It was an exciting time to be in Hong Kong because the following year the British territory was to be returned to China.

The factory trip was a fascinating cultural awakening. What I saw were new warehouses built in guarded, gated compounds. Employees were primarily female between fourteen years of age and their late twenties. In their long pigtails and blue uniforms they assembled in rows to work assembly-line style. In 1996, school in China was compulsory until the age of fourteen, so working in a factory after graduation was quite an honor for rural families, for it provided needed income for the entire household. Most of the money earned by the girls was sent home to their parents. After working several years they were able to keep an amount for their dowries. I shared a meal with managers, noticing that the food we ate was nutritious and tasty. Fresh fish was drawn daily from a one hundred foot long pond on-site. I was bothered by their bedroom conditions. During the busy season the girls lived ten to a room, sleeping on thin mattresses. There was little storage space and they had to duck under wet clothes that were hanging everywhere. The young ladies worked six days a week and were only allowed to leave the compound on Sunday to go shopping in the local outdoor market. Thousands of people wanted these coveted jobs.

Each January, through 2013, I returned to China, taking note of the transformation occurring across the vast swaths of land we crossed on our ride to the factory. For a great many years, the countryside looked like a war zone. As soon as villages were vacated and walls bulldozed, box-like apartment buildings started to rise. It reminded me of how the boardwalk in Atlantic City looked when wrecking balls lined the ocean front, demolishing hotels to make way for the new casinos. Massive Chinese revitalization replaced the outdoor latrines and wells that had been there for generations with water, electricity, and indoor plumbing. These new towns are certainly not picturesque, but the sanitation is much better. Unfortunately, pollution in the new factory towns is unbearable.

On the last visit to my primary factory, I observed that operations had expanded tenfold. A golf cart was needed to get around to the many new buildings erected on the site. Gone were the pigtailed, uniformed fourteen-year-old girls; in their place were young men and women in Western attire. With more stringent education requirements, workers do not get hired until the age of eighteen. Long assembly lines have been substituted with team-building areas. Expensive and sophisticated die casting and cutting machines were imported from Japan and Germany, requiring employees with advanced skills.

China's rapid growth has produced difficulties for manufacturers located near the South China Sea, where the industrial boom started. With increased prosperity throughout the country, many small towns now have industry located nearby. It is increasingly difficult to find young people willing to travel great distances to work. In response, salaries have escalated affecting the cost of products.

There are other issues that also confront Chinese factory owners. Over the past two decades the government has subsidized electricity. That support has eroded and electric power is no longer available every day. Politicians in this centralized government have shifted their priorities away from toy manufacturing and towards solar energy and pharmaceuticals. The recession of 2008 put an added burden on toy manufactures, and many started diversifying their product line. The company I originally visited now produces most of the biological models used in hospitals and medical schools.

It will be interesting to see if toys will ever be manufactured in the United States again. Some companies are trying to bring manufacturing home, but expenses are still so high that volume production remains less expensive in Asia.

Home as Museum

You can easily substitute home for museum and live in an environment made inspiring. Instead of exhibits, consider decorations, furniture and personal treasures. Architecture, use of space, selection and arrangement of furnishings, collections, and the way they are displayed all define you. How you move about your home, share treasures with friends and family, and teach your children to understand their cultural heritage becomes your way of passing on values.

Ray, my life partner, is a maker of totem poles and Northwest Coast masks. Outside of our home, there is a seventeen foot pole that has become a neighborhood marker. "Go to the totem pole and turn left," is an oft heard direction given by acquaintances. The lower level of our house has both indoor and outdoor shop areas where carving and painting are pursued much to the enjoyment of nosey friends and those hiking an adjacent trail. Strangers who hear the tap, tap, tap of a hammer stop by wanting to know what is going on, and Ray gladly shows them his carvings, entertaining them with stories of Raven and Beaver. Our home is filled with his carvings, my collections of pottery and masks, canvases that I paint, and art purchased while traveling. Our furnishings are arranged in a restful way, though presented as eye candy for our visitors. I enjoy living surrounded by the items Ray and I have either made or collected. Sharing them with friends lets them into our souls and initiates many conversations about culture, art, and even politics. Our friends often say when entering our home that it looks like a museum, only warmer and more welcoming.

Many children are first introduced to a cultural institution by visiting a children's museum. These institutions are unique because the ingenuity they apply to educating the young is more than just exciting—it is engaging. Children spend hours engaged in activities such as playing in water (learning physics and hydrodynamics without realizing it), dressing up in period costumes (a study in history), constructing and plumbing buildings (engineering), and a host of other activities that involve physical as well as mental effort. Young visitors often are seen crying as their parents pull them from the building to go home. A secret to their success is that they are centered on the child and organize their spaces in a way that permits freedom of movement. Displays are built to withstand hard use. They encourage learning by using a variety of cleverly hidden techniques.

I encourage parents to think like a professional and start their own museum at home. What better place to inspire your own child than the relaxed environment of a play area or living room? According to The American Association of Children's Museums, "A children's museum is defined as an institution committed to serving the needs and interests of children by providing exhibits and programs that stimulate curiosity and motivate learning." They encourage parents to interact with their children while in the museum in order to make the experience more meaningful.

That definition fit my family to a "T." When we moved to Lexington, Massachusetts, a community without a hands-on museum, I decided that I could make my own home into one. The Boston Children's Museum was much too far to travel to on a regular basis. Part of the challenge of my home operation was one of organization. I decided to set up my children's basement playroom with a Montessori approach.

Maria Montessori was a 19th century physician turned educator who became involved in designing Casa dei Bambini, a school for low-income children. As she experimented with curriculum and classroom design "she began to see independence as the aim of education and the role of the teacher as an observer and director of children's innate psychological development." She believed that young children were sensitive to order, enjoyed doing activities repetitively and were happiest doing practical things. She developed an environment that was kid-size so that materials could be easily reached and put away when completed. Over time, very sophisticated materials were designed for Montessori schools with teachers specially trained in her methodology. These materials are quite expensive since they have to withstand use by hundreds of children.

I discovered that toy manufacturers have duplicated most Montessori materials and make them available at more reasonable prices.

I did not have the training or money to set up a Montessori school, but I did have the ability to develop a child-sized, child-centered environment. I started by organizing locations in our play area for various activities and I spent time showing my kids how to properly use their toys. Once they succeeded in mastering the toy's challenge they were encouraged to be creative with their materials before returning them to their original storage locations. There were construction areas, a place with math manipulatives, a book nook, one for puppetry, a puzzle area, dress-up stations and a craft center. I also added a carpentry area filled with safe tools. In my living room we installed a music pole with clips to hold percussion instruments.

Successful use of a home playroom includes training children to put items away. This task is accomplished effortlessly if training begins when your child is quite young and if you are consistent. Keeping the environment clear for the next project not only made my job as parent manageable but it ensured that the child's space was more accessible for daily projects. Part of the secret of a successful "home museum" is to introduce toys (activities) one at a time. After first demonstrating how the product is to be used, I observed my child in action. Cleaning up was an expected part of the cycle. The goal was for my young ones to master the activity, gain satisfaction from success, and become motivated for the next challenge.

This home/museum environment takes careful planning, but once it is operational, the task becomes uncomplicated, because the system is in place for your child to select his or her own activity, concentrate on the task at hand and move progressively from one skill level to the next. Toys are not jumbled one on top of another and hard to reach. Again, independence is the goal.

A child of about two and a half years old is ready for a home museum. In the beginning, it is best not to have too many toys available, making sure to have them easily accessible. If there are several children using the space, then each child needs to understand which items he or she has earned the right to use. This system works for older children as well as preschoolers, with older children shown how to use the materials more creatively. Older siblings can also be encouraged to help their younger brothers and sisters.

A while ago I read about a pioneer family that homesteaded in Colorado in the 1800s. The book featured the life of a ten-year-old who assisted his father in putting up their prairie home, barn, fences, and sheds and even to dig a well. There was no need or time to play with blocks or spend an afternoon using clever toys when real things needed to be built and serviced. Construction and household skills were passed down from parent to child and experimentation was rewarded by improved designs they both worked on.

My partner grew up in a second-generation pioneer family, living adjacent to a gravel pit. His father owned the operation, and from a young age, Ray was crushing rock, fixing machines, and even driving tractors. Today, Ray can repair most small engines and is a very useful man to have around the house.

Children raised in cities rarely have opportunities that come from living life on a farm or in the middle of a gravel pit. Public schools could contribute greatly by providing a basic understanding of construction techniques, electricity, plumbing, small engine repair, and automotive care. A bit of physics thrown into the mix will give children a rudimentary knowledge that may help avoid costly mistakes. Boys and girls engaged in these subjects are using kinesthetic or tactile skills and by doing so are exposed to an alternative way of learning. There are advantages of participating in a hands-on education for it has been shown to enhance creativity, curiosity, and language.

Learning history from a book may not capture a child's imagination. It is a difficult subject to teach because children are more involved in the here and now and do not have a sense of distant time. Doing or making rather than reading is more likely to garner success. I observed a teacher introduce the industrial revolution to his class by having students develop an assembly line simulation that started with a model steam engine. Each child along the line had to add one gizmo to the end product.

Roman architecture and philosophy came alive for me when I visited Italy and saw beautiful pottery and mosaic tiles. Children in the classroom or home who are taught to make tiles and paint vases have a chance of becoming equally intrigued. Study of medieval cathedrals built to reach the sky and early bridges designed to span wide rivers can be introduced with construction toys rather than history books. Once engaged in hands-on activities, reading for information often follows.

Families who live in confined spaces like an apartment or small home can acquire smaller construction kits or arrange for outdoor park activities. Play areas at home can still have building toys, machines to take apart and tools that encourage imagination but they may need to be rotated in and out of storage.

One way to reinforce construction play is by encouraging children to observe workmen who build or fix appliances. My kids and grandchildren always loved being taken on construction site visits, and I still find it fascinating to observe large cranes hauling supplies sixty stories in the air. As my children got older, they were enrolled in physics and chemistry classes to complement their humanities selections. Though I am not a physicist, my high school course was eye opening because in addition to giving me a basic understanding of mechanical advantage and machines, it made me curious, and curiosity created a lifelong love of learning.

After interviewing Jeff Gottfried, OMSI's former education

director, and Barry Eichinger, past exhibit director at Charlotte's Discover Place, I realized why these men managed to raise their own creative children. The clue came from Barry who said that when walking in the woods, he would encourage his children to explore, wander, and wonder. On family excursions, both Jeff and Barry would talk animatedly to their children about what they were doing and seeing. They would bring home rocks, buckets of bugs, and samples of stream water to view under microscopes. The local flora and fauna would stimulate hours of discussion. Their excursions were informal, intuitive, and without structure. These men incorporated inquiry-based education in their families' lives. Parents, grandparents, aunts, and uncles who turn their homes and outings into exploratory experiences contribute a great deal to educating the next generation of thinkers.

Thirty years later when I decided to start my own company, I organized my catalog just like our home playroom, making it possible for buyers to purchase a range of materials to educate mind, body and perceptions. My goal was to make it effortless for parents to set up a mini-museum for their children. There are many wonderful products on the market today that are downsized versions of exhibits found on the floors of science centers and children's museums. These educational toys provide comfort for those parents who choose to develop a museum at home.

PROGRAMMING IN ACTION
FOCUS ON DAVID HEIL: PBS HOST *NEWTON'S APPLE*

I worked side by side with David Heil and watched him grow as an educator, television personality, and consultant to museums throughout the world. This dynamic, self-made man has a burning passion for learning and is a strong proponent of parent involvement in the educational process. David is a whirl-wind always on the go. His energy is contagious, and his mind is always devising clever ways to help people implement their goals. As an informal educator, David concerns himself with the entirety of the education process that includes classes, museum exhibitions, and informal learning experiences.

"Oh, shit!" The words popped out of David Heil's mouth as he leaped—his first parachute jump. For obvious reasons, PBS could not air that first take, and unfortunately for David,

David

he had to repeat the jump several times. As host for ten years of the nationally televised *Newton's Apple,* David found himself in all manner of peculiar situations, trying to explain the science behind the adventure. His excursions took him all over the world, from Antarctica to the Arctic Circle, high in the Andes Mountains and in low-lying deserts. He was Mr. Reality TV before the phrase was coined. At first the station wanted stunt

338

doubles to conduct some of the more dangerous capers, but David said no. He wanted his audience to experience the exploit along with him and feel his emotions as he explained the science behind each experience. The only time he did use a double was in a piece on skateboarding because, despite practicing with world-class skateboarders, he could not quite master the high-flying 180-degree twist of an Alley Oop. In 1989, *Newton's Apple* won a Daytime Emmy for an outstanding children's series. The show the judges viewed included that very first segment with David as host, jumping out of an airplane to explain the physics of skydiving.

David's TV career started when he was employed by the Oregon Museum of Science and Industry (OMSI) as head of education programs that included enrichment classes, programs for schools, teacher education, and overnight camps and adventures. One morning early in David's OMSI career, a panicked producer from the local ABC affiliate, KATU Channel 2, called to see if OMSI could provide someone to fill in for a four o'clock talk show spot that had just had a cancellation. David immediately said sure and gathered up materials for making a gooey substance with unique qualities known as Ooblek. If you punch the substance with your fist, it feels like a solid, but if you push your fingers in slowly, it behaves like a liquid. The term for this property is thixotropy, which is fun to say, let alone put into practice. Oobleck's unusual name comes from a Dr. Seuss book called *Bartholomew and the Oobleck*, a favorite from David's childhood. With his enthusiastic manner, David managed to intrigue the television audience, and by the time he had returned to his office, OMSI's phones were ringing with people asking for the recipe. KATU quickly asked him to become a regular on the show and continue to bring science experiments into the homes of its audience.

Less than a year later, Ira Flatow, decided to end his *Newton's Apple* hosting duties, and KTCA, the Minnesota PBS affiliate that had created *Newton's Apple* began contacting stations across the country in search of a potential successor. Without informing David, KATU forwarded several tapes that vividly featured him as a television science demonstrator. The executive producer for *Newton's Apple* was intrigued and immediately called David, inviting him to Minnesota for an audition. Having only recently been introduced to studio TV production, David had never used a teleprompter or choreographed his demonstrations with a three-camera crew.

The daylong audition included a range of "think on your feet" scenarios and requests for scientific explanations in everyday terms. He remembers one request where he was given a large bowl of water as a prop, and asked to talk for five minutes about why skin wrinkles in the bathtub. Without hesitation, he plunged his hand in the water and began explaining the various properties of water, skin cells, and osmosis. When his long explanation ended he raised his hand with hope that it would indeed be wrinkled. He got the job and for the next decade the show attracted large audiences.

While working with PBS, David continued to develop new programs at OMSI, serving as the associate director until 1996. He was employed during my tenure, and I got to know his ambitions well, but I did have to protect him from occasional disgruntled staff who found him to be less collaborative and willing to listen to their ideas than they were used to in a leader. Though all celebrated his television success, I always suspected a degree of jealousy. David needed extra leeway because of his travel schedule, and some staff assumed that all of the attention he was getting was making him prideful. I did not agree with their assessment and just thought of David as a smart go-getter and an asset to OMSI because we had on staff a television celebrity with a weekly audience of 1.5 million, larger than any other museum outreach program at the time.

What made David the forward thinker and risk taker

that he was? He claims that it was another favorite childhood book that opened his eyes to possibilities. Dr. Seuss's book *On Beyond Zebra.* Yes, as the book professes, we can all learn the alphabet from A to Z but why stop there? Why not invent new letters and fantastic creatures that are born from imagination? This insight, that we are not trapped by what already is but have the ability to think beyond boundaries, is what makes David so effective. It brings us to his first lesson.

— — — — — — — — — — — —

David's Lesson #1: Learn the basics so that you can compose something new and unique: think cognitive jazz.

— — — — — — — — — — — —

David Heil was born in The Dalles, Oregon, a town that at the time of his birth boasted a population of fifteen hundred. He was the middle child with an older and younger sister to keep him grounded. His mother, Eunice, felt at home in their small community, having come from rural British Columbia to study at Willamette University. His father, Bob Heil, was enrolled in Willamette University's law school, having selected the school "in order to get as far away from St. Louis as he could." The two students met, fell in love, and decided to reside in the bucolic foothills of the Coast Range where Bob started a title insurance company and served as city judge.

Eunice introduced her children to the wonders of the outdoors and the enjoyment of gardening and camping. Their home was adjacent to a large city park that, at that time, had acres of undeveloped land, providing the children with a backyard playground to build forts, explore streams, meadows of wildflowers, and climb tall trees. When David was in elementary school, the park manager would often come by and request that he and his older sister help with trimming bushes and clearing trails in the park. Judge Heil introduced more urban elements to the children's lives, taking them on trips to Portland when funds allowed, introducing them to fancy restaurants and first-class hotels. He introduced David to the world of business and civic duty, which helped him feel at home with both city and small town life.

During his junior year in high school, David took an opportunity that greatly affected his future. His chemistry teacher made him aware of a select summer education experience. The National Science Foundation (NSF) was funding universities across the country to bring curious youngsters on campuses to participate in science and math enrichment programs. David was accepted to a program at the University of Utah and for six weeks was immersed in mathematics and the philosophy of math. He discovered that he had a passion for the topic.

When it was time to go to college, though, David was not sure what he wanted to do. At the time, he held a wonderful summer job as a counselor and camp caretaker on the edge of the Mt. Jefferson Wilderness and considered wintering over. While solitary living and the encroaching winter weather did not deter his plan, long conversations with Henry Kaiser, the father of a fellow counselor, did persuade David to come off the mountain and enroll at Oregon College of Education in Monmouth, Oregon, where Henry was an adjunct professor in the Natural Sciences.

This industrious seventeen-year-old, determined to demonstrate his ability to be independent and self-reliant, applied for federal grants and worked several jobs to sustain himself through college. Some of the jobs were quite challenging and directly in line with his interests, such as the four years he spent working as a biological aide at a nearby national wildlife refuge. In the research arena, he first worked with a professor of plant biochemistry and later held an assistantship in radiochemistry that provided him with an office and lab space of his own. When he graduated, David earned multiple bachelor's degrees, one in natural science with a major in biology and a minor in chemistry and the second in secondary education with an emphasis in biology, advanced mathematics, chemistry, and physics. He received teaching certificates in all of these subjects and took a job as a high school science teacher in a small district outside of Salem, Oregon. It appeared to be a perfect profession for a man who loved to innovate, experiment, study nature, and share his passion for learning.

The reality of political maneuverings and bureaucratic barriers appeared during his first year on the job. Our enthusiastic science teacher recognized that there were students who were not being challenged by the standard curriculum, and he asked the superintendent for permission to start a talented and gifted program. The school board agreed. To jumpstart the program, David secured a grant from the Oregon Department of Education, and for the next three years, the program saw rapid growth and recognition, eventually leading to the placement of over a dozen students in NSF summer programs similar to the one David himself had attended as a high school student. As part of his science teacher duties, he developed another class called Natural History of the Pacific Northwest, which included weekend trips to three different habitats across the state to study nature through immersive experiences like trapping small mammals, hunting for reptiles and amphibians along stream beds, and collecting and preserving native plant specimens. When student enrollment requests climbed to fill three sections of the class in the upcoming spring term, the principal shut it down. Money concerns were cited at the time, but internal jealousy over David seemingly bucking the system seemed to be the real issue at hand. David the educator was devastated and decided to submit his resignation, committing to finishing out the school year, but in search of his next challenge. Bad news for his high school students but good news for his next employer.

Dr. Mary McConnell was director of education at OMSI at the time and served on the board of directors for the Oregon Science Teachers Association, an organization of which David had recently been elected president. When she learned that he was available, Mary lobbied hard to have David join her at OMSI, eventually including the ultimate enticement by telling him that he could write his own job description. "Just come," she implored. He took the job of managing the museum's education programs with the caveat that he could be entrepreneurial in his approach. David wanted the museum to emphasize the Oregon in its name and was determined to have the education offerings develop in a business-like manner that would be self-sustaining.

Within his first year on the job, his trusting mentor discovered that she was dying of cancer. Over the next two years, David found himself carrying her load as well as his own and becoming exhausted. It was about this time that I arrived on the scene and, realizing the scope of possibilities, split the department in two. One focused on in-house education classes and programs and the other addressing outreach opportunities, including camps and outdoor adventures. David became the outreach leader, which eventually led to one of the nation's largest museum outreach programs, serving a seven-state region and thousands of individuals annually. During this time, he began hosting *Newton's Apple.*

David's Lesson #2: The world itself is the best teacher.

Learn from your surroundings. See how your community works. Be observant and pick up on nuances, like how to combine existing resources with new innovations to meet public interests and needs. No matter what he does or where he goes, David pays attention to details and learns from the experience.

Over a ten-year period, David and I worked well together, building an institution to serve the greater Northwest. I left OMSI in 1995 to start the *Museum Tour Catalog,* and one year later David also decided it was time to move on, and he started an independent consulting company, David Heil and Associates. His first contract resulted from talks with the National Audubon Society about raising the quality of their education programs. Though the organization wanted to hire him as executive director of Audubon Centers, he explained that he had just started his own company and would prefer to work as a consultant. They agreed to the arrangement, and David went on to develop a master plan for multiple centers across the country characterized by four key elements: accessible natural habitats, innovative curriculum resources for teaching and learning, exciting public experiences and education programs, and sustainable operating plans that included both staff and volunteers. Within two years, David's plans were being implemented nationwide, and his reputation grew. He was subsequently hired by a group representing small border towns on the Rio Grande between Mexico and Texas. The economically challenged communities were looking for an attraction that would boost regional employment and local revenues. After extensive research, it was determined that birding showed the greatest promise. These communities are located in one of the richest flyways of the world, birds flying south toward Mexico and those going north toward Canada all stopping within and near these border towns. Under a comprehensive business plan developed by David and two other consultants that he recruited for the task, the World Birding Center was born, composed of nine experientially linked sites envisioned like pearls on a string along the Lower Rio Grande River. Today, the year-round attraction brings thousands of birders from across the globe to view more than five hundred bird species in strategically restored habitats of palm-fringed resacas, rare thorn forests, riverside woodlands, and gulf water shorelines. The development is a wonderful example of both successful

345

ecotourism and David's inclinations toward coalescing science, human curiosity, and entrepreneurism.

David's company has grown in size to include between eight and twelve consultants, depending on the project load. They have worked with such notable museums as the Great Lakes Science Center, Pacific Science Center, Cranbrook Institute of Science, California Science Center, and Bishop Museum; leading scientific corporations like Merck, Bayer, Bristol-Myers Squibb, and Intel; as well as prestigious federal agencies such as the National Science Foundation, National Aeronautics and Space Administration, National Academy of Sciences, National Academy of Engineering, and National Oceanic and Atmospheric Administration. Today, the company focuses primarily on nonprofit business planning, research and evaluation, and innovative program, exhibit, and new enterprise development.

What David often discovers when called in to fix a dire situation reinforced what I heard from many of the museum directors I interviewed. Consultants and architects consistently over-project attendance for new and expanding museums, and when this single source of revenue for sustenance and projections aren't met, institutions get into trouble. David helps organizations think outside of the box by first researching their local and regional markets to determine what their prospective audiences want and need and then suggesting a variety of programs, products, and services to diversify their income from sources other than just donations and admissions. Science centers and museums need to encompass this type of thinking. Long-range business plans with a diversified model for attracting both philanthropic investments and earned revenue is the only way to ensure sustainability.

— — — — — — — — — — — —

David's Lesson #3: Observations need to be both macroscopic and microscopic in scale.

— — — — — — — — — — — —

In order to fully analyze a situation and understand the world we live in, it is necessary to constantly observe lots of small details very closely and then pull back in order to see those details in the context of the larger ecosystem. The process repeats again and again as the "pull in, close up, and push out for context" cycle continues throughout life. David applies this natural process as he analyzes science programs, nonprofit business models, and educational institutions. He considers one of his greatest challenges to be that of managing creativity and the flow of creative energy. Consistently looking for these attributes in others, he finds ways of helping innovative thinking to blossom.

I asked David what he thought of the state of hands-on science education today, and he responded that he believes that it is challenged. In the post-Sputnik days of the '60s, '70s, and into the '80s there was huge attention given to science education. The United States put a man on the moon, and NASA was in its heyday. The need for scientists was great, and teacher education programs as well as science centers were developed as places to discover, tinker, and experiment. The '90s brought in high-stakes testing, and in the decade that followed, the Common Core Curriculum. The original goals of these reform efforts were well intentioned—better accountability with all students having equal opportunities. Unfortunately, emphasis on testing has become a huge damper on learning. A test is meaningless if there has not been meaningful, authentic learning first. What developed was a system where learning is of secondary importance to the test, with only two subjects being stressed—reading and math. As a result schools have decreased the time allowed for science and the arts, stunting students' desires and natural inclination to explore, ask questions, create, and solve problems. Funding for hands-on materials for science as well as the equipment and facilities to support hands-on learning has declined. Schools stopped taking field trips to local museums and nature centers, and an entire generation of children has been growing up with minimal experimental science and problem solving experiences.

David is hopeful, though, and is seeing the pendulum swing once more. Persistent demands from the private sector for stronger workforce skills in science, technology, engineering, and mathematics (STEM) are finally resulting in increased public and private investments in STEM education. The Next Generation Science Standards, released in 2013, include standards for K-12 engineering education, which will eventually lead to an integration of scientific inquiry with problem solving and a return to more hands-on, experiential learning. There is a movement called STEAM that adds the arts as a way to motivate children to be interested in STEM subjects. Music and art have many connections to electronics, computers and mathematics.

— — — — — — — — — — — — —

David's Lesson #4: Inevitably people want to fix a problem when and where they see it.

— — — — — — — — — — — — —

"By the time a disease shows itself, it is often too late to treat," insisted David. We need to be more proactive and apply a wellness approach to education. If we want to change the way we teach and learn, we need to begin the intervention before the problems appear. "You need to start at a young age." He addressed this issue in an early program he developed at OMSI, *How to Grow Science in Kids.* Start when the children are very young because they are natural scientists and explorers. Keep the channels open by nurturing and cultivating the children's naturally scientific minds with a behavior of inquiry. Harness the energy of youth by tinkering, trying, succeeding, and failing. David loves to watch parents and children doing science together and has been a big proponent of family science and family engineering, writing books to address these subjects.

"Nerds are in," said David. Burning Man, which combines art and technology, attracts seventy thousand people to its annual gathering and stimulates year-round workshops where groups of friends gather to create "techie" sculptures for the event. The Maker movement, with its emphasis on crafts and technology, is growing in response to the deprivation felt by many who have limited chances for creative play.

Increasingly, people David works with are turning their emails and mobile phones off for part of the weekend, as he has for years. He observes that those in their twenties and thirties are starting to realize there are other things in life besides their cell phones and computers that seem to demand 24/7 attentiveness. These ambitious young millennials are now developing an alternative culture that is more grounded in the physical and natural world. It will be interesting to see if some of David's ideas and ways become realized and more widely spread. I do hope they will.

A Hong Kong Gerbil

SECTION VI
SUMMARY AND CONCLUSION

Summary

Over the course of this book, I explained how the environment of the '60s and '70s impacted the growth of science centers. Leaders who ignited various social movements inspired a belief that each person is in charge of his or her own destiny. There was a strong assumption that a scientifically literate populace could solve the world's problems. Brains were taken to the limit by challenging imbedded ideas and creating new educational paradigms.

During these "can-do" times, decisions were thrust on us about whether to burn draft cards, ride freedom buses, or live environmentally clean lives. The Cold War stimulated competition in space exploration, and our country cheered as a man landed on the moon. Space exploration in turn created new technologies such as freeze-dried food, now in common use. Scientists such as Robert and Frank Oppenheimer, Albert Einstein and George Tressel turned away from military uses of the atom toward exploring nuclear power for clean energy. Rachael Carson, with her publication of *Silent Spring*, awakened the country to the hazards of DDT and Lady Bird Johnson tried to clean up America. Soft-shelled chicken eggs, rivers on fire, and thousands of dead fish floating in streams polluted by industrial waste and raw sewage became the focus of national outcry leading, in 1970, to the birth of the Environmental

Protection Agency. Feminist writers such as Betty Friedan, Tony Morrison, and Erika Jong challenged women to become more independent. Researchers Master and Johnson gave us a better understanding of our own bodies, and advances in birth control provided freedom from unwanted pregnancies. In addition to highlighting African Americans, the civil rights movement brought attention on all who lived in poverty. The agitation of freedom fighters also set fire to the passions of women tired of living with unequal rights under the law. Gone were gray-suited men to be replaced by long-haired and paisley-skirted hippies dedicated to living and working communally, trusting that anything they set their minds on could be accomplished.

My friends and I spoke of a caring community, love, and individual expression. Vietnam energized those of us on the home front to attend rallies focused on peace. Armies of activists joined in civil disobedience marches to Washington the likes of which have not been duplicated since. Their cries were heard in the rock musical *Hair* and in the songs of Joan Baez, Pete Seeger, and Bob Dylan. To avoid the draft, many already-educated men stayed in college, studying for advanced degrees in critical scientific fields. Others accepted jobs working in rural, poverty-stricken communities as Vista or Peace Corps volunteers.

In response to growing public concern, science centers burst forth on the scene, becoming sites for disseminating information and educating visitors. Tuned into issues of the day, they developed exhibitions centered on controversial subjects such as human reproduction, global warming, and the environment. For a great many, these museums provided an introduction to a scientific world about which they were ill informed. They took up the call by embracing Earth Day and becoming leaders in environmental education. Civil rights issues were taken to heart by making museums more inclusive for all levels of society. Women's health was addressed through exhibitions and education classes and nuclear issues became a regular part of energy displays and added to lecture rosters.

The ethics of the times produced organizations like Synergy, where sitting for hours on the floor, I imagined Impression 5 Science Museum. In Frank Oppenheimer's case, being banned from University research because he was deemed a communist resulted in him teaching high school in rural Colorado where he gave birth to the Exploratorium. Words like colorful, free, inventive, experimental, and creative became beacons marking the decade.

Well-studied men and women contributed greatly to developing an interactive educational pedagogy. As schools became desegregated, young children of every race were taken on visits to the new science centers, where lively approaches involving hands-on exhibitions provided a welcome contrast to classroom instruction. In these institutions large numbers of children and teachers alike were exposed to inquiry-based learning techniques. My contribution to the emerging field was to tie exhibits to social issues, a departure from the phenomenon based approaches developed in museums like the Exploratorium.

Movements do not last forever, and the public's interest in education has always been a roller-coaster ride. Once the Cold War ended, the nation's focus on science started to wane. The Bush administration initiated the No Child Left Behind school accountability movement, with standardized tests and penalties for not meeting certain goals. This was followed by the Next Generation Science Standards in literacy and math. Though the ideas were well intentioned, the results have been discouraging. Teaching to a test, rather than testing what is taught, became a criticism that rallied teacher unions and parent groups alike. Penalizing teachers of students who live in poor, dysfunctional neighborhoods by comparing their students' scores to those in wealthy suburbs with lots of support was seen as grossly unfair. Policy makers realized that No Child Left Behind (NCLB) needed quite a bit of adaptation and compromise for it to work. In December of 2015, legislation was signed by President Barack Obama that replaced NCLB with the Every Student Succeeds Act which has a more flexible approach. The new act focuses on improving teacher quality, developing a clearinghouse of what works, giving parents more choices, and increasing funding of Charter Schools.

Science did not fare well during this decade of high stakes testing where reading, literacy and math came to dominate nearly every hour of school time. Labs were closed, and the science curriculum, if taught at all, became textbook driven. The deep recession starting in 2008 saw governors juggling budgets and school funding suffered. Fights between political factions, increased poverty, a real estate bubble, and shaky banking practices led to destabilization. Over that past twenty years the can-do excitement of young college students fizzled as the number of recent graduates without jobs increased. From 2000 onwards school field trips to museums declined.

The technology community did not take the public's disinterest in science without pushback, and decided it was time to exert their influence. Jobs of the future need the critical thinking of trained engineers and scientists. Scientists and educators united to revise science standards and in 2013 published a new set known as STEM that added technology and engineering to science. They refocused on inquiry-based learning and the practices of science and engineering with growing recognition that children needed to get back into experimenting, and teachers needed to relearn how to facilitate open-ended hands-on activities. Dependency on textbooks and computer directed programs will not suffice to train leaders and visionaries for the twenty-first century.

There are current trends I do find exciting, for they are opening gates to innovation. Growing from grassroots swell, enabled by the Internet, young adults gather in tinker, craft, and maker evenings to combine traditional arts with computing and new technologies. The movement, started in 2005 by *Make* magazine, is driving innovation in manufacturing, industrial design, engineering, hardware technology, and education. Involved are amateur hobbyists and students enthusiastic about creating new products and art that bring value to their community.

Lego Corporation also spurred hands-on learning by funding creative problem-solving activities that promote technology through play. Informal education institutions such as museums embraced this approach to art and science by developing maker centers within their walls. Their hands-on enrichment classes focused on invention and "making things" are booming, with camps and classes filling to capacity.

There is growing recognition that industrial jobs require people with knowledge of chemicals, waste disposal, electronics, computers, and health hazards, and schools are being challenged to provide a work-ready curriculum with high school graduates able to read manuals and do mathematical computation. As a result school vocational programs, once in decline, are again gaining popularity with more sophisticated offerings than in past. Practical studies emphasize internships and hands-on approaches to learning.

Science Centers are more involved in cooperative ventures than ever before. Though the exhibit collaboratives were the first to be formed, other joint ventures have created new ways of working together. For example, the Nanoscale Science Network, dedicated to helping the public understand nanoscale science, technology and engineering was launched in 2005. Funded by the National Science Foundation, it involves fourteen museums and universities across the nation committed to educating the public in how medicine, computing, materials science, energy production and manufacturing are being impacted. Its collaborative model is a major leap forward in demonstrating how a group of organizations can benefit the country by acting synergistically.

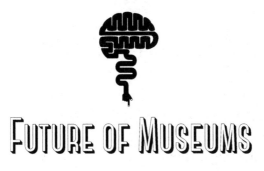

FUTURE OF MUSEUMS

During the past few years I have observed a reimagining of science museums in response to static attendance, even as populations have increased. Funds from the National Science Foundation have dried up for the agency is no longer interested in stimulating the expansion science centers. In the United States small community children's museums represent the area of greatest growth for hands-on education, though throughout the third world science centers continue to be built in record numbers. Large institutions constructed during the heyday of the building boom face pressure to earn their way without government subsidies. Many of them find program budgets being downsized because of aging facility issues.

Changing social pressure is contributing to these centers becoming places for communal gathering. Young adults are enticed to adult-only evenings with a pub-like atmosphere. They are presented with wow-factor lectures, large-screen movies and planetarium shows that turn visits into fun date nights. Multigenerational programs bring grandparents together with their grandchildren for overnight camp-in experiences are also flourishing. Erik Larson, present director of Impression 5 shared that they have adopted a new way of doing things in a Play, Create, Challenge space. Believing "the family unit to be the most powerful learning group ever created," Erik promotes that families need a place to play with

STEAM (science, technology, engineering, art, mathematics) together. "The family unit is social, multigenerational, and trusting, providing the essential environment for people to take the risks necessary to learn."

Children remain the primary audience for experiential classes and camps, though museum staff see many campers having poorer coping skills and lower self-esteem than those they taught even ten years ago. These youngsters, often products of good meaning parents, have lost much of their childhood freedom by being hovered over during their daily activities. Instead of gaining confidence by overcoming mistakes, they are protected, and wind up developing a sense of entitlement to the good things in life without effort. Author and licensed psychologist Dr. Ann Dunnewold labels these adults as "over controlling, overprotecting and over perfecting, in a way that is in excess of responsible parenting." Yet failures and challenges are what teach children new skills. Programs in museums continue to be designed to permit missteps, without making the individual feel like a failure.

To stay relevant, science centers are constantly changing. Indoor exhibits, influenced by the maker movement, use expanded approaches to encourage experimentation. This flexibility has helped them survive downturns in the economy, though it has not always been easy.

Tight funding has meant cutbacks in risk taking. Worrying about new ventures failing is opposite to their mantra of trial-and-error experimentation. Staff creativity is constrained by daily responsibilities being piled on fewer people. Programs previously developed with national goals in mind have dwindled, with focus shifted to local concerns. One of the biggest budgetary challenges museums face has to do with keeping the roof over their heads. As museums mature and struggle with maintenance it is urgent that increased funding become available. The electric bill alone is enough to make any director hiccup.

The public has become increasingly distrustful of science. Unfortunately, this has spawned a plethora of unprepared teachers who in turn produce scientifically illiterate students. Scientific skepticism is found in a Congress that ignores research and a public afraid of immunization shots. Museum board members are more cautious and careful not to invite political controversy. Issues such as global warming, fracking, and genetically modified food are handled gingerly. Museum directors have to be mindful to place scientists on their boards to balance those trustees who may be scientifically naïve or biased by business interests.

Four decades after the start of the science center movement, education remains too focused on the expository distribution of knowledge. Educators still teach children what to learn rather than how to learn. Critical thinking, innovation, problem solving skills and social context are needed to empower a society to be more knowledgeable, respectful and ready to move on in harmony.

COMMUNICATION AND PUBLIC INTERESTS

Ways of reaching new audiences have also changed with social media having a monumental impact. Twitter, Facebook, texting, apps, gaming and e-mails rule the day. Getting a person's attention is more difficult than it was years ago, though certain subjects remain popular and are easier to promote. Dinosaurs, space exploration, and brain science top the current list of public interest. Yet current research in subjects like epigenetics are likely to be of growing importance, and there needs to be better ways of communicating their merit. Why is it important? Because poor nutrition during pregnancy might be passed on genetically to the infant, creating long-term concerns for society. That is a difficult topic to advertise.

Space exploration is getting a new boost from the media. Astronomy nights are booming, with families attending in large numbers to use the telescopes provided by volunteer amateur astronomers. Young employees are as excited and energized as they ever were, but unfortunately, because of salary limitations, the work they are doing is seen as a stepping stone to other jobs in the greater community. Yet retaining long term personnel is a challenge with limited budgets.

I am hopeful that the distancing from science witnessed over the past decades is part of a societal swing and feel confident that interest in scientific breakthroughs and inventions will keep centers strong. Curious visitors will continue to be lured into these experimental playgrounds in order to fill in gaps in their understanding of new technologies.

Though it has been many years since pathfinders such as Piaget or Howard Gardner made their marks, there are new educators and researchers at universities today studying the impact of combining science, math, engineering, and technology and more recently the arts. They realize that past social upheavals are challenged by technological innovations, scientific discoveries, the environmental, and population issues and are learning ways of dealing with difficult subjects and incorporating them into museum studies curriculums.

With so much excitement and innovation, museums continue to be strong advocates for an engaged public. As long as there are men and women enthusiastic about informal learning, concerned about science literacy, and willing to engage the public in lively debates, science centers will continue to be a vital force in our communities. And, as long as parents remain committed to education, there will be children to carry on the creative act of inventing the future. They too will think outside the box and become *Museum Junkies*.

LOOSE ENDS

With each museum venture I lost a husband. Ron, the man of my youth, remains in Michigan having won accolades as a professor and dean of the College of Engineering at Michigan State University. East Lansing is a stimulating community, but for a coastal girl raised in Philadelphia and Boston it was too confining for my ambitions. As my four children graduated from high school, and Impression 5 became stable in its new location, I asked myself if I wanted to spend the rest of my life in the Midwest.

After twenty years I left Ron to marry Marty, a man closely aligned with my interest in the arts. In many ways he helped insure Impression 5's success by convincing me to become his landlord while helping build exhibits. Marty also wanted to leave East Lansing so when the president's position at OMSI became available I applied, was hired, and we never looked back. I am so pleased that Impression 5 is doing so well and nearing its forty-fifth anniversary, but OMSI offered the opportunity to operate a larger institution in a major metropolitan area. I fell in love with Portland. Unfortunately the demands of the job made it difficult to help my husband in his career as a sculptor. In this I failed, and after bringing one beautiful boy into the world our eighteen year marriage ended.

Realizing that I enjoyed new ventures, I resigned from the helm of OMSI, concluding twenty-five years of managing museums. The *Museum Tour Catalog* was started with support from board members and twenty-two national museums interested in bringing hands-on educational toys into the nation's homes while contributing to the financial support of these institutions.

Ray and I met at the Unitarian Church as my new venture started and we immediately bonded. For more than twenty years he has helped me on numerous occasions with my business and I have been able to assist him in promoting his northwest coast masks and totem poles.

My life has been long and productive. I am fortunate to have realized so many dreams. As a retiree I have turned my attention to another crisis in our society. After Ray and I adopted a homeless teen I became concerned with the increasing numbers of disenfranchised youth running towards a life of hopelessness. Through interviews with youth organizers and conversations with a variety of street kids I am beginning to form a few hypotheses that will be shared in my next book *Over the Peanut Fence*. As always, I do believe that hands-on learning opportunities will be part of the solution to educating these children.

Riding a Gyroscope

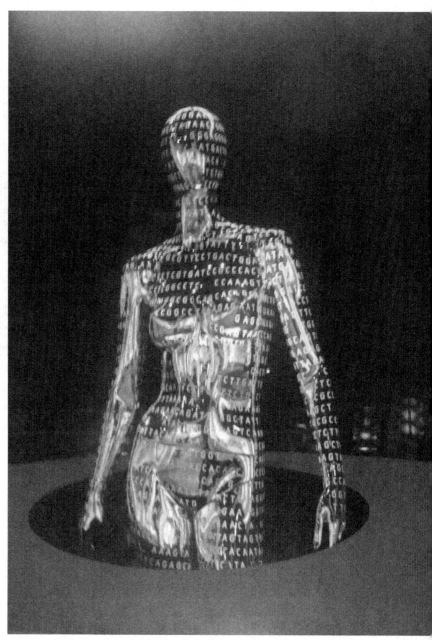

Genome: Unlocking Life's Code
(A Smithsonian Traveling Exhibit)

SECTION VII

REFERENCES

REFERENCES

pxii: *Our passions were fired by psychologists, educators, and scientists such as Jean Piaget, Maria Montessori, Jonathan Kozol, John Hart, A. S. Neil, Carl Rogers, and Frank Oppenheimer.* Rogers, C. R., Stevens, B., Gendlin, E. T., Shlien, J. M., & Van Dusen, W. (1967). **Person to person: The problem of being human: A new trend in psychology.** Lafayette, CA: Real People Press.

p14: *According to a 2013 Popular Science article, there is renewed interest among scientists in studying the use of pharmaceutical grade hallucinogenic drugs in psychiatry.* **Popular Science** "Why Doctors Can't Give You LSD (But Maybe they Should)" 04/16/2013 By Shaunacy Ferro.

p36: *In addition to the Cold War and the civil rights movement, the Vietnam War was just starting to escalate.* **Against the Vietnam War, Writings by Activists,** edited by Mary Susannah Robbins, published by Rowman and Littlefield Publishing Group, Inc., Maryland 20706, c 1999 by Mary Susanna Robbins, Reprinted 2007.

Turbulent Years: The 60s, Time-Life Books, 1998, Richard B. Stolley, https://books.google.com/books?id=sK9aAAAAYAAJ.

p38: *First Nixon and then Reagan promoted the policy of emptying the beds of mental hospitals;* **Ronald Reagan's Shameful Legacy:**

Violence, the Homeless, Mental Illness. Dr. E. Fuller Torrey September 291 2013 for Salon, an online news service. An excerpt from **American Psychosis.**

p41: *Ever since 1964, when Robert Rosenthal, a Harvard Professor did an experiment at South San Francisco, High, there have been studies demonstrating that teacher's expectations can influence how students perform.* **Teachers' Expectations Can Influence How Students Perform** by Alex Spiegel; NPR Morning Edition story, September 17, 2012 : Robert Rosenthal and Ralph L. Rosnow's Classic Books - Artifacts in Behavioral Research, Oxford University Press, Inc, New York, c 2009.

p61: *Maharishi Mahesh Yogi (1918-2008) gained popularity by introducing a mantra based meditation technique that was adopted by many celebrities.* For more information about transcendental meditation go to http://www.tm.org.

p61: *It has been renamed as a modern movement called "mindfulness."* **Psychology Today** article about Mindfulness, a state of active, open attention to the present. https://www.psychology-today.com/basics/mindfulness.

p62: *When I began I often started with, "All children are not created equal."* **The Lansing State Journal**: All Children are Not Created Equal by Marilynne Eichinger: blog.www.museumtour.com, *May 2013.*

p63: During the last thirty years there has been an increased epidemic of kids being diagnosed as attention deficit (ADD) and ADHD. **Ritalin use for ADHD children Soars Fourfold** – The Guardian.com - May 5 2012, **Raising the Ritalin Generation** – The NY Times.com Aug 18,2012, **The Ritalin Explosion** Harvey Parker on Frontline, OPB.

p71: *Maria Montessori was an Italian early childhood educator and physician who in 1907 started a school in for children of working parents called Casa die Bambini.* For an introduction the the Montessori Method go to http://amshq.org/Montessori-Education/ Introduction-to-Montessori.

p71: *As a Montessori parent I was, I was also swayed by the work of Jean Piaget (1906-1980), a Swiss developmental epistemologist who investigated childhood behavior.* **Piaget's theory of Intellectual Development: An Introduction** by Herbert Ginsburg and Sylvia Opper, Prentice-Hall Series in **Developmental Psychology**, Englewood Cliffs, New Jersey c 1969.

p72: *I attended lectures by Dr. Papert who demonstrated Piaget's conclusions to Montessori School parents.* **Papert on Piaget** by Seymour Papert in **Time Magazine's special issue on "The Century's Greatest Minds**," March 29, 1999.

p75: *Piaget's theories, though profound, do not tell the entire story of human development incorporated by museums. Another component comes from the work of Harvard educator Howard Gardner.* **The Unschooled Mind** by Howard Gardner, Basic Books a member of Perseus Books Group, New York, NY, c 1995,2004.

p79: *Frank Oppenheimer(1912-1985) stands out as the individual who has had the greatest influence on the modern science center movement.* **Something Incredibly Wonderful Happens, Frank Oppenheimer and the World He Made Up** *by K.C.Cole, Houghton Mifflin Harcourt, c 2009.*

p87: *In 2012, a young social work student at the University of Rochester was featured in national publications as a most unusual entrepreneur.* www.thesnuggery.org/snugglers.html; **She's Got the Touch** by Shane Dixon Kavanaugh, **Oregonian** November 13, 2013: http://www.scientificamerican.com/article/infant-touch/ - How Important is Physical Contact with your Infant, May 6, 2010 by Katherine Harman.

p106: *On October 23, 2013, the American Academy of Pediatrics offered guidance on managing children's use of media..* **Managing Media: We Need a Plan** 10/28/2013 **American Academy of Pediatrics** offers guidance on managing children's and adolescents' media use - See more at: http://www.aap.org/en-us/about-the-aap/aap-press-room/Pages/Managing-Media-We-Need-a-Plan.aspx#sthash.WSYfblU6.dpuf.

p107: *Who in the world comes up with such strange ideas?* **Time Magazine special Double Issue**, November 25, 2013 – 25 Best Inventions p.69.

p112: *In my thirties I took my first class in creativity.* **Can Creativity Be Learned?** Blog, www.museumtour.com, October 10, 2012.

p113: *Known as image streaming, this approach to problem solving works well for me and I turn to it whenever I am at a loss of how to proceed.* http://www.creativethinkingwith.com/Image-Streaming.html .

p116: *Another rapidly growing craft trend is the maker movement.* http://time.com/104210/maker-faire-maker-movement/; http://www.huffingtonpost.com/brit-morin/what-is-the-maker-movemen_b_3201977.html.

p120: *What is the secret of life?* **The 75 –Year Study that Found The secrets To a Fulfilling Life, Huffinton Post** , The Third Metric, 8/11/2013 , on –line; **The How of of Happiness** a Scientific Approach to Getting the Life You Want, Sonja Lyubomirsk, Penguin Press, New York 2008.

p121: *Providing opportunities for children to play freely is an important part of parenting.* **Imaginative Play.** *blog, www.museumtour.com;* Science writer Melinda Wenner writes about imaginative play: http://melindawennermoyer.com ; https://

www.psychologytoday.com/blog/freedom-learn/201206/
free-play-is-essential-normal-emotional-development.

p125: *In my early Portland days I brought Otto Piene from Boston to town to lead a workshop with exhibit staff and educators from OMSI and the Portland Art Museum:* About Otto Piene - *http://www. nytimes.com/2014/07/19/arts/otto-piene-german-artist-of-new-modes-dies-at-85.html?_r=0.*

p149: *A few words about homeschooling;* research about homeschooling - http://www.nheri.org/research/ research-facts-on-homeschooling.html; *http://www.edweek.org/ew/ issues/home-schooling/*; pros and cons -http://school.familyeduca-tion.com/home-schooling/parenting/29861.html?page=2.

p157: *In 1972 most businesses, public institutions and museums were run by men.* Women in the 1960s, what they could not do - *http://www.cnn.com/2014/08/07/living/sixties-women-5-things/* ; Board makeup today- **Catalyst** , May 31, 2013 Women on Boards ; about the feminist movement - *https://tavaana.org/en/ content/1960s-70s-american-feminist-movement-breaking-down-barri-ers-women.*

p172: *My favorite quote by Rita Coolidge: //www.brainyquote.com/ quotes/quotes/r/ritacoolid335198.html.*

p173: *Psychologist and Harvard faculty professor Jeff Brow and assis-tant professor, Mark Fenske, of the University of Guelph in Ontario, used cutting-edge neuroscience to study attributes of successful people.* **The Winner's Brain: 8 Strategies Great Minds Use to Achieve Success**, Perseus Books, March 22, 2010.

p204: *There are lots of crises that face directors of public institutions;* About Mayor Guiliani and the Brooklyn Museum- http://partners.nytimes.com/library/ arts/092499brooklyn-museum.html; http://ncac.org/resource/

decency-arts-and-the-first-amendment-the-case-of-rudy-giuliani/.

p221: *During the early 80s, a communal experiment was started on a 64,229 acre parcel of land not far from OMSI's Camp Hancock in central Oregon.* Rise and Fall of the Rajneeshpuram -http://www.ashe-prem.org/two/davisson.shtml.

p230: There is a controversial Harvard University author by the name of Charles Murray who with Richard J. Herrnstein wrote "The Bell Curve" and more recently "Coming Apart, The State of White America, 1960-2010." **Bell Curve: Intelligence and Class Structure in American Life** by Richard Herrnstein and Charles Murray, Free Press Paperbacks, Division of Simon & Schuster, c 1994.

p231: *Henry Ford required those who worked in his factory to participate in a training program promoting American values.* About the Ford English school: http://www.autolife.umd.umich.edu/Labor/L_Overview/FordEnglishSchool.htm.

p273: *Fund-raising events are often used as friend-raisers.* **Relationship Fundraising: A Donor-Based Approach to the Business of Raising Money** by Ken Burnett, John Wiley and Sons, 2002. **Fundraising for Small Museums** by Salvatore G. Cilella, Jr., AltaMira Press, division of Rowman & Littlefield Publishers, Inc, c 2011.

p286: *There is a juicy read called the Medici Conspiracy. . .* **The Medici Conspiracy** by Cecilia Todeschini and Peter Watson, 2007.

p287: *The return of several finds, including that of Kennewick Man in Oregon and a ten-thousand-year -old spirit Cave Man discovered in Nevada, were held up in court for years.* http://archeology.about.com/od/kennewickman/a/introduction.htm.

p355: *Once the Cold War ended, the nation's focus on science started to wane.* The following articles are about inspiring interest in science.

http://www.usnews.com/education/best-colleges/articles/2011/05/23/combating-students-disinterest-in-the-sciences:

http://www.washingtonpost.com/blogs/the-fix/wp/2013/04/02/polls-suggest-publics-interest-in-climate-change-is-waning/.

p355: *The Bush administration initiated the No Child Left Behind school accountability movement, with standardized tests and penalties for not meeting certain goals.* **The Politics and Practice of Accountability** by Martin R. West and Paul E. Peterson, c 2003, the Brookings Institution.

About a National at Risk and No Child Left Behind: **National Education Goals and the Creation of Federal Education Policy** by Maris A. Vinovskis, Teachers College Press, c 2009.

p256: *Scientists and educators united to revise science standards and in 2013 published a new set known as STEM that added technology and engineering to science.* **STEM Education: Concepts, Methodologies, Tools, and Applications** Edited by Information Resources Management Association , Published as Information Science Reference an imprint of IGI Global, C 2105. *d*

p357: *Science Centers are more involved in cooperative ventures than ever before.* About the Nano Scale Informal Science Education Network. http://www.nisenet.org/about.

p360: *These youngsters, often products of good meaning parents, have lost much of their freedom by being hovered over during their daily activities.* Difficulties caused by helicopter-parenting. *http://www.parents.com/parenting/better-parenting/what-is-helicopter-parenting/*

FOR GENERAL INFORMATION ABOUT MUSEUMS:

The National Council of Nonprofits is a resource and advocate for America's charitable nonprofits. Through a network of State Associations and 25,000-plus members–the nation's largest network of nonprofits–they serve as a central coordinator and mobilizer to help nonprofits achieve greater collective impact in local communities across the country. See more at: https://www.councilofnonprofits.org/#sthash.gQodwcEm.dpuf.

The Association of Science and Technology Centers(ASTC) is "a global organization providing collective voice, professional support, and programming opportunities for science centers, museums, and related institutions, whose innovative approaches to science learning inspire people of all ages about the wonders and meaning of science in their lives." http://www.astc.org.

American Alliance of Museums. The Alliance since 1906, helps by developing standards and best practices, gathering and sharing knowledge, and providing advocacy on issues of concern to the museum community. They represent the entire scope of the broad museum community. http://www.aam-us.org/about-us.

ABOUT THE AUTHOR

Marilynne Eichinger has been an active supporter of hands-on learning throughout her career as both a mother and museum professional. Graduating magna-cum-laude from Boston University with an emphasis on anthropology, she went on to receive a master's degree in psychology from Michigan State University. In 1972 Marilynne founded Impression 5 Science Museum in Lansing, Michigan in order to share the wonders of science that she was introduced to as a child at the Franklin Institute in Philadelphia.

After thirteen years she left Impression 5 to become president of the Oregon Museum of Science and Industry, one of the nation's oldest and most renowned science center. There she spearheaded building a new 250,000 sq. ft facility and workshop on the Willamette River in center city Portland, acquired a submarine from the Navy and installed a large format theater. Under her presidency she cultivated a traveling exhibit service developing displays that travelled internationally. She oversaw science classes, camps and education programs that serviced a five state region.

Marilynne's concern for children's education led her to move to her next venture in 1995. With the involvement of 22 museums and private investors she established the nationally distributed *Museum Tour Catalog* which provides hands-on investigative materials that compliment school curricula. Her business sold in 2013, providing more time to spend with her five children and eight grandchildren. Marilynne remains an active painter, blogger, and traveler. She is the author of books that benefit the education of young children.

In 2010 she and her partner Ray Losey adopted a nineteen year old homeless boy. His story, both personal and poignant inspired Marilynne's interest in impacting the lives of disadvantaged youth. **The True Story of Streetwise: Overcoming Homelessness and Beating the Odds** is available as an ebook on Amazon. She is currently engaged in research for a comprehensive treatment of youth homelessness. **Over the Peanut Fence** is scheduled for publication in 2017.

To receive updates about future publications and special offerings you are invited to join her mailing list at http://eepurl. com/bLznrP.

CPSIA information can be obtained
at www.ICGtesting.com
Printed in the USA
FSOW03n0142120816
23518FS